D0375598

ALSO BY BETHENNY FRANKEL

Naturally Thin

The Skinnygirl Dish

A Place of Yes

Skinnydipping

Skinnygirl Solutions

Your Straight-Up Guide to Home, Health, Family, Career, Style, and Sex

∽

Bethenny Frankel

with Eve Adamson

Illustrations by Bunky Hurter

A TOUCHSTONE BOOK

Published by Simon & Schuster

New York   London   Toronto   Sydney   New Delhi

Touchstone
A Division of Simon & Schuster, Inc.
1230 Avenue of the Americas
New York, NY 10020

First Touchstone hardcover edition August 2013

TOUCHSTONE and colophon are registered trademarks of Simon & Schuster, Inc.

For information about special discounts for bulk purchases,
please contact Simon & Schuster Special Sales at
1-866-506-1949 or business@simonandschuster.com.

The Simon & Schuster Speakers Bureau can bring authors to your live event.
For more information or to book an event contact the Simon & Schuster Speakers
Bureau at 1-866-248-3049 or visit our website at www.simonspeakers.com.

Illustrations by Bunky Hurter/Mendola Artists

Manufactured in the United States of America

10   9   8   7   6   5   4   3   2

Library of Congress Cataloging-in-Publication Data
Frankel, Bethenny.
    Skinnygirl solutions : your straight-up guide to home, health, family, career, style,
and sex / Bethenny Frankel with Eve Adamson ; illustrations by Bunky Hurter.
      pages   cm
    "A Touchstone Book."
    1. Women—Life skills guide.   I. Adamson, Eve.   II. Title.
    HQ1221.F723 2013
    646.70082—dc23   2013016625

ISBN 978-1-4516-6739-4
ISBN 978-1-4516-6744-8 (ebook)

Dedication

This book is dedicated to women. We struggle every day just to find balance, even when we rarely master it. We strive for fairly simple things: love, sex, health, family, work, sleep, time, water, and trying not to look like a total hot mess while attempting to achieve them. You have given me so much. Every day I learn something from you, whether it is something as simple as removing a stain or something as intense as coping with divorce. I wrote this book to try to give you some of the solutions that keep me sane under the most difficult of circumstances. I love you and I am so proud of you for all that you endure and strive for every day.

Contents

Skinnygirl
Solutions

Introduction

I haven't been in your lives, or your living rooms, for a while.

It's been interesting adjusting to a private life. No cameras in the house and nobody following me around, catching my intimate moments. I still get snapped by the paparazzi when I go outside, but it's different not to have you in my living room or kitchen with me, not to have you following me around to my events or even hanging out with me while I talk to my therapist. You've missed a lot of important changes in my life, and I've missed you.

But I have to be honest. I left reality television, and I haven't looked back. I don't miss it, although occasionally when something funny happens, I have a fleeting thought that the cameras should have been there to catch it. (Humor is still very important to me.) I'm so grateful for all the opportunities I've had in television, but by the third season of *The Real Housewives of New York City*, I was kind of through with it. The word "toxic" was tossed around very freely back then, but I have to admit that it was definitely an accurate term for that situation. When you're in an experience like that, you think about things you normally wouldn't, you fight about things you probably shouldn't, and you say things that you couldn't possibly imagine you would ever say. Then there was *Bethenny Getting Married/Bethenny Ever After*, which was stressful to say the least, but I decided at the beginning that if people were going to take time out of their busy lives to tune in, I would give them the truth. Three seasons of truth—and the truth can hurt.

I can admit that I bit off more than I could chew with the fame game. I have become very recognizable and pursued by photographers. I thought fame would be fun, but it changed me a little. I opened up Pandora's box, and once you do that . . . I've had to become more careful, a little more suspicious, and I've had to tighten my inner circle. It's taught me that I have friends I really can trust, but maybe not as many as I once thought. That's the reality, but in a world where people sell you out all the time, I'm proud to say that my friends haven't sold me out, my business partners haven't sold me out, my colleagues from television haven't sold me out, and everyone on my team has been loyal and stuck by me.

All along, I just wanted to be happy. I wanted a normal life with Bryn. I wanted to be able to wake up in the morning and have breakfast together and play with puzzles and Legos and then take her for her daily activities, whether it's school or ballet or the park. I've had a taste of that this year, as I've been out of the spotlight (except for the divorce drama, of course). Some days, I almost feel like a regular stay-at-home mom, but my life has never been entirely "regular." Every fashion decision, hairstyle, even expression on my face I dare to make in public gets plastered online. (No complaints here. Just explanation.) I'm also running all my businesses and writing this book. One moment, I can feel like nothing exists in the world besides Bryn, me, and the art project we're doing or the cupcake we're decorating or the slide we're about to go down. Just a few hours later, I might be in the depths of editing my book or making decisions about my product lines or on a flight across the country. Fortunately, I now work with some incredible people who support me so I have as much time with Bryn as possible, but I wouldn't exactly call it a year off.

Yet, it has been a year off in many ways. Unless I was doing an appearance on *Ellen*, I haven't been on television. I've been dealing with my personal life instead. That's been a full-time job. If you watched my show *Bethenny Ever After*, the last time you saw me, I was slogging through an extremely difficult time. I was completely in love with my daughter but struggling to keep my relationship with my husband positive. As you may have heard, that hasn't worked out so well.

I know a lot of you want to hear about the divorce. I don't like to talk about it or be public about it because it's a private issue, and every relationship is 10 percent what everyone else sees and 90 percent what only the people involved know about or understand. It's the same with me as with anyone, but it just so happened that I was on television during this time in my life. I was totally open with my life and you saw a lot, but nobody saw everything. You saw what I could show you, but that wasn't the whole picture. Relationships are complex and private and never simple, but people thought they had the whole story. That made the entire situation even more difficult and stressful.

After I suffered a miscarriage last year, in some ways I was actually relieved because I was scared that I wasn't in a happy place. I didn't want to fail, so I forced myself to make things good. I tried very hard. I went to therapy. I obsessed. I lost weight. I was terrified. But I made the choice, and it was the right choice. I ripped off the Band-Aid and I definitely found clarity.

Right now, my personal life is very uncomfortable. It feels frightening and unnatural but my priority is to be the best mother I can be and make sure that my daughter knows how much she is loved. It's not ideal, but it's the best solution right now.

I know many of you criticize me for my failure, and I totally get that. I criticize me, too. I feel embarrassed and ashamed that I tried so hard to live the fairy tale in front of everyone, and it didn't work out. I guess life is full of disappointments and I take the bad with the good. I've learned about myself, and I'm heartbroken, but I'm still here. I'm a little wiser, and most important, I am certain. I know many of you have gone through the same thing. You've been divorced, or are going through a divorce now, or are thinking about it. Or you've just had a bad breakup or had your heart broken. This is life. It's not perfect, but it's full of beautiful moments nevertheless. It's a rose with petals and thorns.

I'm slowly learning that maybe divorce doesn't have to suck. There are advantages to being the only adult during the times when you are with your child. That time is all your own and you get to make it as quality as you can. You can really be present with your child, without focusing on anything else, because you appreciate that time so much more. You're really in it. When your child is with the other parent, that's when you get alone time and do things for yourself. The point is to look on the bright side. Easier said than done.

It's a long road. The torment comes first, then the fear, then the action, then the clarity, and then the mud. And hopefully, there's a certainty that you've done the right thing. But when you're in the mud, everything is a little bit harder. I expect there to be sunshine after the mud, but I'm not there yet. I'm still in the mud. I'm working my way out.

Right now, nothing has to be anything. I have no expectations. I'm not trying to find someone else. I have enough in my life. If I meet someone new, I can talk to him like he is a human being, not some prospect. I don't care about getting set up. I don't care about getting married again. I just want to be happy with myself. I just want to enjoy my life.

In the meantime, when I'm not with my daughter, I've been coping by throwing myself into work and being more social. I say no to many things, but if my little girl is with her father, I will say yes to almost anything because I need to get my mind off being away from her and get out of the house. I used to dread traveling for business, but now I welcome it. If I need to go to L.A. to do Ellen's show, I get excited because it's an escape.

I've also thrown myself into working out a bit more. I usually only do yoga or fun exercise like surfing or snowboarding when I'm away, but lately I've needed something more intense, for those days when I feel like I need to beat something up. Other days, I only need yoga or a massage. Every day is different, and I take the days one at a time. I used to stay home every night, but now I try to go for business dinners or out for drinks after Bryn goes to sleep. Other than that, I am immersed in my work, and that's one of the best things in my life right now.

One of the things I've been doing this year has been writing this book. You asked me a lot of questions, and I've always wanted to take the time to sit down and answer them all. This is that book. I am obsessed with finding solutions for the little issues women have in their lives: eating, dieting, cooking, trying to stay healthy while enjoying life, exercising, organizing, decorating, cleaning, being environmentally responsible, finding better ways to reuse things, dressing well, traveling, entertaining, and of course parenting, not to mention all the ins and outs and complications and joys of having an exciting career. We all find every one of these issues challenging on occasion, and I've devoted my life and my work to finding solutions and presenting them to you. I could go on and on, and in this book, I do. It's been exciting for me to get to share all my ideas, and I hope you love them and use them the way I do.

In the past year, I've been relying on Twitter and Facebook to have a conversation with you, but now I'm coming back into your homes. I can't believe it has finally happened, but my new talk show, *Bethenny*, will air right about the time this book comes out. We have a lot to talk about, and this time, it's not going to be about me. It's going to be about *you*. We can talk about all the things girls talk about when there are no men in the room. We can be truthful and we won't have to feel ashamed of who we really are. Divorce is the worst thing you could ever go through in your life, but part of the silver lining is that I can experience it with people. We can talk about it and help each other. We can talk about anything and everything.

Doing this talk show makes me feel like I'm finally a success. There was a time when I had anxiety about the talk show. Did I really want to do that every single day? Then the lull came, and the divorce, and I realized that this is what I was meant to do. I was made for this. It doesn't even feel like a choice anymore. It feels like a calling, and it's all because of you.

I'm so grateful to you. I wouldn't have the talk show without you. When we had our trial run last summer on Fox, in just a few cities, you could have gone to the beach, but you stayed in and watched my show. You proved to Fox that I was worth betting on, and now I can hang out with you every day. Let's make next year a great year for us all.

I can hardly wait to see you again.

Part One

Skinnygirl Wellness

- ✦ How do you stay so thin?
- ✦ Were you always so thin?
- ✦ Do you just have good genes?
- ✦ Aren't you just naturally thin? Don't you just have a fast metabolism?
- ✦ You seem to be able to eat anything you want. How do you get away with that?
- ✦ How did you lose your baby weight so quickly?
- ✦ Do you starve yourself? Is that what I have to do to look like you?
- ✦ Do you eat? What do you eat?
- ✦ What do you drink? How much do you drink?
- ✦ How much do you exercise? What do you do?
- ✦ What do I do to lose weight?
- ✦ How did you stop binge-eating?
- ✦ I can't diet anymore. Is there any hope for me?

Chapter One
. . . .

Living Naturally Thin

I get asked questions all the time: by e-mail, Twitter, letter; politely asked at a signing or at my show; and sometimes just screamed from passing cars. Although many of them are about business or work-life balance, most are about how to get or stay naturally thin. How do I do it? And how can you do it? That's why I'm starting this book with some of the questions I've received since writing *Naturally Thin.* Because you want solutions.

You worry about your weight. I get it. You want to be thin and in shape, but you also want to live your life. You want to get off the virtual treadmill. You feel like you're white-knuckling it all the time, trying to keep your weight under control. You feel like food is your obsession. You're always on a diet. You're always hungry, or guilty, or thinking about what you will or won't eat next. You look at food and gain weight. You swear that tomorrow, you'll be "good." I know that feeling and that anxiety. I know what it's like to go on one diet after another and to spend money you don't have on a gym membership you don't use. With every new diet or exercise plan, you think that finally, *this will be the one.* It gives you false hope of a new beginning. Or you've already given up. You hear about the latest diet everybody is trying and you think, *I just can't do it again. I just can't do another diet. I guess I'm just not meant to be thin.*

I know what it's like to feel like food is your consolation, your best friend, your enemy, your hobby. If you have a dysfunctional relationship with food, getting to your ideal weight can seem like a dream that's slipping away, especially as you get older. Or you look great but it's an eternal struggle, like a horrible job that you're never going to be able to quit.

I've been there and done that again and again and again. It's maddening and it feels hopeless, when how much you weigh or how much you eat or how you fit into your clothes can make the difference between a good day and a bad day. The old me would tell myself that I was bad if I ate food and good if I starved myself. The old me would promise myself that I would be good tomorrow. The old me thought that avocado was the devil, that I could only eat vegetables if they were steamed, and that salad had to be plain, with dressing on the side, or the whole salad was ruined. Alcohol was forbidden or strictly rationed until the deprivation tipped me into drinking too much. I would be "good" for days at a time until I couldn't stand it anymore, and then I would binge-eat myself into a food coma of bloating and self-loathing. It was madness. It really was a prison, and the rules were: forbid, restrict, and deprive, followed by crave, explode, and binge.

All that changed when I realized no food was "bad" or "good" and that nothing was off-limits. I stopped feeling obsessed and compelled to overeat by lifting all the restrictions I'd been living with for years and replacing them with some general principles I could live with for the rest of my life. This inspired my first book, *Naturally Thin*. The basic concepts are these:

- No obsessing, extremes, or yo-yo dieting
- No forbidden-food lists
- No meal plans
- No counting calories
- No counting fat grams
- No counting carbs
- No measuring
- No eliminating
- No denial
- No dieting ever again

I am very proud to hear that *Naturally Thin* helped many women lose weight and, even more important, regain control over their eating and their relationship with food, so food is no longer an obsession, a frenemy, or an addiction. I maintain that this is my greatest work accomplishment to date. It showed me what I was made to do—help other people with their struggles, and especially help other people to break free from being tormented by food. Because it's just food—one great part of life, but not the meaning of life. It can be hard to see that when you're in the middle of it, but I'm extending a hand to help pull you out.

I am not a nutritionist and I'm not an expert. I'm just a woman who played the weight game for years and lost, but who finally figured out how to win. That book busted out of me. It practically wrote itself. Those ten rules changed my life forever, and I was so passionate about the principles that I wanted to scream them from the rooftops. I wanted everyone to know what I had discovered. I wanted to lend everyone a hand, because when I was there, I needed one.

Dieting doesn't work and it has never worked and it will never work because it's about restriction. I don't want to be restricted. That's how you end up in diet prison: fighting yourself all the time and then rebelling and wrecking yourself. All of that is over. It ends now. You can be the person who doesn't obsess about food, who enjoys life and looks great and feels great.

I used to spend all my energy focusing on what I ate and how much I exercised and loathing myself if things didn't work perfectly, because I didn't have a healthy relationship with food. All the parts of my life suffered. No more. Now I spend my energy being creative, being a mother, running my business, and enjoying my life. Pretty much every day I have a small bowl of baked or regular chips and an ice cream with sprinkles. I eat things like French fries, pancakes, and candy once or twice a week and I enjoy a cocktail at the end of a long day. I pick my spots and I don't go crazy at meals. It's about quantity, not which foods are "good" and which foods are "bad." When you understand that, it changes everything about your relationship with food.

I know that there are so many of you out there who are still struggling the way I did. You don't want to fight yourself anymore. You want to be free. You want to eat the foods you like and still be healthy and feel good about your body. You want to indulge, but you don't want to take food so seriously. You want to unleash your Skinnygirl. This is the way. This is the answer. My whole philosophy is allowing and indulging, not restricting and depriving. *Naturally Thin* was the beginning of that journey, and this is the continuation of the story.

Naturally Thin Evolves

When I wrote *Naturally Thin*, I'd only been living the principles for a few years. Now, when I look back at that book, I realize even more how proud of it I am. It says exactly what I still believe today. The ten principles in that book are still relevant and adaptable to every stage of life.

But I've gained some insights over the past five years as I've continued to *live* naturally thin over the long haul. Every day, I come up with new tips and ways to underline and clarify and highlight those same concepts. I've realized that you don't have to use all the rules all the time. Different rules will become relevant in different situations and at different times in your life. Whether you're single or dating, married or a parent, at home most of the day or on the road for work, on vacation or just running around the city, the rules are your toolbox. You take out what you need and use what's appropriate for the situation you're in.

The more you use the tools, the more they become second nature to you. This is how you become that person who can indulge without damage, that girl who eats French fries and pizza and ice cream and bread, who doesn't have to worry about food, even at a party or on vacation or when she really wants a cocktail.

If you've already read *Naturally Thin*, this chapter will be a refresher course, but it also contains new information and additional insights about how to nurture your healthy food relationship. If you haven't read *Naturally Thin* yet, this chapter will start you on the journey to being diet-free. There will be lots more help in my first book. So I hope you will give it a read, if you haven't already. The principles work. They are real. They are effective. They will finally quiet your food noise, and they will change your life forever.

You Know What to Do

Look, I know if you are reading this book, you probably already have a basic knowledge of health and diet. You know what you should be doing. It's just a matter of figuring out how to do it. You see the island but don't know how to swim to it. I'm not going to insult you with rudimentary information you already have. Instead, I've got twenty-five simple strategies that can get you where you want to be with your body and with the way you think about food.

These are your tools and this is your cheat sheet: the principles you can draw on as you go through your day. These are twenty-five short, sweet calls to action. This is *Naturally Thin* crystallized. When you internalize these principles, you won't have to think about them anymore. You'll just do them. You'll eat like a naturally thin person, and you'll be free.

The Naturally Thin Twenty-Five

1. Balance Your Diet

This is the guiding rule, and if it's the only one you remember, you'll be ahead of the game. You can eat anything you want in moderation, as long as you keep it in balance. In *Naturally Thin*, I say, "Your diet is your bank account." This is the same principle. When you invest in something decadent, you balance that with something healthy, now or later.

Balance big meals with small meals, sugary meals with protein and vegetables, rich choices with lean choices. If you eat cheesecake, you know you indulged. Pull back at the next meal. If you ate a giant muffin the size of your ass, you know you just ate a ton of sugar and carbs. Don't fool yourself. Instead of pretending it didn't happen or using it as an excuse to keep going with sugar and carbs, balance it at the next meal with a salad and lean protein. Check yourself.

You don't need to measure. You don't need to eat fat-free fake food. Eat what you want, and be calm and okay with it when you indulge. It's just like money. You make a big purchase when it's worth it, but then you've got to skimp a little to balance that indulgence. You might get upset with yourself if you spend too much on something stupid, but that doesn't let you off the hook. Balance is everything. Know it, face it, and live it every time you make a food choice. Pretty soon, you won't even have to think about it anymore.

2. Listen to Your Food Voice (Not Your Food Noise)

Food noise is what I call that anxiety-fueled noise in your head that tells you that some foods are "bad" and some are "good," or that you are "bad" or "good" for eating particular things in a particular way. Please remember: Nothing is fattening in small portions. Nothing! Recognize food noise for what it is: useless. It makes you think you're not the one in control, and that's not true. If life is a party, food noise is not invited, because it spoils all the fun.

Your *food voice*, on the other hand, is the part of you that knows what you really want and what your body really needs. It comes from a calm place where you call the shots. We all have a food voice. My food noise might encourage me to keep eating cookies, but my food voice tells me when I've had enough to enjoy the food but not overdo it or regret it. It's just hard to hear until we learn to tone down the food noise.

3. Pick Your Spot

If you really want something, you should have it, in a reasonable amount. If you don't care as much about it, skip it. In *Naturally Thin*, I say, "You can have it all, just not all at once." It's the same thing, but now I tend to say, "Pick your spot." For example, if you really want dessert, skip the cocktail. If you really want the cocktail, skip the dessert. If you really want the pasta, skip the bread. If you really want the steak, have a vegetarian lunch that day. In other words, you can and should indulge, as long as you pick the spot where indulgence means the most to you. The rest of it is just calories without a cause.

4. Make Food Moments Meaningful

When you eat, pay attention. Don't just shove it in. When you make food moments meaningful, you can appreciate and enjoy eating. If you're having sushi at home, use chopsticks. Put your sushi rolls on a nice platter. Put the soy sauce in a little dish. If you're having pizza, make a nice salad to go with it and put it on a good plate. Notice each bite. I just ate half of a hot-fudge sundae, but I enjoyed every spoonful, so it was worth it. I wanted it and I made it count because it meant something. Because of that, I didn't have to finish it. If you don't pay attention to your food, what's the point of eating something really good? You might as well eat the steamed-vegetable plate. If you're going to indulge, make it count.

5. Stop at the Point of Diminishing Returns

The point of diminishing returns is the exact moment when a food doesn't taste as good as it did at the first bite. You can eat anything— truffle fries, nachos, cake. Take a bite and relish every part of how delicious it is. Then take another. Is it just as good? By the third bite, if the experience has peaked and it's not quite as good as the first bite, that's the point of diminishing returns and it's your signal to stop eating. (Pay attention or you'll miss it!)

6. Keep It Moving

If you feel you're about to get derailed and you can't stop eating something, then move on to a different taste. When you switch the taste, it can interrupt the rampage and make you realize you've had enough food. If you can't stop eating cookies, then have some cheese or chips or something salty to interrupt the sugar bender, and you'll be more likely to realize you're actually full. Then you might stop, but just to be sure you don't drift back to the cookies, keep moving on to something else. Move on. Going back to those cookies ain't worth it, and you know it.

7. Don't Let "Good Enough" Be Good Enough

Never settle when it comes to a food indulgence. Only go for the special things that are really worth it. "Mediocre" is no longer in your vocabulary. If you choose to eat it, it's only because it is totally worth it. It's not the last cookie you're ever going to see, so unless it's the *best* cookie, skip it. Period. The end.

8. Taste Everything, Eat Nothing

When you just can't pick a spot to indulge because there are too many choices, then taste everything, eat nothing. This means taste just a little bit of everything you really want. Use this rule at a buffet, an indulgent restaurant, a party, or any place where you know there will be many fattening choices. Make yourself a perfect little plate with small bites of the most tempting foods. If you want to go back and have a few more bites of what was really worth it, fine. This rule allows you to participate in any event and not have to feel anxiety that you missed something. You didn't miss anything because you tasted everything.

9. Know the Differential

What's the differential between a cheeseburger and a veggie burger with cheese? If both would taste roughly the same to you, especially if you dressed the veggie burger up with mushrooms, onions, ketchup, mustard, pickles, lettuce, and tomato for the whole burger experience, then the differential is small. That's when you go for the healthier choice—the veggie burger.

When the differential is great—for me, a fat-free brownie would never be as good as a regular piece of red velvet cake, and sugar-free frozen yogurt doesn't come close to the real thing—then go for the more indulgent choice. If you genuinely like the fat-free version, great. If not, have what you prefer. You don't have to go crazy. Have a handful of fries and walk away. Have one or two cookies or a small scoop of real ice cream or a small piece of fried chicken and enjoy it without guilt, then move on. If you truly allow, honestly and fully without guilt and food noise and beating yourself up, then you won't ever binge.

10. Spot the Knockoffs

If it's artificially sweetened, fat-free, or some other "fake" version of a real food, beware. There is evidence that artificial sweetener actually makes you crave sweets because it confuses your body, and people tend to eat more of fat-free foods because they aren't getting that full feeling. If you really want something, a little bit of the real stuff—even soda sweetened with sugar—is better than gorging on the knockoff. (Full disclosure: I love veggie burgers, veggie nuggets, and all those "fake" meat products, because to me they are genuinely satisfying and definitely lower in fat and calories than hamburgers and chicken, and I think they taste just as good. I know that they are pretty much junk because they're so processed, but I also like that there are no animals in them.)

11. Know Yourself

What do you really like to eat? How hungry are you? If you skip a meal, will you be fine or will you binge? If you don't know yourself, you won't be able to plan or balance your diet or make the right choices, so have a heart-to-heart with yourself and figure out who you are when it comes to food (and everything else).

12. Downsize

The portion sizes in this country are disgusting. People from Europe come here and they can't believe how much people eat. Gigantic iced coffees at Starbucks, tubs of soda, huge entrées in restaurants, slabs of cheesecake—we think we get value because of the money we save, but we end up spending even more on diets. Instead of giving in to overconsumption, start downsizing. Always order the small. Use small plates. Take small portions. If you start with too much, you're more likely to eat more than you really want. If you start with just a little, you might be surprised at how little it actually takes to satisfy you. And if you're still genuinely hungry, you can always get another small portion.

13. Sharing Is Caring

Sharing your food makes every meal nicer. Share with your kids, your partner, your friends. You'll eat less, enjoy the meal more, and save on the bill. Most restaurant portions are equal to at least two servings, so sharing is a good way to eat a more rational amount of food. I especially like sharing with Bryn. We tell kids to share their toys, so why don't more people encourage kids to share their food? When you share with your children, they'll eat healthier food because kid menus are typically junk. Your child will feel more grown-up, and you'll eat less, too. Recently, I was at Starbucks and Bryn wanted lemon pound cake. I knew she would only eat half, so I didn't order anything. I ate the other half, and we both got to enjoy a treat. It's win-win. Ordering a separate thing for every person is a trap. Share, and cut your losses.

14. Contain Yourself

Never eat out of the large bag (chips, pretzels, candy) or full-sized box (ice cream, cookies). That container is a bottomless pit of empty calories and you won't realize how much you're eating until the whole thing is gone. Unless it's a single-serving package, portion it out on a small plate or bowl every time. Make this a no-exceptions rule for yourself: The container is *not a serving dish*. I like to use individual-sized ramekins or dessert plates for my snacks. Enjoy what you've decided to eat, and if you really want more, you can decide to go back for seconds, but do it on purpose. Then it's your choice, rather than being mindless.

15. Don't Clean Your Plate

In *Naturally Thin*, I say, "Cancel your membership to the clean plate club." Some people automatically eat everything in front of them so the food isn't "wasted," but overeating and feeling lethargic and too full is the true waste of what could have been an enjoyable, guilt-free meal. Get in the habit of not quite finishing your food, even when you are downsizing your portions. "Healthy" is no excuse to lick the plate. Truthfully, I don't always leave something. There are exceptions to every rule, and when I have a small portion, I sometimes eat it all. Sometimes I go back for more. But my aim is to limit my portions to a sane amount. If you're paying attention, you'll notice when you don't really need any more, clean plate or not. (Unfortunately, you'll still have to do the dishes.)

16. Only the Good Die Young

Why spend your life feeling deprived? You should be able to enjoy your life, your friends, your family, and your food, as long as you pick your spots. If you really want something, have it. Just don't overdo it, and more important, don't feel guilty about it. When Bryn and I go to a diner on the weekend, we'll order a giant blueberry pancake the size of a mattress. It's fun! We share one or two, and we certainly don't finish the whole thing, but we want it and so we have it, exactly the way we like it (with a little maple syrup). As long as you don't inhale everything, you can enjoy decadent foods without guilt or regret. Being virtuous all the time is boring.

17. Check Yourself Before You Wreck Yourself

Here's the bottom line: No bingeing. It's my only unbreakable rule. I used to binge and now I never, ever do. Know the signs that it's starting and do whatever it takes to stop it. If you can't, you might need to seek professional help, and there is nothing wrong with that. If you often go off the rails because of your emotions and you don't have the ability to stop yourself, that's not hunger. That's a problem. Everybody has emotional days and starving days, but constant food obsession and self-loathing is what I'm talking about. You absolutely have to stop this, in whatever way possible. I feel you. I know what it's like. But I conquered it, and so can you.

Now I can't imagine bingeing anymore, but for a time, I had to design some tricks to stop myself. One of them was thinking of a stop sign. When I know I've eaten enough and I start getting the feeling that I want to keep going for reasons other than hunger, I imagine the stop sign popping up. If you take this stop sign as seriously as you would take a stop sign on the road, consider yourself checked and unwrecked. Every single time you don't binge, it's a victory, and it means you are slowly training your brain out of going into bingeing mode. It really does get easier with each successful check. I urge you to make a commitment right now to stop. If you are a binger, then checking yourself should be your number one most important food goal and priority before you worry about anything else. Fix that, and the rest will fall into place.

18. Think Outside the Box

If it comes in a box, a bag, or a package, pause before eating it and determine how badly you really want it. Processed food isn't as good for you as fresh food, and it usually doesn't taste as good. It's probably full of preservatives for a longer shelf life. Canned foods can contain aluminum or chemicals from the can lining, and foods packaged in plastic might contain residual chemicals, too, especially if you microwave them in the containers.

Not all processed food is bad. Just because it's in a package doesn't mean you shouldn't eat it. Some packaged food is very minimally processed, like frozen vegetables and staples like brown rice, whole wheat pasta, dried beans, and quinoa. To determine how processed the packaged food you want to eat is, read the label. If something has an ingredients list that covers the entire back of the box and is full of chemicals, artificial coloring, and things you can't pronounce, reconsider. I have a box of butternut squash in my freezer, and the ingredients list says: *butternut squash*. I feel fine about that. Even Fritos, surprisingly, contain just corn, oil, and salt. I'm not saying you should have a whole bag of Fritos, but if you're going to eat salty chips, there are much worse options. Bottom line: If it came from a factory, make a conscious decision before putting it in your mouth.

19. Listen Up

Are you hungry? Are you sure? It's important to listen to yourself so you know the real answer to that question. You should be able to tell the difference between real hunger and a mood that makes you want to eat for emotional reasons. A good way to start practicing is to notice how you feel when you first wake up in the morning. Are you in the habit of immediately eating breakfast, or do you even want breakfast? Maybe you want it a little bit later. Are you snacking out of boredom? Do you eat when you're depressed, or late at night, or because of anxiety, or because you're in love and feel free? Do you eat when you're out with the girls or when your boyfriend is being a jerk? Know thyself. It's common to eat out of habit or anxiety, but the only really good reason to eat is when your body tells you it's time, and you won't hear the cues unless you are listening.

20. Make a Plan

Before you start stuffing your face, take a beat and make a plan. Take a moment to figure out what you want to eat and what makes sense with what you already ate and what you're going to eat later. If you're going to a party later, eat smaller but regular meals. If you're having a snack, balance it with your earlier eating. If this is your big eating moment for the day, make a plan for the best, most enjoyable choices. Then execute your plan—put the food on a plate and enjoy it.

This rule is about never having to say, "Why did I just eat that?" or "What happened to the rest of the chips in this bag?" or "How could I have possibly eaten that much?" Eating shouldn't be Russian roulette. Even if it's decadent, you should be able to say, "I ate that because I wanted it, I enjoyed it, and I'm okay with it." You should be able to say, "I ate that because I have PMS and I'm really hungry. I'm allowing it." You are the one in charge, not the food.

21. Be Prepared

If you get caught starving with no option but fast food or junk, you're more likely to eat things you'll regret later. Never get caught without healthy snacks in your purse, desk drawer, car, and especially at home. Always have nuts, dried fruit, fresh fruit, half a sandwich, a can or box of healthy soup, or a Skinnygirl Daily On-the-Go bar handy (I'm never without one) so you're never desperate and ravenous.

22. No Shotgun Snacks

If you do get caught unprepared, no matter where you are or what you're doing, you can find something healthy to eat. Don't rush into a relationship with the first snack you meet. There are always options. Just take an extra minute. Go to the next counter at the mall, look into the aisles at the gas station or convenience store, scan all the options in the vending machine, or take something out of the cabinet and cook it. If you just work a little extra to get what you need, you can find a snack to make you feel good about yourself.

23. Cook Creatively

There are a million ways to make the foods you love lower in fat, sugar, and calories without sacrificing taste. My book *Skinnygirl Dish* has many: substitute egg whites for eggs; substitute applesauce or pumpkin puree for half the oil in baking; use veggie burgers and veggie bacon instead of the meat versions; eat more seafood than red meat; try low-fat or soy cheese instead of full-fat cheese; cut creamy dressing with half low-fat vinaigrette; and add as many vegetables as you can to your pasta, rice, soup, and salad. Make small changes every day, and they will add up.

24. Be Good to Yourself

Love yourself. Work on yourself. Play to your strengths. Wear things you feel good in. (Almost nobody actually feels good in a bikini, so don't sweat it.) Accentuate the positive. Do you have great arms? Great legs? Great hair? Great eyes? Make the most of your assets, especially your attitude. Confidence is the most attractive feature you can have—it's much more important than those five or ten pounds you're obsessing about.

25. Be a Skinnygirl

Stay calm. Be sensible. Find what works for you, and don't let life get you down. Make the choices that feel right to you. Indulge without bingeing. Invest when it matters and hold back when it doesn't. Being a Skinnygirl doesn't mean being "skinny" by any objective measure. It means being the best girl you can be, having confidence, and owning your own life. When you can do that, you are a Skinnygirl, even if you don't know it yet. When you've finally unleashed your power, you'll be changed forever.

Chapter Two
• • • • • • • • • • •

The Naturally Thin Quick-Start Plan

Don't let the title of this chapter fool you. I want you to find your own way and feel empowered to eat what *you* want to eat. That's why I've never believed in diets or "plans." When I first wrote *Naturally Thin*, I was pressured by my publisher to make a "diet plan," even though diets don't work. I refused.

But I do understand that sometimes, you want a little more guidance and structure. I'm never going to tell you to eat X on Monday for breakfast and Y for lunch and Z for a snack. That goes against everything I believe about naturally thin eating. I will, however, tell you what strategies can work to help you eat the foods you love and stay naturally thin.

I will also give you some examples of how I use these strategies and what choices I would probably make in a particular situation. It can be inspiring to see what someone else does, and it might help you see where you're going wrong if you're having trouble losing weight. This chapter's purpose is to help you know yourself better as you learn naturally thin habits. Old habits are hard to break, and while the twenty-five naturally thin principles are your tools, this chapter is about the structure you're building with those tools. This is a way to start letting the naturally thin principles become second nature to you.

This quick-start plan is easy and intuitive. It's about paying attention and reclaiming your life from the grip of food obsession. It's about how to eat on any given day, no matter what life throws at you.

Morning: Are You Hungry Yet?

Eating like a naturally thin person starts the moment you wake up. Is your first thought about food? Do you start eating before you're fully awake? I used to do this because I was obsessed with the idea that people who eat breakfast lose more weight, because I'd read that somewhere. My first thought of the day was always about food, and I decided that if breakfast was the most important meal of the day, like everybody says, then I should eat it. I ate it mindlessly without assessing my own hunger. That's not the way to start the day like a naturally thin person.

The only rule you need to remember in the morning is this:

Don't eat until you're actually hungry.

This can change your whole morning. It might feel wrong to you, but here's the truth: Breakfast *isn't* the most important meal of the day. Whatever meal you're eating in the moment, when you're genuinely hungry and ready to eat, is the most important meal of the day. It doesn't matter what time you eat breakfast. It doesn't even matter if you *skip* breakfast (unless you know yourself and know you will overeat later without breakfast).

If you're not hungry: Don't eat yet. Wait until you're hungry. Have some coffee or tea, if that sounds good to you. (But don't overdo it—too much caffeine can spike your insulin, causing excess hunger later.) If you have to get to work, bring something with you for later, like a banana and some Greek yogurt or something more hearty like a PB&J on whole wheat. Keep it in your desk or purse and eat it only when your body tells you it's ready for food. And if you aren't hungry until lunch? Have a small, protein-rich snack, like a small handful of nuts or a piece of cheese, to tide you over. I'll probably catch flak for saying that, but in my opinion, you don't need to eat breakfast every single day. People say it slows down your metabolism, but I don't believe that having a handful of nuts at ten A.M. rather than having a whole bowl of cereal with milk and fruit at seven A.M. will mess with your metabolism. What really messes with your metabolism is bingeing all day, then starving yourself the next day out of guilt.

Just remember that if you know that skipping breakfast, even when you're not hungry, will result in major overeating at lunch (I see this happen a lot with men in particular), then you need to eat something in the morning. Respect your own tendencies and work with them instead of against them.

If you are hungry: Eat breakfast. Do it deliberately, not randomly. Don't grab the first thing you see. Take some time to assess what you really want. Are you in the mood for eggs? Pancakes? A granola bar and a glass of milk? Whatever it is, make yourself a nice small plate, sit down, and enjoy your choice. Whether you're at home, a diner, or a deli, a small portion of what you really feel like eating will make you feel good and satisfied.

. . . .

MAKE A PLAN

If you don't want to think about what you want every morning, especially on mornings when you're in a hurry, it's fine to have a loose, adaptable plan for yourself that you usually follow. Choose something easy that you like, such as oatmeal or a hard-boiled egg and a piece of fruit. On your indecisive days, you won't waste time trying to figure out what to eat because you can default to your plan. Just remember it's okay to deviate from your plan when you want something different.

. . . .

What I Do

Some days, I have pancakes at seven A.M., and some days I have nothing but green juice until about ten A.M., when I finally get hungry. Before I had a baby, I usually slept until about eight o'clock. When I woke up, I would typically have a medium-sized coffee with soy milk. I eased into the day slowly. Around ten A.M., I would often have something light, like a scooped-out toasted whole wheat bagel with a little bit of real butter, or some cottage cheese and fruit.

Now I usually eat breakfast with Bryn, but every day is different. Some days, I'm not hungry. I might have coffee or juice. If I am hungry, I'll have a small bowl of cereal or a muffin. Bryn and I might go to a diner, or I'll cook eggs and veggie bacon or make pancakes. On the road, I might pick up oatmeal at Starbucks or, if I'm in the mood, eat half of a muffin from a bakery. Sometimes, all I want is fruit.

. . . .

DOWNSIZE

Bagels used to be small but now they're huge. Nobody needs all that starch or that many calories. My solution is to scoop my bagels. To scoop out a bagel, pull out some of the bread from the bagel, pinching it out with your fingers. Throw the extra bread away. It's the bagel experience for half the calories.

By the way, "whole wheat" is BS. It's marketing. Whole wheat bread is just a white-flour loaf with a little bit of whole wheat flour thrown in so it looks healthier. I eat it because it makes me feel better and I like the taste, even though I know it's not really doing anything for me. If you really want the benefits of whole grains, you have to find something that says "100 percent whole grain" and only contains whole-grain flour on the ingredients list. You'll know it's whole-grain if it's brown and coarse and you actually see grains in it. The only place to find really good whole-grain products is in a health-food store, but don't sweat it. Just do your best and have what you like. If you prefer the taste of the plain white bagel, just scoop it and you'll be fine. A white bagel isn't going to kill you.

. . . .

Midmorning Snack: Are You Sure You Need It?

A lot of plans and programs encourage snacking, and some require it, but I disagree with that. Don't just assume you need a snack. Your body will tell you if you're hungry or not. Listen to your food voice. Don't be a slave to the idea of snacking, but don't forbid it, either. Only you will know on any given day whether you really want or need one. It should never be automatic.

If you are genuinely hungry before lunch, have something small and healthy. Sometimes I'll have a few bites of a muffin, a small handful of nuts, a few crackers with hummus, or a Skinnygirl Daily On-the-Go bar when I'm out. Other days, I don't need a snack, so I don't have one. Free yourself from snack tyranny by giving yourself permission to forget about snacks if you're really too busy or breakfast was enough to hold you.

• •

CARB CONFUSION

I tell you to trust your body and tune in to what you really want to eat, but sometimes people tell me they can't trust their cravings because they'll just binge on carbs and sugar all day. Some people say that when they eat extreme amounts of carbs, they crave more carbs, and it can trigger a binge. Before I was naturally thin, I used to eat candy at night, right before I fell asleep. I would wake up wanting something sweet for breakfast, like a muffin or frozen yogurt. If this is you, you don't have to give up carbs. In fact, I think refusing to eat carbs is ridiculous, and low-carb diets are unhealthy. Instead, just remember that you personally need to go easy on the carbs (so-called good carbs as well as so-called bad carbs) and make sure you have some protein along with anything sweet or starchy. Some ideas:

- Mix a teaspoon of mini chocolate chips into Greek yogurt
- Have peanut or almond butter with your apple, crackers, or whole wheat toast
- Have milk or yogurt with your cereal
- Have a small handful of dark chocolate almonds

Protein with your carbs will help keep your blood sugar more level, so you don't have a crash and end up eating everything in the house later.

• •

Lunch: Balance It

It doesn't matter what time you have lunch. It doesn't have to be X number of hours from breakfast and you definitely don't need to force yourself to eat every three hours, or whatever people say. Eat lunch when you are hungry.

I know this doesn't work every day because you can't always control the time of your lunch. You might have a set lunch hour at work or a lunch meeting or a lunch date. Some days, you might not even get lunch. It's all fine. I'm not advocating skipping meals, but the fact is that on some days, lunch might not happen. Grab some green juice or a small snack when you get the chance, and don't freak out. When lunch happens, stop, take a breath, and make a deliberate choice that considers two things:

- What have you already eaten today?
- What do you want to eat right now?

The first question will help you balance your diet like you balance your bank account. If you had a sweet, starchy breakfast (pancakes, cereal, toast), then balance that with a more protein-vegetable lunch, like a salad with some lean protein or a hearty vegetable soup without noodles or rice (or just don't eat much of the noodles/rice).

If your breakfast was protein-rich (like eggs or turkey bacon), then it might be time for some carb energy. Maybe you'll choose a sandwich, a slice of pizza, noodles with lots of veggies, or something light like hummus with crackers and raw vegetables.

Also consider what you really want, not what you "should" have. Beyond the balancing part, the choice is up to you. Do you love sushi? Pasta? Mexican? A simple PB&J or a salad from the deli? Knowing yourself and how different foods are likely to make you feel, choose wisely but also choose what will taste good to you. You should enjoy your lunch.

What I Do

No two days are ever the same with me. Typically, after a morning out at the park, Bryn and I come home and eat lunch before she goes to preschool. We might have salad with some kind of protein, soup with a sandwich, whole wheat pasta or healthy mac and cheese, a white-meat turkey burger, tuna on whole wheat and some raw vegetables and dip, a gyro, pizza, or a Subway sandwich with all the veggies. It's always something different, based on what I had for breakfast, what I have in the house, or where we are if we're out.

. . . .

MOM TALK

I never understood the childhood obesity issue until I was a mom and going to the playground. Michelle Obama is right on track. I often see moms giving their kids chips and fruit snacks and smoothies all day, then forcing them to eat meals they're too full to eat. Kids scream, and they get cookies. They fall down and they get ice cream. They clamor for the chicken fingers and French fries, then when they don't eat them all, they get lectured for not finishing their lunch. It's so warped and bizarre and it's setting up the next generation to have serious food noise. We shouldn't be forcing our kids to overeat. We shouldn't be feeding tantrums with juice (although don't think I haven't done that twice this week already—a cup of juice is the new pacifier).

I'm not obsessive about how I feed Bryn. She eats a lot of different things because I present her with variety. She eats mac and cheese, ice cream, pizza, cookies, and Popsicles, but not all the time, and in small amounts. I never, ever force her to finish her food and when we go out, I order something from the regular menu that I know we will both like, and I share it with her. She never orders off the kids' menu.

I don't get why children's menus are full of junk. Because it's cheaper? Feeding our children nothing but chicken fingers and French fries is irresponsible. Why can't restaurants make better kid menus? They could add pureed zucchini to tomato sauce, make baked sweet potato fries, or use whole wheat crust on pizza or whole-grain pasta in macaroni and cheese. It wouldn't be that hard to do.

The seemingly insignificant habits your kids adopt now can get them addicted to sugar, make them think they don't like vegetables, or teach them to eat more than they really need because you force them to finish. It could take them years to break those habits. Instead of dooming them to a future of food dysfunction, make healthy choices for yourself and your child, at home and in restaurants. Share large portions, add vegetables and whole grains to meals wherever you can, and set a good example by the way you eat in front of them and with them. Introduce new healthy foods as often as you can. If you don't want them to eat something, don't have it in your house. Don't reward tantrums with food—they will stop crying when they realize their tactics don't work with you. You can have a huge impact today on who your children become, and you can start by ignoring the kids' menu.

· ·

Midafternoon Snack: Hunger Check

Are you genuinely hungry or just in the habit of a midafternoon snack? If you're fine, skip it. You don't need it. Don't cave in to snack anxiety. If you're genuinely hungry, have something that will carry you through until dinner. Snacks with some protein are best.

Dinner: Balance It!

Whether you have dinner early or late, be sure to ask yourself the same two questions you asked yourself at lunch:

- What have you already eaten today?
- What do you want to eat right now?

And additionally, ask yourself:

- Do you want to have dessert?
- Will you be drinking?

A day of eating is like a puzzle, especially as you're still learning to eat like a naturally thin person. What are you still missing? Look back over your day. Have you had enough vegetables today? Have you had enough protein? Could you use some more whole grains? Do you need more fiber? Are you starving? Craving something in particular? Are you thirsty? Are you feeling toxic and you just want something light, or ravenous and ready for a good hearty meal? Choose your meal based on an assessment of how your day has gone so far, what you have in the house or what's on the menu, and what sounds good to you. Consider whether you're likely to have dessert and whether you will be drinking alcohol. All these things help you decide where to put the last pieces of the puzzle. If you're not that hungry, eat something light. You can have a salad for dinner. It's not against the law. But if you're hungry, you can eat until you're satisfied. Just do it consciously and in balance with reasonable portions, and pick your spot with the decadent things like dessert and cocktails, and you'll be fine. And remember that a lighter meal leaves room for an evening snack!

MOMENT-OF-TRUTH JEANS

How do you know when you're on track? Forget the scale. I hardly ever weigh myself and I don't even own a scale. A much better measure of how you're doing is your moment-of-truth jeans—that pair of jeans that fits you perfectly when you're at a good weight and gets uncomfortable when you gain a few pounds. Try them every few weeks, to know for sure whether you're in the zone or off the rails. When you can't button them, that's your moment of truth. Caveat: Don't try them on if you already know they will be tight—it could backfire and make you self-loathe. If you do try them on and they are too tight, just breathe and work through it, and think about how you can get back into balance.

What I Do

Dinner is not necessarily a well-balanced or an entree/potato/vegetable meal every night in my house, and that's fine. Sometimes I pick my spot and have one great thing. Sometimes I taste everything, eat nothing. Sometimes I cook, or go out, or order in. Sometimes I eat light because I know I'll want a treat later. It all depends on what I've done so far that day, what I want, and what my schedule demands.

I often meet up with my friend Hoda Kotb for dinner. We like to taste a lot of different things and she has a similar "taste everything, eat nothing" philosophy, so we order appetizers. We might split a kale salad, crab cakes, and a grilled octopus appetizer. I'll get a side of Brussels sprouts, which of course are swimming in butter, but it's fine. They're vegetables. We also usually get an order of fries. I'll take a handful and put them on my plate and not keep going back for more. For dessert, we love to get apple crisp with ice cream. We'll each have a couple of bites, but we don't finish it. And we each have a martini. It is a filling and decadent-seeming meal, but in the end, neither one of us is stuffed. We really enjoy the variety, and we taste everything, eat nothing.

. . . .

DOWNSIZE

Sometimes, it's just the idea of a small portion that freaks people out. If you catch yourself having anxiety because you think your portion isn't big enough, maybe your eyes and your stomach aren't aligned. A small cupcake, a small scoop of ice cream, a small bowl of cereal, a small bag of chips, or a regular-sized muffin can seem inadequate next to the giant portions you're used to seeing. Try it anyway. Sometimes, a small portion is surprisingly satisfying, but your *eyes* give you anxiety when you see it: *Oh my God, just one cookie? I can't eat just one cookie!* It can also help to combine the cookie with a yogurt or a small latte, just something to make the cookie feel and look like a more substantial portion.

Trust me, there are plenty more cookies in your future, so having just one is fine. Take a deep breath, pay attention to how you feel *right now*, and remember that your eyes might be deceiving you. When you get comfortable with smaller portions, that anxiety will disappear.

· ·

Evening Snack: Just a Little

Dinner is often my smallest meal, which leaves me room for a treat in the evening, like a little bit of ice cream. It's what I enjoy, but I never gorge. I keep my portions small because I've learned that a small scoop of ice cream or a few bites of cake are enough for me.

I don't have an evening snack every single day. Nothing is automatic. If I had a big dinner, I won't need or want anything later because I've had enough. Before you plop down in front of the TV and grab the first bag of something, consider once again whether you really want it. Don't obsess about it, but if you need a snack every single night, you're not listening to your food voice.

And that's it's. That's the Naturally Thin Quick-Start Plan. It couldn't be easier. Nothing's off-limits. No anxiety, no pressure, no habits. Just genuine hunger, balance, and small portions. This is how I eat every day, and it's intuitive and natural for me. It's a habit. It can be for you, too. If you want more inspiration, pick up a copy of *Naturally Thin*.

If all this seems unnatural at first, don't worry. Just keep going. You'll consciously assemble the puzzle of your day of eating to keep it balanced. Just remember that you can go back for more if you need it, and if every choice doesn't exactly balance, it's okay. Do the best you can. Sometimes you'll have days where you're really hungry and you naturally need to eat more. Some days, you'll naturally need to eat less. If you have a carb-heavy day or a fat-heavy day, just pull back the next day. Balance can happen over the course of a week. It's not just day by day.

Most important, let go of your anxieties and learn to listen to your body. That's what naturally thin people do. Feed your body what it requires and what it desires—no less and no more. Remember that no food will make you fat in small amounts, so let yourself have what you really want, rein it in, and trust yourself. Soon, you'll do this without thinking and you'll be eating like a naturally thin person. You'll be free.

Chapter Three
. . . .

Troubleshooting Your
Weight-Gain Traps

Life is unpredictable. Some days, you're going to make good choices, and some days . . . not so much. You can have the best intentions in the world and be working hard to integrate new habits into your life, but then you get too busy to eat regular meals, your significant other tempts you into too much pizza and beer, you do too many shots and eat too many tortilla chips, or your kids talk you into fast food and you give in because it's easier. Maybe you just had a long, hard day and you really want another cocktail. Then there's just good old stress.

This is life, and food is a part of it. Just remember that no single meal will wreck you. However, eating the way you want to eat can be more challenging in certain situations. This chapter will give you some strategies for staying naturally thin even when it feels like you have an excuse not to.

Trap #1: "I'm Too Busy to Eat Well!"

Hey, if I'm not too busy to eat well, nobody is. I have days where I never stop moving from dawn to dusk, and I know all too well that when you're working all the time, it can be hard to find a good meal, let alone find the time to sit down and enjoy it. When you don't eat all day, you're going to be ravenous at night and you could set yourself up for a binge.

Instead, be smart about your day. You can handle any situation as long as you're prepared. If it's a stressful time, you don't have to be actively losing weight. Coast and maintain, and you won't gain. You'll get back to more fruits and vegetables and cooking your own dinner when you have more time. Here's how to keep it under control right now:

- **Snack smart.** Snack on what's in your purse or desk, not out of the candy jar, or you'll crash later. If you have to resort to the vending machine, there are smart choices in there. You don't have to get candy. Try a package of crackers with peanut butter, baked chips, or pretzel crisps. Just keep it under about two hundred calories. Occasionally, maybe you'll get something sweet, like licorice or even chocolate. No worries.

· ·

NOTES FROM JACKIE

Sometimes, I feel like I'm in the dungeon—I'm so busy that I can't leave the office for lunch, or I know that as soon as I leave, all hell will break loose. There are days when I don't get a chance to use the bathroom until four P.M.! For those crazy days, I keep a snack box in the office with food I can eat while I'm working, like almonds, fruit, pretzel crisps, dried mangoes or raisins, and Skinnygirl Daily bars. I was so excited when the Skinnygirl Daily bars first came out. It's my favorite product because I can break into it when I'm starving. I think I went through three boxes a week when we got our first shipment. I was like, *Thank God she's making food!*

· ·

- **Try not to skip meals.** When I was on *The Apprentice: Martha Stewart*, everybody else was living on street food and energy drinks, but I took time to make myself something quick and healthy, like soup or a sandwich. It's how I kept going without crashing while others were dropping like flies. If you bring your lunch to work, you will avoid this trap completely. Keep it uncomplicated if you have to eat on the run or in the car. A cheese sandwich on whole wheat, peanut butter and jelly, fruit—these simple foods will hold you over until you have time for an afternoon snack or dinner. Or make up a little box for yourself like I make for Bryn. It has dividers and I fill each section with a little bit of something: cheese, apple slices, edamame. It's purposeful and fun to eat. But if you don't have time for that, just do the best you can.

. . . .

ONLY THE GOOD DIE YOUNG

If I do go out for lunch (which is rare), I might have one glass of wine or a light cocktail. I'm not going to start swilling martinis at noon when I've still got work to do, but I'm not going to be a teetotaler just because it's before five P.M. I want to enjoy lunch! Of course, how much you drink during the day depends on your job. It's my job to taste the new flavors of Skinnygirl cocktails, so if margaritas are on the to-do list for my afternoon, what choice do I have? It's a tough job, but somebody has to do it.

. . . .

• **Manage your after-work hunger.** When you get home at the end of the day and you're starving, it's tempting to have a glass of wine and eat a pound of cheese while you're cooking dinner. If you know you're at risk for mindlessly snacking on a full meal and then eating dinner, too, have a quick snack before you start cooking. Choose something high in volume but low in calories, like a can of organic soup or a quick salad. Or, if you know you can compensate for it at the table by eating less, then snack while you cook and taste as you go. Some people prefer to cook this way. There are no rules, as long as you know yourself.

Truthfully, when you're trying to lose weight, being busy and on the go all the time can be a blessing. Use it to your advantage. When I'm on the run, I often forget all about food until it's time to stop and have a meal. When I'm not busy, I eat more because I'm bored. As long as you stay just slightly organized so you have something healthy on hand to eat, be glad you're too busy to spend the day thinking about food.

. . . .

WHEN YOU WORK AT HOME

When you work at home like I do, sometimes eating is a great temptation. The kitchen is right *there*, and food may be more attractive than finishing up a project that's difficult or boring. There are a million ways to avoid shoving something in your mouth. (I could make a joke here, but I'm a mother now.) Some alternatives:

- Get up and do a few yoga poses or stretching.
- Take a bath.
- Give your dog or cat some attention.

- Organize your closet for fifteen minutes.
- Listen to a song or watch a video you really like.
- Take a walk, or just step outside and get some sun on your face and breathe the fresh air.
- Have sex. Or masturbate. Why not enjoy a little "afternoon delight"?
- Take a beat and consider whether you're actually hungry or just looking for an excuse to procrastinate. If you buckle down and just finish, you can knock off sooner.

Trap #2: "My Significant Other Sabotages Me!"

Sometimes I think men are robots fueled on protein. They all think they're lumberjacks and they need enormous slabs of meat or they'll drop dead. Why do men have this idea that dinner has to be a huge event? Years ago, I spent many Sundays tailgating with a former boyfriend. We mainlined steak sandwiches and Bloody Marys for hours, and after the game, he was ready to go out for Chinese because he always went out for Chinese on Sundays and needed "a real meal." Are you kidding me?

Most of the women I know are perfectly happy to have a light dinner if they aren't very hungry, like a can of soup or a hummus sandwich or a little bit of leftover pasta or rice. Sometimes you just don't want to wreck the kitchen and have to clean it up. I really don't get the whole meat-potato-vegetable-dessert-event mentality surrounding dinner, like life is one big Hungry Man TV dinner. Dinner doesn't have to be the biggest meal of the day. It's not even a crime to skip dinner if you're really not hungry. The next time your guy demands a big dinner when you don't want one, point him to the nearest diner and tell him to knock himself out.

Of course, maybe your partner isn't like that, and maybe your partner isn't even a man. That doesn't mean you won't still feel sabotaged sometimes, because not everybody has the same hunger at the same time. Most dates revolve around eating, and sharing a meal is a nice way to touch base with someone during a busy day. When you live together, of course you will share meals, but eating with someone else can make you feel like you aren't able to eat the way you want to. Here are some strategies for keeping it together without being one of those girls who can't have a good time:

- **Do your own thing.** You don't have to make a big deal about it and you shouldn't feel you have to make up some fake food allergy just to keep yourself from being "forced" to eat something. You and your date don't have to eat exactly the same things. So your date wants to share a hot dog or pizza or beer at the ballpark? Have a few bites, have a few sips, and move on, or tell him (or her) you'd love a pretzel and some mustard. At a movie, share a popcorn and have a few handfuls. You don't need to make any excuses. Don't say you're on a diet. That's a mood killer, and if you're naturally thin, you don't diet anyway. Nobody's paying as much attention to how much you eat as you are, so participate in your own way without gorging and all your date will notice is that you're fun.

- **Don't be a salad bitch.** That's the girl who only orders salad and constantly bothers the waiter with special requests about dressing on the side, no cheese, no croutons, no olives. That's called a pain in the ass. I used to be a salad bitch, especially on dates, because I didn't want to gain weight, but then I'd go home and binge-eat because I was starving. You should be able to get what you want, but guys will go running for the hills if you're going to be that high maintenance on a first date, and he definitely won't think you're good in the sack if you're that constricted about a salad. It's an indicator. Instead, you can be the cool girl—

the girl who actually eats and enjoys it. When you enjoy your date instead of having an anxiety attack about how many fat grams are in the salad dressing, maybe you'll actually get to enjoy the person you're with. He's certainly more likely to enjoy you.

- **Disguise healthy food.** Whether you've invited a new love interest over for the first "I'll cook you dinner" date or you're living with or married to someone, and especially if you have kids, you should be able to cook food you like to eat. You don't have to be a short-order cook, making different meals for everybody. Solve the problem by making the foods everyone likes, but with small adjustments to reduce fat and calories and increase the nutrition. For example:

  ° *Mix ranch dressing 1:1 with light vinaigrette.*
  ° *Make red meat less often, in favor of chicken, salmon, or roast turkey. Every date meal or Sunday dinner doesn't have to be a steak dinner.*
  ° *Include side dishes like a big salad, fruit, veggie soup, roasted vegetables, brown rice, or whole wheat pasta. When you indulge in man-eater-style meals, just serve yourself a small portion and fill up on the side dishes.*
  ° *Remake comfort food to be healthier. Try turkey or veggie lasagna, turkey meatloaf, healthier ziti with vegetables, veggie chili, stews, stir-fries, one-pot dinners, and homemade desserts with reduced fat and sugar. (See my cookbook, Skinnygirl Dish, for hundreds of ideas.) As long as you don't make a big deal about it, nobody will notice.*

Trap #3: "But I'm a Food Lover!"

I'm a food lover, too, but that's no excuse to be a glutton. In fact, it's more of an excuse to be choosy and selective. A true food lover will savor and relish the very best foods, and healthy foods are some of the best. But I get what you're saying—you like the decadent foods. The foie gras, the truffles, the fancy cheese, the Belgian chocolate. No problem. There is a line between enjoying an indulgence and overindulging, and you know where it is. Your line might be in a different spot than mine, but if you are paying attention to what you eat and how you feel, you will know automatically when your behavior crosses the line. You might still decide to cross it, but know you crossed the line and be prepared to balance it at the next meal.

To me, crossing the line is eating things like deep-fat-fried Oreos. Did someone invent those just to prove how disgusting they could be? A Paula Deen recipe for bread pudding with condensed milk, canned fruit salad, and Krispy Kreme doughnuts? It's just vile. Injecting foie gras into hamburgers? It's true gluttony. It's food porn. It's not gourmet, it's gross. Do you really want to go there?

I cross the line sometimes. I'm not going to lie. I'll have a peanut butter Rice Krispies Treat with chocolate frosting. Hell, I'll eat frosting with a spoon right out of the can. I'm that annoying person who eats a cupcake and then eats the icing off three other cupcakes. Frosting on a spoon is over the line, but I know that, so I compensate for it. There's a restaurant in Miami Beach called Prime One Twelve that has decadent chocolate peanut butter s'mores with vanilla cream and fudge. I live for those s'mores. I want to do naughty things to those s'mores. They are completely over the line, but I just take a few bites. I'm not scraping the plate with my spoon.

You want to enjoy life, and so do I. You don't want to miss a great new restaurant or the signature dish of a city you've never been to before, and neither do I. I'm right there with you. I love to explore food and cook food and go on food crawls. I want to eat out and bake desserts and *live*, and I can do all those things and still be naturally thin. So can you.

You just need to stay focused, pay attention, listen to your body, balance what you eat, and never settle for less than the very best. No guilt. No regret. Keep it moving and you can be a foodie who also happens to be naturally thin.

Trap #4: "But It's Girls' Night Out!"

Friends can be a bad influence. When you're all out together, you'll probably laugh about how you'd rather be fat and happy and how you'll be good tomorrow, but then you're going to wake up feeling bloated and guilty. Bingeing on girls' night out is just an excuse. Misery loves company. If your girlfriends have bad eating habits, you can be subjected to peer pressure, or what I call "portion pressure." Friends with overweight friends are more likely to be overweight, but I'm not telling you to ditch your friends or be the girl who spoils all the fun because she can't have another four-calorie asparagus spear.

Girls' night out can be an opportunity instead of a liability. How often do you get to order eight different appetizers and try them all? This is what I call friends with benefits. When I go out with a group of friends, we order several things and we all share. Everybody chimes in with what they like, we have a cocktail or two, and we all get the experience of tasting everything while eating nothing. Nobody gets weighed down by a whole entrée and nobody has to be envious about someone else's order. If it's not enough, you can order more, but if you focus more on your friends and having fun and where you're going to go dancing next, you probably won't have to.

Trap #5: "But My Kids Won't Eat That!"

People often complain to me that they can't lose weight because of what their kids eat. I don't understand this at all. What's good for the goose is good for the gander, and why would you give your children anything to eat that you wouldn't eat yourself? In fact, there should be nothing in your house you wouldn't eat. If it's junk food, nobody should be eating it. That doesn't mean you and your child can't enjoy the occasional cookie, candy, or chips. You don't have to be militant about it, but if it's neon or full of artificial ingredients, skip it.

I serve my daughter plenty of "fun" foods, but I make them healthier. For example, we make veggie nuggets that taste like chicken, and the only thing juvenile about them is that they might be in fun shapes. I eat those sometimes. I make her macaroni and cheese with soy milk and mix butternut squash into it. We'll have whole wheat waffles for breakfast, or whole-grain cereal. She eats regular pizza (which, by the way, is perfectly healthy in moderation) and French fries and pretzels and tortilla chips and most things other kids eat, but in a mostly healthy way. I don't obsess about it. Most of the time, her food is nutritious, like it should be for anyone.

I never push her to finish her food. Nobody is going to starve if they don't eat every bite. I also don't jump to finish her food myself. If she doesn't finish something, I wrap it up and put it in the fridge for her to finish later. If I know I'll finish what she doesn't eat, I anticipate this by eating a little bit less—I'll pour myself less cereal knowing she might not finish her waffle, or I'll just have a salad, knowing I'll probably eat the last couple of veggie nuggets. In a café, if she wants a muffin or a cookie, I know she'll only eat a little, and I can enjoy it, too. Why waste food by ordering something for everyone when kids don't eat very much? Most important, never force your children to finish every bite of their food! It's better to throw away a few bites of something than teach your children that they can't trust their own food instincts. If she's full, she's full. Period. The same goes for you.

Disguising healthy food works for kids, too. If your family already has some bad habits, start ditching the junk but transition the food you make or order gradually. Add pureed vegetables to macaroni and cheese, spaghetti sauce, or even smoothies. Switch to whole grains. Reduce meat consumption. My daughter is not on any kind of diet and she has full-fat dairy because kids need fat for growth, but you can put skim milk or soy milk on your own cereal. And remember, sharing is caring.

The bottom line is that your children aren't old enough to be in charge of what the whole family eats, so why do you think their tastes should govern the meal planning? You're in charge, so step up.

Trap #6: "I'm Starving After I Work Out!"

Ironically, exercise can be a fat trap because it makes you hungrier. I exercise to stay lean and for peace of mind, but it has nothing to do with the scale. I used to overexercise, and then I'd be starving and I would overeat. Just because you're exercising doesn't mean you have a license to eat everything. Exercise without overdoing it and you won't feel compelled to overdo your meals, either. (For more about exercise, see chapter 5.)

Trap #7: "But Eating Makes Me Feel Better!"

Nobody eats just for fuel. Food is more complex than that. It's tied up with our feelings and our past, in both negative and positive ways. We eat to calm ourselves, cheer ourselves up, or celebrate. That's normal. What's not normal is when you binge-eat or overeat because you are trying to fill up something with food that really needs some other kind of attention.

If you are prone to emotional eating, if you are a secret eater or a closet eater, or if you feel like you can't eat what you would normally eat in front of other people, then there is definitely a problem. Tell somebody that you do it. Talk about it. Find an online support group. You might need to talk to a professional. Explore the emotions behind it and think about why this happens to you. You have to get ahold of this kind of behavior. It will wreck your health. You have to understand that you're not bad.

If you're more the person who just tends to eat when you're stressed or depressed or anxious, that's very common. It doesn't mean you have an eating disorder, but you have to pull yourself out of those moments and step back. You will be more depressed or have more anxiety or stress if you overeat. Look at the big picture. Find something else to do that will make you feel better instead of worse later. Remember my only unbreakable rule: Do not binge. Emotional eating is a habit and it's hard to break, but you can replace emotional eating with something else, like emotional walking or emotional talking on the phone or emotional listening to music. You'll be healthier and it will be worth the effort.

. . . .

TO TELL OR NOT TO TELL

Trying to lose weight can put you in a hyperemotional state. If you tell people you're on a diet, it might create a source of support. They can encourage you. Or it might make things worse if you feel like everybody is wondering, *Are you doing it? Are you losing weight?* It might be too much pressure. You have to know yourself and know whether it's a good idea for you to tell people you're trying to lose weight, or not tell. Working on weight loss can be your own thing, and that's okay. If you're eating to be naturally thin, you're eating normally anyway, so what is there to talk about?

. . . .

We all associate strong positive feelings with certain foods. Hot cocoa in winter, chips and margaritas on vacation or at a Mexican restaurant, candy and sweets during the holidays, ice cream when you break up with someone, barbecue in summer. All these events in life are linked with food, and they can all be great in moderation. They make life sweet. But they aren't the only parts of life to enjoy. In winter, you can celebrate by buying a fluffy sweater. On vacation, you can sightsee or lie on the beach. On holidays, enjoy being with friends and family. When you break up with someone, escape with a good movie. There are so many ways to enjoy life and celebrate without resorting to overeating. Expand your horizons. Think outside the box. There is more to life than food.

Chapter Four

What to Eat

People always ask me what I eat, and they also want to know what they should eat—on certain kinds of days, in certain situations, on holidays, at restaurants. In this chapter, I'll give you a glimpse into what I eat, in case you need inspiration, motivation, or ideas for those days when you have PMS or a hangover, when you go out for Chinese food, or when you panic because you're at an all-inclusive resort and you can eat everything for "free." I've got tips and menus and strategies for every situation.

I've personally eaten all these things and in all these combinations, but truthfully, I'm not always so balanced. Some days, I might eat an entire bowl of fried rice for lunch. Another day, I might skip breakfast. These are just my ideas for what might work for you in a variety of situations, based on what has worked for me.

Your Basic Feel-Bad Day

On a feel-bad day, I want to make myself feel better, and I usually do that with comfort food. Whether I'm depressed, anxious, irritable, sleep deprived, or just had one too many the day before, on a basic feel-bad day I usually crave salt, sugar, and fat, and I tend to eat things like eggs, salty snacks, and ice cream. Dinner is often pasta because it's comforting.

Portion control is very important on these days, so I really watch how much I eat of these decadent foods. Especially when I had too much to drink the night before, I know my body is trying to replenish and hydrate, so I also keep at hand a full glass of club soda with a splash of juice. Here's what I'm likely to eat:

BASIC FEEL-BAD DAY	
Breakfast	Breakfast burrito or wrap with egg whites and a whole-grain tortilla. Keep the additions on the light side—salsa and vegetables, and only a little if any cheese and sour cream.
Lunch	Half of a sandwich or a piece of pizza.

Afternoon	A small bag of baked barbecue chips.
Dinner	Comfort food like angel hair pasta with red sauce and maybe a glass of wine.
Evening snack	Small cup of ice cream or frozen yogurt with sprinkles, or a few more handfuls of chips.

On a Famished Day

Some days, you just wake up really hungry, so focus on volume. High-volume, high-fiber foods fill you up without the dense fat and calories in more decadent foods that need more portion control. You can eat more and still end up in balance. You might also be famished on days when you work out a lot or have demanding physical activity, whether work or play. On days when I'm snowboarding, I'm famished. Here's what I might eat:

FAMISHED DAY	
Breakfast	Whole wheat pancakes or an egg-white omelette with a lot of veggies. On the run, oatmeal is a filling option. Add soy milk and fresh fruit for volume.
Lunch	Whole wheat veggie sandwich with cheese and avocados or tuna salad, or a Cobb salad or Caesar salad. I might or might not eat the whole thing—if it has a lot of bacon and blue cheese, I probably won't finish it. On a ravenous day, I might just tear right into a big bowl of fried rice because I can't wait.
Afternoon	A Skinnygirl Daily On-the-Go bar or half a brownie.
Dinner	Two spicy crab sushi rolls and a salad, or crab cakes with a green salad. I might just make a mishmosh, like a bowl of soup, a sweet potato, a salad, and some hummus and crackers.
Evening snack	If I'm still craving something sweet, I might have half of a large chocolate chip cookie.

On a Sick Day

When you wake up with a sore throat or a queasy stomach or that all-over feeling that things just aren't right in your body, pamper your system in an easy way. When I'm sick, I'm not very hungry but I'll drink juices and smoothies and eat soup to flush out whatever virus is trying to take hold. It's good to hydrate when you're sick. When I want something sweet, Popsicles are perfect. Sometimes I just want comfort food and salt. This is what I'll typically eat on a sick day:

SICK DAY	
Breakfast	Fruit smoothie.
Lunch:	Vegetable noodle soup, Popsicle.
Afternoon	Green/apple juice, or watermelon.

Dinner	Chinese food, like vegetable mu shu, steamed dumplings, brown rice, and spicy sautéed broccoli.
Evening snack	Another Popsicle, or maybe fresh fruit.

On a PMS Day

Hormonal PMS days aren't egg-white-and-salad kinds of days. These are salt-sugar-fat days, so I keep my portions down but I have whatever I'm craving. I don't hold back on dairy during PMS days either as I've found that calcium is good for PMS symptoms and cramps. If I'm feeling bloated, I'll eat lighter than this, but this is a typical hormonal day of eating. Here's an example of what this might include:

PMS DAY	
Breakfast	Homemade blueberry pancakes with real maple syrup, or whole-grain cereal and a Starbucks decaf misto with soy milk. (To be totally honest, one morning I had PMS and I ate half of a gigantic piece of chocolate cake with lots of icing.)
Lunch	A veggie burger or a turkey burger on a whole wheat bun with low-fat cheese, ketchup, and mustard, or if I'm craving something sweet, maybe just a peanut butter and jelly sandwich on whole wheat and a cup of soup.
Afternoon	A kiddie-sized cup of ice cream or frozen yogurt with sprinkles or a few dark chocolate almonds. (PMS days are sugar-craving days for me.)
Dinner	Whole wheat pasta with pesto sauce. If I'm going out, I might want the salty/spicy taste of Thai food, or I might order in Chinese and eat it on the couch with a heating pad and a side of Advil.
Evening snack	A small cookie or a few bites of a brownie or chips and a glass of wine.

On a Super-Busy Day

On many days, I literally have no time to cook. I need to make things fast or grab something when I'm out, but there are good options for those super-busy days. Here's what I might do:

SUPER-BUSY DAY	
Breakfast	Blueberry muffin from Starbucks or oatmeal with dried fruit and coffee with soy milk.
Lunch	Veggie nuggets and a salad with chickpeas, cucumbers, lettuce, and tomato.
Afternoon	Skinnygirl Daily On-the-Go bar from my purse or pretzel crisps and hummus (these come in a kit).
Dinner	Miso soup, salad with ginger dressing, edamame, one spicy scallop sushi roll, and one spicy crab avocado roll.
Evening snack	When I finally get home, I might relax with a small cup of ice cream to unwind.

On a Kid Day

When I spend the day with Bryn and we're eating together, I think it's nice if we can eat the same things and share. I focus on foods she likes (and that most kids would like), but I make them healthier for both our benefit. I know Bryn will get crazy on too much sugar, so I limit that, but I never limit fat or her portion sizes. Kids need healthy fat, and I want her to eat as much as she wants—no more, no less. Here's what I might make for both of us on a day we spend together:

KID DAY	
Breakfast	Multigrain squares (cereal) or a whole wheat waffle.
Lunch	Edamame, whole wheat grilled cheese sandwich, and steamed broccoli, or whole wheat macaroni and cheese with butternut squash puree mixed in and veggie "chicken" nuggets.
Afternoon	Baked chips, homemade granola, or a small scoop of ice cream.
Dinner	Cheese pizza, salad, strawberries.
Evening snack	Small cookie, glass of soy milk.

• •

MOM TALK

Kids need plenty of calories for growth, but I want Bryn to get her calories from healthy sources like avocado, peanut butter, full-fat yogurt, nuts, and milk, rather than junk food.

• •

· ·

COOK CREATIVELY

This is a nice alternative to a fattening Cobb salad that you can make at home for a fraction of the price. Try my healthier version. On top of chopped romaine lettuce, add chopped turkey breast, crumbled veggie bacon, hard-boiled egg whites, a few avocado cubes, and a side of ranch dressing mixed with half low-fat vinaigrette. Top with very small crumbles of blue cheese to make a little go a long way. It's the Cobb salad experience for a fraction of the calories.

· ·

Eating Out

I get many questions about what to order in different kinds of restaurants. You should never feel like you can't go out to a restaurant because there won't be anything healthy. There is *always* a healthy choice. However, remember that restaurants only care about taste, so restaurant food is usually high in oil, butter, cream, bread crumbs, etc. If a stick of butter makes their customers happy, they'll use it! Just keep in mind that portion size is everything. Here's what I tend to choose in different kinds of restaurants:

In a Japanese Restaurant

Japanese food can be really healthy or really fattening, depending on what you order. Beware the tempura and sushi rolls with mayonnaise and "crunch," which is just bits of deep-fat-fried batter.

- Edamame is a great high-protein snack and a way to fill up before your entrée. Also fill up on miso soup and seaweed or green salad with ginger dressing.
- Ask for brown rice or a half portion of rice and/or light mayo in your sushi rolls. You can be very specific because

sushi rolls are made to order. Rice paper is the new craze, but I'm not into it because I love seaweed. Maybe you'll try it and like it.

- My favorite sushi rolls are the spicy crab, spicy shrimp, and spicy scallop. They are made with mayonnaise, but I ask them to leave out the "crunch" and I keep my portions small. You can also ask them to go light on the mayonnaise or rice.
- Watch the soy sauce, just because it's high in sodium.
- Sashimi is free. Knock yourself out. You can also request no rice in your hand rolls.
- If you want dessert, try green tea ice cream, lychees, or orange slices.

In a Chinese Restaurant

Chinese restaurants are usually pretty good about making your food the way you want it, but although the entrees seem healthy, many foods are fried—fried rice, wontons, egg rolls, spring rolls, crab Rangoon, shrimp toasts, etc. Pick your spot and fill up on the vegetables and protein. I usually ask them to skip the sugar, MSG, and cornstarch, and I avoid eggplant because it's a fat sponge. Some things I do order:

- Brown rice (if they have it).
- Egg drop, hot and sour, or wonton soup. The soups are salty, so stick with a small. It will still be filling.
- Sautéed vegetables—this is where you can really fill up.
- Chicken, shrimp, or beef with white sauce on the side. I've found white to be the least heavy Chinese sauce. You can also choose a tofu entrée, but they often fry the tofu so ask for it steamed instead.
- Mu shu is mainly shredded cabbage and vegetables, but go easy on the pancakes and condiments because it already has a sauce.
- Steamed vegetable dumplings.
- If you really love fried rice, ask for light oil, egg whites only, and brown rice if possible.

- For fried appetizers and entrées with a lot of oil, just have a few bites and move on.
- If you love the noodles and meaty dumplings, just have a few bites. They are treats.
- Remember not to eat out of the container. Put your food on a real plate.

In a Thai Restaurant

Thai food is similar to Chinese food but lighter. They have great salads and summer rolls, which aren't fried but are instead wrapped in soaked rice paper and filled with veggies, and Thai salad contains papaya, which in this salad is not a fruit but more like a crisp fresh cucumber. The spicy sauces can be high in sugar, salt, and fat, but if you keep your quantities down, you don't have to worry about it. Watch the noodles, though. Everybody wants pad thai, and that's fine, but eat the chicken or tofu and vegetables out of it and just have a little bit of the noodles and peanut sauce. Cellophane or glass noodles are lighter.

· ·

TASTE EVERYTHING, EAT NOTHING

Asian restaurants have so many tasty options that tend to be high in fat and salt that they are ideal places to practice "taste everything, eat nothing." Order family style and share with a group. You'll get to try a few bites of a few different appetizers and a few different entrées. You can pace yourself while you're in the experience of the meal and come out of it still feeling good.

· ·

In a Mexican Restaurant

It's easy to go through a whole basket of chips before you've even ordered. If you love the tortilla chips with salsa and guacamole like I do, you should have them. Put a handful of chips on your plate and don't dip back into the basket after they're gone. If you know you can't control yourself with the chips, ask for a tortilla. Break that into pieces and use that instead of the chips. When it's gone, you stop. Salsa is a healthier choice than guacamole, even though guacamole is fine in small amounts, so have a few dips of the guac and focus on the salsa, or mix them together. Ceviche is a great low-fat Mexican dish. I hope your restaurant of choice carries Skinnygirl Margaritas!

- Salads in Mexican restaurants aren't great choices when they come covered in cheese and sour cream in those big fried tortilla shells, but if you love them, pick your spot. Do you want the shell? Stick to the vegetables and cheese. Do you want the guacamole and beans? Skip the cheese and sour cream and use salsa as the dressing.
- Fajitas are a good choice, but they often come with rice, cheese, beans, and sour cream, so fill up on the veggies and some protein. Do you really want to wrap it in a tortilla? Then pass on the rice. If you don't care about the tortilla, have a few bites of the beans and rice.
- Veggie burritos are another good choice, but they are huge, so cut them in half. Do you need rice and beans and cheese and sour cream? Pick the ingredients you like the most but have it filled mainly with vegetables.
- The big lure at a Mexican restaurant is the frozen-drink machine. Who doesn't want a margarita? Here's my solution: Order a clear (white) tequila on the rocks and ask them to put just a splash of the frozen concoction in the glass. Add a squeeze of lime, and you get the fun effect without all the calories. You're participating, but you're doing it your way. (If this is too strong, add some club soda.)
- Dessert at a Mexican restaurant? What's the point, unless you're into flan? I'm not, so for me, it's not worth it. I'd rather drink my dessert, and if you had a margarita, that's what you did. My one exception: I might have a few bites of a really good churro.

In an Italian Restaurant

Italian restaurants are all about comfort food and I love them, but I have a few ground rules:

- Have one or two bites of bread with butter or olive oil, then save room for the rest of the meal. Even if it's the best bread I've ever had, I take that as a sign that the rest of the meal will be great, too. Be the person who can have bread, move on, and enjoy the main attraction.
- Stick to one or two drinks. At an Italian restaurant, it's all about the food.
- Pick a green side dish like broccoli rabe or spinach, one appetizer, and any healthy entree like seafood or grilled chicken.
- A small Caesar, seafood, or arugula salad with lemon and olive oil will fill you up before the meal. Hold the croutons unless you're skipping the bread. You can also fill up on a good minestrone or pasta fagioli. These soups are thick, so you only need a small cup.
- If you order pasta, stick to tomato-based sauces or olive oil and garlic and keep portions small for sure, especially if your pasta is dripping with oil. Pasta with cream sauce only warrants a bite or two, at most. Add some protein, like chicken or shrimp, and as many vegetables as you can. Some restaurants will give you a half order, or you can share with someone. You can also wrap half to go.
- Watch out for the chicken dishes, which are mostly dipped in flour, eggs, and butter, and fried. That includes Milanese, piccata, Marsala, and Parmesan. If you can find roasted, broiled, or grilled chicken, that's a healthier choice, but these still likely contain a lot of oil, so just watch your portions.
- Grilled lamb chops and sautéed shrimp dishes are good options. Anything roasted is good.
- Treat dessert like you treated the bread basket: Have a few bites and move on. One perfect bite of tiramisu is better, in

my opinion, than a big bowl of boring berries or sorbet. (By the way, if your date orders sorbet or berries, he's either gay or boring in bed. Beware the berries!) I might also get an after-dinner liqueur. The sugar can give me a headache, but I like the vibe.

• •

TASTE EVERYTHING, EAT NOTHING

I hate being stuck with one entrée, thinking, *I have to look at you all night?* I'd rather order multiple dishes so everyone at the table can try a little bit of everything. I'll choose flavor over volume every time. Some women prefer to have their own entrée, just like they prefer to stay with one man for life. I'm sure they'll be very happy with the chicken, but I say, why not have a couple of one-night stands with the calamari and the French fries?

• •

In a Steakhouse

If you like steak, enjoy it. Don't worry about the fat, but you don't need the meat covered in butter or sauce (if you love the sauce, get it on the side). Most steaks are huge and one person doesn't need more than four or five ounces, so split one or ask for a small steak. Ask them to slice it, so you can have little pieces. This might make it easier for you to decide when you're full, because you can pause after each piece. Some more tips:

- Start with a salad. Steakhouse foods are rich, so it's good to fill up with raw veggies first. Steakhouses have a lot of really high-fat salad options, so if you have to have the wedge with blue cheese and bacon or a Caesar salad, share it with someone. If you're really hungry, get a big mixed-green salad so you can eat more.
- Try one or two bites of the bread with butter, then move it away. You tasted it. Now move on.

- Order one decadent side dish and have a few bites of it. I like the potato, fries, creamed spinach, or macaroni and cheese.
- Order one healthy side dish, like sautéed vegetables.
- Shrimp cocktail and oysters are great options because they are low in calories but feel decadent and special.
- If you can't resist the restaurant's "famous" dessert, have a bite or two so you can say whether it really was worth all the hype.

. . . .

TOPPING OFF

I almost always have a drink when I go out to eat, and I prefer cocktails because you know how much you're drinking. The problem with wine, especially if you get a bottle, is your waiter (or your date) might keep filling up your wineglass when you've only had half of it. This constant topping off can mean you think you've had two glasses when you've actually had six. Then you stand up and realize you can't walk out of the restaurant in your five-inch heels.

. . . .

At Brunch Buffets

Brunch buffets are dangerous and one of the most important places where you need to make a plan. Don't bullshit yourself with the "This is breakfast and lunch" line, because you could easily eat more than two meals' worth of calories at a good brunch buffet. Know yourself. But if you really want to get into the brunch experience, don't try to do everything. You can have it all, but not all at once. Pick a lane and stay in it:

- The egg lane: Get an egg and some turkey bacon and maybe one piece of whole-grain toast. If you go back, only go back for fruit. Or do the omelette station—egg whites and veggies.

- The pancake lane: Pancakes with a little syrup and fresh fruit. If you go back, only go back for more fruit.
- The grain lane: Have some whole-grain cereal or oatmeal and a slice of whole wheat toast. Don't go back.
- Forget the buffet and order off the menu. So the giant buffet is only $3 more than ordering off the menu? So what? Save the three dollars, and the hundreds of dollars it could take you to get the extra pounds off, and order the oatmeal or an egg-white frittata with vegetables. Or do what I do— let your child get the buffet, you order off the menu, then have a few things off your child's plate.
- Rules are made to be broken, but if you don't start out with some rules, you could lose control completely. Rules can help you keep your wits, so if you do break them, only break them a little.

• •

MOM TALK

We recently took Bryn to Disney World on a kids' vacation on my birthday. We started the day at one of those character breakfasts, hosted by the Disney characters. The buffet had things like apple pie filling and blueberry filling, candy toppings for pancakes, neon-colored cereals, brownies and Rice Krispies Treats, and cheese grits. No whole wheat anything, no turkey bacon. The eggs were dripping in butter and the fruit was sugar laden. I knew if I let Bryn fill up on Froot Loops and apple pie filling and whipped cream, she would be manic later. However, a buffet usually has something you and your children can eat. Some ideas:

- We often have whole-grain cereal or Cheerios at home, so when Bryn sees the neon cereal at a buffet, she gets excited. On a special occasion, I let her have a little of it on top of some raisin bran, like sprinkles.

- Look for the things that actually look high quality. At Disney, there was one salad with grapefruit and orange slices that looked good, so we had some of that, along with some oatmeal. Even with a little butter and milk, oatmeal is usually a decent choice.
- A waffle or pancake from a buffet can be okay, if you don't drown it in canned pie filling. Instead, use a little butter and a sprinkle of powdered sugar or a little syrup.
- You can almost always find whole wheat toast, sometimes with peanut butter and jelly.
- It's not obsessive parenting to realize how you and your child are going to feel after poor food choices. You'll both spike and crash. It's not worth the price, so stifle your urge to pile the plate high.

. . . .

At a Diner

Pancakes or waffles aren't a bad choice, unless you load them up with sugary toppings. Diners are also good for egg-white omelets with vegetables or oatmeal. If you want lunch or dinner, you can usually get good soup or a big salad, a veggie sandwich on whole wheat, or fun foods like peanut butter and jelly on whole wheat, if you're sharing with your child (or even if you're not and you just want peanut butter and jelly).

At a Fast-Food Restaurant

Even fast-food restaurants have healthy choices in between those stacks of triple bacon cheeseburgers.

- At a sandwich shop like Subway or Quiznos, get all the veggies—lettuce, spinach, tomatoes, olives, peppers, avocados—so your sandwich is more like a salad. Now they even offer veggie patties and egg whites. I usually ask for all the veggies except red onions. Now that I'm newly single I can't have bad breath!

- Most fast-food restaurants have salads. Some have soups. If I was at Wendy's, I would get a baked potato with broccoli or a salad.
- At a random deli, I would see what soups they had or get a veggie sandwich on whole wheat.
- At Chinese fast food, stick with vegetables and protein that isn't deep-fat-fried, like chicken with broccoli or shrimp with snow peas.
- One slice of pizza with veggies on it isn't going to kill you. Order it with a salad to fill up on fiber.
- At Starbucks, I would get a breakfast wrap and a decaf soy misto.
- If the fast-food menu was pretty bereft of healthy food, I would probably just get a small order of fries or a small milkshake and balance it out later. If I was craving something sweet, I might get a small ice cream or the animal cookies.

• •

MOM TALK

When I'm out with Bryn and she wants to have something decadent, I rarely say no because I don't want her to think anything is forbidden and therefore more desirable. However, she usually just has a small amount because that's all she wants. I try to keep healthy things in the house so she eats good food most of the time. There is no food noise and there are no food extremes.

• •

At a Resort

All-inclusive resorts seem like a great way to have a relaxing vacation, but they can also give you anxiety because you can eat all the food you want and drink all the drinks you want for "free." It's too easy to feel like you have to get your money's worth by eating as much as you can at every meal, but this defeats the whole carefree, relaxed purpose of an all-inclusive because overeating can make you feel bloated and guilty. You want to feel good and energetic so you can enjoy yourself and do fun noneating things like snorkeling, swimming, and lying on the beach without feeling like a beached whale. Just remember: *You can have it all, just not all at once.*

Even if your husband or partner has that get-my-money's-worth-in-food-and-liquor mentality, you don't have to get crazy. Don't let the buffet suck you in. Instead, look over the menus and all the choices at the resort. Some have multiple restaurants or specials on certain nights, like lobster night or Caribbean night. Make a plan for your whole stay. Maybe the first night you'll do the Italian night, the second night you'll try the local fish, the third night you'll do the Asian restaurant. One night, you'll have that dessert everyone is talking about. Figure out which restaurants to go to or which foods on the menu to try on each night, so you can look forward to every meal without panicking because you think you're going to overdo it or miss something. Instead, you can calm down and think about how much you're looking forward to lobster night, and how much you're going to enjoy sushi the next night and steak the night after that.

You should never have to feel like you need to try it all *right now*. When each meal is a new adventure and you don't blow your wad in any one place, then you'll never have to backpedal and try to make up for anything. Portion it out, then have fun!

Also make a plan for drinking. It's really hard not to let the bartender keep the rum punches or piña coladas flowing, but you can unknowingly chug down hundreds of calories at the pool bar before you've even thought about dinner. Just because the liquor is top shelf doesn't mean you have to drink it from mimosa to nightcap. Have clear rum on the rocks with a splash of the frozen mix or punch. Have one drink during the day, maybe one at happy hour, and one at dinner. Normally I say stick to two drinks, but you're on vacation. Live it up! If you want three drinks, make room for it by skipping the dessert or cutting back on the bread or chips. Pick your spot and you'll feel better in your bathing suit the next morning.

• •

GOURMET MOMENT

The fruit at resorts in tropical climates is usually fantastic and you might even get to taste some fruits you've never tried before. Take advantage of this culinary opportunity because it also happens to be good for you. Fill up on that.

• •

About Cleansing

Occasionally what you ate and drank yesterday or for the last few weeks will have you feeling draggy and heavy. A lack of sleep can also make you feel low on energy. Maybe it's time for a cleanse.

I get many questions about cleansing because I do it sometimes, and I have a cleansing product (Skinnygirl Daily Cleanse and Restore). There are many misconceptions about cleansing out there, and there are ways to do it that aren't safe, but in general, it should be a gentle way to reboot your system and purify you after you've been overindulging. A cleanse is an opportunity to let your body rest from the rigors of intense digestion, so it can focus instead on removing toxins. It's not about weight loss, although that can be one result if you have weight to lose. It's really more about cleaning everything out so your body can work better.

There are plenty of reasons to cleanse:

- *If you ate a lot the day before.* Eating heavy foods like meat in particular taxes your digestion. The machine is straining. A cleanse is like giving the machine of digestion a rest so your body can focus on other things, like healing and repair.
- *If you're sick.* People are naturally less hungry when they are sick because their bodies know they need to focus on healing instead of digestion, so on those sick days when you

have a cough or a cold, support your body with nutrient-rich but easily digestible cleansing foods, especially green juices.

- *If you've been living it up on vacation.* You might want to cleanse for a few days to get back on track.
- *If you've got an event coming up,* like a wedding or a class reunion or just a first date. You might want to cleanse so you feel good and look good.
- *If you are tired.* You might just be feeling more tired and low on energy than usual. A cleanse can invigorate you.

When I cleanse, I eat foods that are comforting but healthy and I eliminate all animal protein. I focus on diuretic foods that flush out water if I feel bloated (like cucumber, asparagus, and melon) and I drink a lot of lemon water with a sprinkle of cayenne pepper to help speed up the release of toxins. I also concentrate on gentle foods like oatmeal, fruit smoothies, vegetable soup, and brown rice. Some days, I might even do a juice cleanse with green juices sweetened with just a little fruit for every meal, or with light food like brown rice, vegetable soup, or raw veggies. Here's what I'm likely to eat on a cleanse day:

CLEANSE DAY	
Breakfast	Oatmeal or a fruit smoothie.
Lunch	Pureed vegetable soup or brown rice with tofu and a cucumber salad.
Afternoon	Watermelon or grapefruit.
Dinner	More pureed vegetable soup and a big salad with diuretic vegetables like cucumbers, celery, artichokes, tomatoes, carrots, and beets, or steamed asparagus (usually I don't like steamed vegetables but they are good for cleansing days). If I really want to reboot, I might just have a green juice for dinner and go to bed early.

If you want to try cleansing, I recommend starting slow and following these guidelines:

Choose your level of cleanse. Will you eliminate meat, dairy, caffeine, sugar, or all of these? Gentle cleanses can be about just eating fruits and vegetables for a day, or just skipping all animal products, or sugar, or caffeine. They don't have to be complicated. Or you could be more extreme. Some people only drink freshly squeezed vegetable juices on a cleanse. I put my Skinnygirl Daily Cleanse product in my water every day. This is a really mild, gentle way to cleanse, without doing anything else. It's just fiber and greens, so it keeps things moving without being extreme. I'm not going to drink it with a Philly cheesesteak. It inspires me to have a light meal, so in this way, I'm continually cleansing.

Choose your length of cleanse. Your first cleanse doesn't have to be for a whole day. You can have green juice for breakfast, then go back to your normal diet for lunch. It's a good way to ease into the practice of cleansing. More experienced cleansers can do a few days, but if you choose to do a juice cleanse with no solid food, don't do it for more than one day without your doctor's consent.

In general, focus on having vegetables, herbal teas, pureed vegetable soups, and fruit, with or without gentle whole grains like brown rice.

Freshly squeezed juices are great for cleanses. Get a juicer and do it yourself, or save yourself the trouble and go to a juice bar. Green juices should be mostly vegetables, with just a little bit of fruit, like green apple or lemon, for palatability. Go easy on carrot juice and beet juice. These are high-sugar vegetables. Also, beet juice is a strong liver cleanser, so it can feel intense. Smoothies are also great for cleanses—they have all the benefits of juice plus the fiber, so they will help get things moving.

Fiber supplements can also help clean you out. Some people also take stool softeners or swear by colonics. These choices aren't for everyone, but your body needs to be cleaning itself out. Only you know what that means for you.

Cleansing also requires mental calm. Don't cleanse on a day where you have a ton going on, need to do intense exercise, or are doing something stressful at work. Choose a day where you can relax, maybe do some yoga or meditation, breathe deeply, take a bath, and let your body do its thing.

You can further support your cleanse by helping your body eliminate the toxins it is releasing during your cleanse. Anything that helps you get toxins out of your pores will help, like taking a sauna or a steam, soaking in an epsom-salt bath, or dry-brushing your skin before you shower.

. . . .

You can monitor the progress of your cleanse by checking out your tongue and using a tongue scraper. You may notice that after a night of drinking or a day of heavy eating, your tongue has a yucky white coating on it in the morning. As you cleanse and your body starts to clean out, this coating may get thicker.

A tongue scraper will scrape it off as it comes out, and over the course of the cleanse, you'll notice that this tongue residue will gradually get lighter, until it's gone and your tongue looks clean and pink again. This is one sign that your cleanse is complete.

. . . .

Don't freak out if you "break the rules" of your cleanse. I know people who do juice cleanses who'll have an anxiety attack because they gave in and had a piece of watermelon. Get over it. The bottom line is that your body is healing, and that's good. A piece of watermelon isn't going to stop that whole process and if you really wanted it, you probably needed it.

When your cleanse is over, go back to your regular diet gradually. It takes just as long to come out of a cleanse as you spent in the cleanse. Never end a cleanse with a big meal of heavy foods. You don't get to break your cleanse with a cheeseburger. This is serious. I've heard about people who break their cleanses with a steak and a martini, and end up in the hospital. If you cleanse for three days, then introduce other foods (like meat and dairy) back into your diet over a period of three more days. Start with raw fruits and vegetables, soups, and whole grains.

Chapter Five

· · · · · · · · · · ·

Fast Fitness

I used to exercise like a maniac. I obsessed about it, just like I obsessed about food. I'd spin for hours, hike the Santa Monica stairs, Rollerblade for fifteen miles. I did everything. I was consumed by it. On the days I didn't do it, I would be consumed by guilt as well. I didn't have a healthy relationship with exercise.

Today, I'm twenty years older, I work out fifty times less than I did then, and here's the kicker: I weigh twenty pounds less than I weighed in those days.

Exercise is a tool and if you want to make it work for you, you have to understand what it actually does for you and what your goal is. If you are using that tool wisely, exercise keeps you fit. It clears your mind, it's good for your heart, it builds your muscles and gives you definition, it gives you energy, it can improve your sex life, it makes you feel stronger and more confident, and it can lift your butt and your mood. It's a great thing to do and I wish I had time to do it more often.

But here's the truth: exercise alone will not make you lose weight. It is my opinion that what you eat is more important. You can't start exercising like a maniac, the way I used to do, and eat like a wolverine, and expect to get thinner. I used to get up every morning for a six A.M. spin class. By ten A.M., I was so starved, I was eating things I would never normally have eaten. I told myself, "Well, I just took a spin class, so I can eat this," or "I'll eat all this now and tomorrow

I'll take a step class." But I wasn't in control. I would come out of an extreme exercise class feeling so happy that I'd managed to do it, and then the hunger would overwhelm me.

That's because exercise done in a manic state becomes a vicious cycle. You exercise too much, so you overeat, so you run to the gym to make up for it, and then you're starving again, and the cycle continues. You're on a literal and figurative treadmill and you can't get off. You're not in control of your own behavior.

Extreme exercise could make you lose weight, but you'll pay a price. If you are engaging in constant intense physical activity, it can be hard to keep weight on. When I was on *Skating with the Stars*, I was up every morning at five A.M. ice-skating and I lost a lot of weight. I was burning extreme calories and I didn't have time to eat enough, but it was hell and I was in a state of high anxiety the whole time. Most people aren't living their lives like this, however, and it's not a weight-loss approach I would recommend to anyone. Under normal circumstances, weight loss happens because of what you eat. Those thirty minutes at the gym three times a week or even every day are not going to keep you thin if you don't get control of your eating.

This is why exercise is not and cannot be a unilateral weight-loss strategy, no matter what you've seen on TV. When you watch what you eat and combine it with moderate exercise, that's the winning combination.

I exercise now to stay fit, look toned, and feel good, but I *do not exercise to stay thin*. It's liberating to realize this. Now I eat like a naturally thin person, pretty much whatever I want, and I exercise simply because I know it's going to make me feel stronger, better, lighter, and brighter. I have a healthy relationship with food, and equally important, I have a healthy relationship with exercise. I exercise not only because I want to but because I don't feel like I have to. That's the sweet spot.

EXERCISE NOISE

In the same way you can have food noise, you can also have exercise noise. You can have a love-hate, obsessive relationship with exercise, where you do it constantly or you don't do it at all. It's like being on an eating binge or a crash diet. I used to obsess if I had to go somewhere on vacation or somewhere for work where they didn't have a treadmill. I would get irritable about early meetings that would interfere with my workout schedule and think the whole day was ruined. Now, if four days go by without a workout, so be it. If four days go by and I can work out every day, that's great, too. I've made peace with exercise. Even if I do something intense like a boot camp class, I make sure I'm breathing and not overdoing it, and if I feel like I'm pushing too hard, I take a break. Just do what you can and be truthful to yourself. Let exercise be in your life.

Never Reward, Never Punish

Another extremely important idea to remember about exercise is that eating and exercise should not be related. *Never* reward exercise with eating, and *never* punish eating with exercise. This sounds counterintuitive to people who have been dieting for years, but you need to separate these two things in your mind. People often say things like, "Oh, you work out so you're able to eat more," but I don't agree.

You will never be able to calculate exactly how many calories you burned versus how many extra calories you can eat, and even if you could, that's not the right mentality to have. Linking exercise and food will only fuel your food noise and your exercise noise. Never have French fries or cookies *because* you worked out. Only have them because you want them, unrelated to exercise. If you really want French fries or cookies, eat them according to the naturally thin principles, not as a reward for thirty minutes on the treadmill. On the other hand, you weren't "bad" because you ate French fries or cookies, and that doesn't mean you have to do a two-hour kickboxing class as penance. Simply try to eat well and exercise when you can. That's the naturally thin way.

. . . .

LIKE THE FRIEND YOU HAVEN'T SEEN IN WEEKS . . .

I like to exercise thirty to forty-five minutes a few times a week, but sometimes my life gets too busy and I'll stop for a time. When I pick back up, my body remembers. Exercise should be like one of those friends you love to see but that you don't get to see every day. When you do see them again, you can pick right back up where you left off.

. . . .

What I Do

I've been all over the exercise map. I do yoga maybe three times a week and I go on long walks with the stroller to take Bryn to the park. When I'm traveling near the water, I will walk on the beach or go surfing. When I'm traveling in the mountains, I'll go snowboarding. Normally, however, it's mostly about yoga and walking, but there are times in my life when I do less, or more.

I'm going through a stressful divorce right now, and I need something to really sink my teeth into that can get my head someplace other than my troubles. Lately I've been doing the Tracy Anderson workout. I have excess energy to spend and exercise is a good way to defuse it.

I used to dread going to exercise classes. I would be panting in the first few seconds and I would hate it and force myself to get through it. The first time I ever tried spinning, I was panting and trying to do what the woman was telling us, but after fifteen minutes, I quit. I got off the bike and went home. I remember my first yoga class—same thing. I was trying to do what everyone else was doing, getting into advanced poses and holding them for so long it was painful and my muscles were shaking. I left that class after fifteen minutes, too. Now, I pace myself. When I did a boot camp class recently, everyone was running around frantically as the instructor screamed at us to be at level 10. Sweat was slinging everywhere. I call this fear-based exercise, and I wasn't playing that game. I was playing my own game. I stayed at level 5, where I was comfortable, and I was just happy to be there. Getting there is half the battle, and staying is the other half. If I'm panting and gasping and throwing up, I'm not going back. If I go to level 5 one day, then 6 the next day, and then 7, then I want to keep going back because I see progress—on my terms. I might not be at level 10 like some of those people, but what I'm doing is still better than sitting at home eating bonbons.

The point is that if you can do something, do it. It can be a little overwhelming or just out of your comfort zone, but don't do something so far out that you hate it. Figure out how to stay consistent with exercise. That's more important than trying to sustain an intensity level that feels miserable. If you commit to the hour or however long the class is and stay there even if you have to back off what the teacher is saying to do, then that is how you keep your relationship with exercise healthy and happy. Start where you are, take it easy, do what you can, and challenge yourself a little bit. If you're just phoning it in, it's not going to do you any good, but don't challenge yourself so much that you quit.

When you go back to exercise after a break, you may not be perfect. It may feel really difficult. You might even start to hate it. That's your sign to back off and take it a little easier. Just be where you are. Do something when you can, even if it's just walking to the store, taking your kid for a walk, or doing some jumping jacks to relieve your stress. No pressure.

Shake It Up

If you want to work exercise into your life or step up the pace a bit, that's great, but I want you to do it successfully, not in a way that you can't sustain. Too many people make a New Year's resolution to start exercising in a way that doesn't fit into their lives. There is nothing special about December 31 or January 1 or even Monday. If you put all that pressure on yourself, then missing one day or missing your start date or burning out three weeks later means you're back to lying on the couch waiting for another magic beginning. There is no magic beginning. Don't wait another eleven months or even six days to start again. Just start. Just do what you can. Don't force it. To help, here are some of the ways I think about exercise:

- **You don't have to exercise every day.** In fact, don't. As soon as you tell yourself you have to do this, you will start obsessing. Knowing exercise doesn't have to be a daily thing is a huge relief to people. I don't exercise every day, and although I could be fitter, I'm still pretty fit and I finally have a healthy relationship with exercise because I never force it on myself.
- **Exercise when you get the opportunity.** There are so many opportunities in life to get out and move in a fun way. Take your kid for a walk. Take a break from your desk and do some jumping jacks. Walk to lunch. Walk to work. Take the stairs. If I'm on vacation at a beach, I will walk for an hour on that beach every day because I love doing that. But if I'm in New York and I'm in meetings or with Bryn all day, my formal workouts might be down to two or three days a week. Just be alert for it. Do tricep exercises on the coffee table when you watch TV. Do a yoga pose to unwind after a stressful phone call. Get down on the floor and stretch or do a few push-ups if you think of it.
- **Exercise changes with your life stage.** Before I was pregnant and a mother, I exercised probably three to four days

a week. I liked yoga in particular. When I was pregnant, I couldn't do as much. I did a yoga video maybe twice a week and walked around the city. When I was on bed rest for two weeks, I couldn't exercise at all. After I first had Bryn, I mainly focused on eating well. Maybe twice a week I'd get on the elliptical trainer, but it took me some time to feel ready to exercise again. Now I get it in two to three days a week maximum, on average, with occasional spurts of more. Your exercise needs and abilities and opportunities will evolve throughout your life, so just go with it. If you're in your early twenties, get exercise ingrained into your muscles so you can come back to it. If you've got PMS, exercise more if it helps, or less if you just don't want to move. Pregnancy, new motherhood, even menopause—they all affect how exercise will fit into your life, and that's natural.

- **Stretching counts.** Sometimes, the thought of an actual workout is just too much, but if you get up and stretch your muscles and do some light yoga poses that feel good, that's better than doing nothing. It might make you feel so much better that you want to do more tomorrow. The more you start to relax and feel good, the more you'll be ready to move and explore and enjoy yourself.

- **There are good reasons to increase your amount or intensity of exercise.** If you want to get in shape for an upcoming vacation or some other special event, then you might want to start exercising more so you will look and feel your best when the event happens. Exercise will make you look more toned and feel stronger and more energetic. If you've been feeling in a funk lately, maybe you need to exercise more, because it boosts your mood and makes you feel better about yourself. Some days, the weather is great and you'll feel better if you get outside and move. Fresh air just feels better if you're breathing it in as you exercise.

EXERCISE FASHION

People get all worked up about what they should wear when they exercise. If buying a new gym wardrobe will actually make you feel better and more motivated about exercise, then by all means, do it. If you want the latest sweat-wicking technology or heart monitor or sports bra, why not? Personally, I wear a tank top with a built-in bra over a sports bra and workout pants I've had for five years or I just work out in my pajamas. I'm not one of those people who wants to spend a lot of money on workout clothes. I won't judge you if you are. All that really matters is getting out there and doing it.

- **There are good reasons to decrease your amount or intensity of exercise.** Sometimes you need to slow down. Sometimes you're better off sleeping or deep-breathing. Know yourself, and you'll be able to sense when you need to do less and when you just need to relax a little more. If you're cleansing, you're getting over a cold or injury, or you didn't get enough sleep, take it easier on your body and focus on something like meditation or just resting. It's okay to take time off.
- **Sleep is more important than exercise.** I prioritize sleep over exercise. That doesn't mean I won't exercise if I'm a little bit tired, but instead of cutting my sleep short to wake up early and exercise, I'd rather take a walk two nights a week after work and then do something on the weekends after I wake up naturally. I love exercise, but I'm not going to lose sleep over it. Sleep is my ultimate goal. If I had a genie in a bottle, one of my wishes would be to get a good solid eight hours of sleep.

. . . .

SEXERCISE

People say sex burns a lot of calories. Honestly, my hat's off to anyone who can get a really good workout from sex. I guess masturbating is exercise, too. If you have the spare time, well . . . "use what you have."

. . . .

- **Be flexible about exercise.** Exercise can be anything, anytime. Don't get stuck on the idea that you can only exercise in a certain place or at a certain time of day. If you have it in your head that you are a "morning exercise person" and you miss a morning workout, you might feel like you can't possibly exercise in the afternoon. Be flexible and fit it in as your day and life permit.
- **Keep changing what you do.** For me, switching it up makes all the difference. Bodies react better to change, and I get bored doing the same thing every day. If you don't want to get stuck in an exercise rut, try to do something different every day, but don't worry so much about what it is. It doesn't have to look like exercise. Pick what sounds fun

or what you feel like doing. Some days, when the weather is nice, you might want to go outside and walk or run or ride your bicycle or just play with your kids. Other days, walk to dinner or go dancing with your girlfriends. It all counts.

- **Let exercise make you happier.** Notice how exercise makes you feel when you do it in moderation. Have you ever seen those people who sweat through an hour of Bikram yoga, then do a spin class, and then lift weights? They look weathered and intense and obsessed. They don't look very happy to me. I'm sure there are exceptions, but in general, moderate exercise boosts your mood and overly intense exercise stresses you out.

• •

MOM TALK

I recently decided that I would do one quality activity with Bryn and one quality activity for myself every day. For example, on Monday, I might take Bryn to a swimming lesson, then I might go for an hour of yoga or a walk by the water. On Tuesday, I might take Bryn to ballet class, and I might go to a museum. Wednesday, maybe it's nice out and I'll take Bryn to a playground so we'll both get exercise. It's never the same thing two days in a row, and it's fun, so that makes me want to stay committed to it. It also just happens to be about getting up and moving, and that's exercise for both of us.

• •

Exercise Solutions

If you aren't in the habit of exercising, or if you only ever do one thing, you might want some new ideas. You can fit exercise into any schedule if you feel like it. Here are my ideas for how to find time and opportunities for exercise no matter where you are:

- **At home:** People can't believe that I don't belong to a gym, but I don't like going to the gym. I'll do yoga classes sometimes if I'm on vacation, but most of the time, I'd rather do a yoga DVD or use my elliptical trainer in the privacy of my own home. There are thousands of good exercise DVDs for just about anything you like to do, from yoga to Pilates to dance videos to more intense boot camp or martial arts workouts. Pick what you enjoy and switch it up when you get bored, even if it's just stretching or walking up and down the stairs a few times or doing tricep push-ups on the coffee table. Or get outside and walk, bike, or rollerblade.

. . . .

YOUR EXERCISE INVESTMENT

Exercise machines are great if you really will use them. I get a great amount of use out of my Schwinn elliptical trainer that I bought at Walmart for about $400. It is a sturdy, quiet, substantial machine. You can spend a little or thousands on exercise equipment, but no matter what you spend, if you actually use it, it will be a good investment.

. . . .

- **At the gym:** A lot of people love the gym. You get access to a variety of fitness classes, cardio machines, weights—whatever you want to do. If you want to forget you're exercising, a lot of those exercise machines have individual televisions. Plug in your earbuds and find my talk show. Health clubs are also likely to have a sauna or a steam room, so you can have a nice reward after exercising.
- **With kids:** Holding Bryn has given me stronger arm muscles. We get a lot of exercise walking to the park and running around, playing on the playground equipment. We also have dance parties. Look silly and make your babies laugh!
- **On busy days:** Running around the city counts as exercise. Sometimes I'll get a couple of miles in just running errands.

Because I live in New York and I know that twenty blocks equals a mile, I like to track how far I walk. It's rewarding to be able to know you walked for three miles.

- **In a hotel**: If the hotel or resort has an exercise class, give it a try. Even if it's too "beginner" for you or you're the only one who shows up or you're the only one your age who shows up, so what? It's something different. You can also swim some laps in the hotel pool or try their workout room. Most hotels at least have treadmills or elliptical trainers or an exercise bike.
- **All the time**: When you're walking around doing whatever you do in your everyday life, get in the habit of squeezing your butt muscles, tightening your abs, and standing up straight. When sitting, maintain good posture, which is exercise in itself. If you're slumping, you might as well be taking a nap. Some people say high heels tone your leg muscles. I think that's a good excuse to buy shoes.

The bottom line is that exercise shouldn't make you feel bulked up, stressed out, manic, out of breath, or starving. It shouldn't be intimidating, and if a gym feels overwhelming or makes you feel bad about it, forget it. Take a walk outside. Work your way up to more advanced exercise. Go at your own pace. Just do something. Keep it moving, change it up, have fun, and don't push yourself beyond your own limits. Don't sweat too much and definitely don't work out hard enough to throw up! Most of all, remember that when it comes to being naturally thin, exercise is a tool, but it's mostly about the food.

My Exercise Routine

Yoga is my favorite way to exercise. It makes me feel relaxed; it works the kinks out of my neck, where I hold tension; and it's like a mental reset. That's why I made a yoga exercise DVD, *Bethenny's Skinnygirl Workout*, and it's the DVD I usually do at home.

Triangle, Plank, and Downward Dog are three of my favorite poses. Here's how I do them:

Triangle

Plank

Downward Dog

Part Two

Skinnygirl Solutions for Daily Life

- ✦ How do you do it all?
- ✦ How do you balance work and being a mother?
- ✦ Do you have secrets for managing your time?
- ✦ What's the best way to keep an organized calendar?
- ✦ Do you still use a BlackBerry or did you switch to an iPhone?
- ✦ How do you prioritize where you spend your time?
- ✦ How do you know when to say no?
- ✦ How do you have time to look good?
- ✦ What's your beauty regimen?
- ✦ Do you ever get to see your friends?
- ✦ Now that you have a baby, do you still spend time with Cookie?
- ✦ Do you take time for yourself?

Chapter Six

Time Management

People often ask me about how I stay organized, how I fit everything in, and how I balance work with my personal life. I won't pretend it's easy. One of my greatest struggles has been work-life balance. Doing it right means managing your time, getting organized, and maximizing your minutes. Phone companies know the world is measured in minutes and that we'll never stop needing more of them. Time management is step one.

I used to think finding time for my friends and myself while building my career was hard, but then I became a mother, and now those days seem like a party. Being a mother equals guilt. You will never have enough time with your family. My friends and I used to count the days until something exciting would happen. Now none of us has time for that, and it feels like something exciting (or challenging) happens every minute. I used to mark my menstrual cycle in a calendar and it really felt like a month between periods. Now I get it every five minutes. Time is whipping by. I'm constantly on the verge of not getting it all done in time, and yet, somehow I do. It's never easy, but it's definitely possible.

How to Manage Your Time

For me, time management is about three things:

1. Being Organized

If you aren't organized, you're going to waste time, period. You'll be looking for things or trying to remember what you were supposed to be doing. If you don't know what's supposed to happen next, you won't be ready. If you don't know where something is, you're going to waste time looking for it. You can be the best multitasker in the world, but if all you're doing is making up for lost time due to disorganization, you're stressing yourself out for nothing. Fastidious organization is the most important way that I save time. Anyone can become organized. Disorganization is just a bad habit. Three seconds of putting something away now can save you an hour looking for it later, and spare time spent organizing a drawer or a closet or a shelf instead of staring at a television will be worth every second you invest.

2. Multitasking

I hardly ever do just one thing at a time, unless it's spending time with my daughter. There are a million ways to get two or more things done at once. As I write this, I'm on a plane to Australia. I used as much time as possible to sleep because that's important, but the minute I woke up, I chose to work on this book instead of staring at a movie.

Multitasking is controversial because people say that nobody can really multitask very well and if you try, you won't get things done as quickly. I'm not sure I believe that, because I'm continually multitasking, and I get a hell of a lot done every day. For me, an idle mind is the devil's playground. This year has been unusual for me because I've had some time off, but when I don't have enough to do, I just torture my staff with new production ideas. I think I do things better if I'm doing three things at once. Multitasking energizes and invigorates your mind, so you think more clearly and sharply and you move more quickly. It seems to me like when I have one thing to do, I get nothing done, but if I have forty-two things to do, I get it all done.

Ideas beget more ideas. If you can get good at it, you'll effectively double or triple the minutes in your day.

Some complex jobs really need your full attention and you need to be able to recognize when that's the case. Writing a book chapter, creating a presentation for work, brainstorming, cooking something complicated, or assembling an entertainment center need all your brain power, so put away your smartphone and get on with it. Also, don't multitask when you're pushing a stroller, holding a baby, crossing the street, using something sharp, like a saw or scissors, or doing anything else that could be dangerous, and don't do stupid things while you need to concentrate, like checking your e-mail every three seconds or obsessively tweeting. That's not multitasking. That's wasting valuable time.

Thousands of tasks you do every day are relatively mindless, so do a few at a time. Here are some examples of how I multitask and how you can get more done, too:

- When you're on the phone, walk around the house decluttering. Put things back where they belong. Dust, or wipe down the counters in your kitchen or your refrigerator.
- When you're waiting for a call or a meeting to start, or you are on hold, organize a drawer or delete contacts from your cell phone.
- When you're watching TV, do your sit-ups and push-ups or a few yoga poses.
- For dinner, make whatever needs to bake first (like bread, cake, or casserole), then make the side dishes on the stove while the oven is going.
- If you're a passenger in a car, write your blog, make your lists, or edit your book.
- When you're waiting in line, answer e-mails.
- Make playdates at parks so you can spend time with your child and socialize with other moms at the same time.
- Get a manicure while you're getting a massage. They can work around each other. You just relax. You can also spend time with your child while getting a manicure. I take Bryn with me and she gets a manicure too, or she colors or plays on my iPad.

- If you have several family doctor's appointments or you need to get your annual physical, see the dentist, and get your eyes checked, bang them all out on the same day.
- If you have multiple appointments in the same area of town, schedule them all for the same day.
- When you're on an airplane, catch up on work.
- If you know you're going to be waiting, stash blank cards and stamps in your purse and write thank-you notes.
- Keep work or a book in your bag or on your phone so if you have a long flight or train ride or a delay, you can use the time to catch up.
- Spend time with your dog while in the car running errands.

. . . .

COOKIE TIME: NEVER WASTED

Anybody who knows me knows how important my dog, Cookie, is to my life. Every afternoon when she gets back from her walk with the dog walker, she flies in wiggling and wagging her tail like a little puppy, even though she's actually a senior citizen. That makes my day. Sometimes a concentrated belly-rub session or a walk together is all we both need to recharge. Sometimes I'll take her with me in the car, and that's our time together. Pets do take time and they need attention, but in my opinion, that's one way to use time wisely. Having a well-behaved pet is good for your stress level and it makes your life richer. While I do agree that once you have a child, your dog becomes a dog instead of a substitute baby, that relationship is still one of the most important in my life.

. . . .

3. Using Time Wisely

How much time do you waste mindlessly Googling things you don't care about, texting, checking your Twitter feed, and staring at TV shows you don't really like? All that bullshit wastes a lot of time. Everybody wastes time sometimes, but it shouldn't be a habit. When you cook, sleep, get online, clean, talk on the phone, exercise, or spend time with your family, make the most of it. Getting organized and multitasking will help, but prioritizing is crucial in knowing how to spend your time. Quality time feels so much better and more satisfying. Sometimes when I'm with Bryn, I realize I'm distracted by something going on in my personal life or in my business. I'm in my head. I never talk on the phone or check e-mails when I'm with her, but sometimes I'm just distracted, and I beat myself up about it. I'm looking at her and thinking about something else. It doesn't feel clean or solid. It's like doing a great workout in a gym when it's a beautiful afternoon outside.

Work comes very easily to me. The rest doesn't, and I really have to try hard, but it's worth it. Every important moment should count. When you're working, work to the best of your ability. When you're playing, play hard and have real, clean fun. When you're with someone you love, give them all your attention. Valuing and focusing on your true priorities will make your whole life better.

. . . .

HOW NOT TO BE LATE

You can't always control your environment. Things like traffic or the behavior of other people can sometimes make you late for an appointment, party, or meeting. However, being chronically late is a huge imposition on other people. It's basically telling others your time is more valuable than theirs. It's rude and a bad habit, but you can stop. Drastically reduce your tendency to be late with one easy trick: backing it out.

Backing it out means taking the time you are supposed to be somewhere and then working backward in your mind, figuring out how much time each thing leading up to that event will take. For example, if you have to be at a meeting at three, think about how long it will take you to drive there. Forty-five minutes? Now you're at two fifteen. How long will it take you to get ready? Thirty minutes? Now you're at one forty-five. How long will it take you to get home so you can start getting ready? Twenty minutes? Now you're at one twenty-five. How long do you know you'll putter around putting away your purse and saying hi to your kids or your pets and maybe having a snack before the meeting? Twenty-five minutes? Now you're at one o'clock. What time is it right now? Twelve thirty? Then you know you need to head home in exactly thirty minutes. Problem solved. If you are a mom, pad it with an extra fifteen or twenty minutes to account for your children pulling on your leg. I'm now often a little late. It just happens.

I back out the time when I've got to get to the airport. It gives Jackie a heart attack but I figure it out this way: Ideally it takes forty-five minutes to get to the airport, so I give it an hour. You're supposed to be there an hour before, but I give myself forty-five minutes because I never check a bag. That means we leave one hour and forty-five minutes before my flight. I've missed flights when I failed to back it out and didn't give myself enough time. Backing it out is having a plan, and having a plan is almost always better than winging it and hoping you'll make it.

• •

My Best Time-Management Tools, Tips, and Strategies

I am obsessed with time management and efficiency. I think about how to make every single aspect of my life more productive. I've accumulated a lot of ideas over the years. These are my best tools, tips, and strategies for saving you time right now:

Use Your Smartphone for Everything

I'm pretty sure you already have one, and if you don't, what are you waiting for? Smartphones are our external brains and society runs on them, so you might as well get in the game. They're not that difficult to use and if you're often on the go, the data plan will pay for itself because it will allow you to get so much done. I don't know how anything happened before smartphones. I rely on mine for everything. All my appointments, calls, appearances, and deadlines, as well as people's birthdays, pop up on my smartphone with an alarm, so I don't forget them. I built a business and I organize my whole life on it. I wrote four *New York Times* bestsellers on a smartphone. It probably saves me hours every day.

I've been a BlackBerry person for years now, but I admit that I recently switched to an iPhone. I've heard about Androids, but I thought those were robots in sci-fi movies so I'm not sure what that's about. I like the iPhone. It's great for photos and videos and organizing everything. However, I'm still in love with my BlackBerry. My BlackBerry is like the ex-boyfriend I can't forget. The touch screen on an iPhone gives me anxiety and I can't type on it. Everything is a typo. I like the keys on the BlackBerry. I may have to cheat on my iPhone with my BlackBerry. I'm not recommending one over the other. Just go with what works for you.

Here's how to use it:

- **E-mail.** I check my e-mail on my smartphone frequently so that when something comes in I can deal with it immediately. Don't double the time it takes to shoot off a one-sentence answer. If you do it later, then you'll just have to read it again. Just do it in the moment. Get it off your plate, check it off your list, and move on.

- **Calendar.** Put every single thing you have to do in that calendar and set alarms on every must-do item so you never forget another appointment, important phone call, or event. Also add reminders for when you have to prepare for things, like "Make restaurant reservations for Friday" or "Draft book chapter today" or "Bake cookies for the bake sale this weekend" or "Call girls to plan night out for next weekend." Use the prioritizing system if your phone has one so you know at a glance what things you have to do and what things you want to do but could skip if necessary.

NOTES FROM JACKIE

I am the master of Bethenny's calendar, and Bethenny has so many requirements that handling this is easily the biggest chunk of my day. I have to set appointments and meetings, move things around, coordinate pickup and drop-off times, and make sure everybody who needs to be in the loop knows exactly what Bethenny is doing. Her schedule and life is a spiderweb.

That's why if I don't put it on the master calendar, it's not happening. We used to send a mass calendar every night to everyone on a long list of people who need to know where Bethenny is at any given moment, but now we just use iCalendar as the master calendar. It's still a work in progress and the way we handle her calendar is constantly evolving, but right now, whenever I add something to the calendar, I notify everyone who has to know every move she makes. This is not only practical but creative. Sometimes the talk show producer might be looking for content and will see that Bethenny is getting her teeth whitened, for example. That might give someone an idea to do a segment about that. When she travels, I'll alert everyone who wants to meet with her. For example, if she's going to be in Los Angeles, I send out a note: "I have her here for three days. Claim your spot now or forever hold your peace." Once the schedule is set, it's set. I'm not canceling an eyebrow appointment because somebody forgot to reserve a spot.

Bethenny can sync the calendar with her iPhone, but she's not good with technology so it's my job to remind her of everything. Every night before I leave, I say, "Can we talk about tomorrow?," then I send an e-mail confirming, and then when I come in the next morning, I remind her again what's happening that day.

- **Notes.** This is where you can store all the information you'll need. Make a list of restaurants you want to try, classes you want to take, movies you want to see, all your frequent-flyer numbers, books you've heard about that you might want to read, passwords for all the websites you visit (you can also find apps for that, which will keep your passwords secure), playlist ideas, the codes to reactivate your car radio and open your garage door, ideas for gifts for specific people, wines you want to try, things to do in cities the next time you visit them, favorite-song lists, ideas for parties, and anything else you think of that you want to remember later. Think of all the paper you'll save. Smartphones are green.

- **Browser.** Your smartphone can look up anything you need to know. Or if you have Siri, just ask it out loud. I don't understand Siri. Siri baffles me, but supposedly you can ask Siri stuff, and she'll tell you the answers. Like, "Siri, where's the closest Starbucks?" So I guess that could be handy, if you don't mind your phone talking back to you. I think that would freak me out.

- **Contacts.** Your smartphone's contacts function is useful, too. Toss your Rolodex and that big pile or folder of business cards. Enter every business card into your smartphone contact list with a note about how you know the person and you'll have the information you need when you see that person again at a party or you suddenly realize you need a product that company makes or a service that person provides (or you just need to remember that hot guy's name). I'm also continuously editing my contacts. Every time I notice a double contact or a contact for someone I'll never see again, I delete it. If you made a business contact seven years ago and you're not even in that business anymore, delete it. If you see some guy in your contacts you slept with in the eighties, delete it. (Although now that I'm getting divorced, I wonder if maybe I shouldn't have deleted those numbers . . .)

- **Camera.** Would I love to use my fabulous camera more often? Yes, but truthfully, I use the camera and the video function on my smartphone constantly. I take pictures and videos of Bryn because it saves time and it's handy. It's my ongoing photo and video record of my life.
- **Writing.** Trust me, you really can write on a smartphone, once you get used to the little keyboard. Some apps will do word processing for you, or just write your great ideas in an e-mail and send them to yourself. If I can write entire books on a smartphone, anybody can write anything on a smartphone.

Keep a Family Calendar

Even with your smartphone calendar, it's good to have a big visual calendar in your home. You can make one on a dry-erase board or buy an oversized one with a lot of space to write things. Use a different-color pen for each family member and keep track of everything so everybody knows what everybody else in the family has to do. Use a different color for events in which all family members must participate, so everybody knows not to make conflicting plans.

· ·

CHOOSE YOUR FRIENDS WISELY

Nothing wastes time and energy like high-maintenance people. I try to have as few of them in my life as possible. High-maintenance people suck your energy and pull you into their dramas. They are always late and make everyone wait for them. They change plans or cancel without warning, and it feels like a part-time job just to know them. They always (according to them) are busier than everyone else, are more exhausted than everyone else, and have it harder than everyone else. They suck all the energy out of a room.

I'm not saying I haven't been this person at times in my life, but I've learned that all relationships are about give-and-take. If you've got friends who only know how to take, reconsider keeping them in your life.

. . . .

Make Your Work Space More Efficient

Whether you work in a home office or an out-of-home office, keep your work space meticulously organized and you'll get your work done in half the time. You should know where everything is. No paper piles. No messy computer desktops. No random stacks of books or disorganized file drawers. Have all the tools you need to organize your office supplies and paperwork: label makers, Ziploc bags, containers. I use fun flowerpots to organize my pens. I put office supplies into a shoe organizer that hangs on the door. (These are also great for cleaning supplies.) It doesn't matter what you use. Just keep it organized.

. . . .

KEEP IT SHORT

I can't stand long rambling e-mails that take forever to tell me just one thing. When sending texts and e-mails, keep it brief. Get to the point so you don't waste your time or anyone else's. Reserve the chitchat for coffee dates.

. . . .

If your office is a hot mess, take a weekend and plow through it. Throw away everything you don't need and make a place for everything else. Then maintain it so you never have to do that again. This will save you hours, even days or months, of time over the course of your career. Don't waste your energy doing stupid things like trying to find a phone number or a contact. Free yourself up for creativity and actual productive work. (I'll talk more about organizing your home office in particular in the next chapter.)

Another huge time saver I learned when I worked for Linda

Bruckheimer, businesswoman and wife of movie producer Jerry Bruckheimer, is to keep the List. The List is a massive comprehensive list of everything that needs to be done, in two columns: "Imminent" and "Pending." "Imminent" is for things like "Cookie is limping, call the vet." "Pending" includes things like "What happened to that nice pen we dropped off six months ago for repair?" or "Fix the leather strap on the red purse" or "Enroll Bryn in ballet class" or "Make up a good grapefruit margarita recipe" or "Look into charity event." It has to be done, but not necessarily *now*.

I've been trying to get this list to happen in my office for five years. First I told my assistant Molly to make one, and she would say she would do it, but for some reason, it never happened. The same thing happened with my assistant Julie. Then I told my assistant Jackie to make one. Whenever something fell through the cracks, I would rip into everybody: "Why the hell don't we have the List? You never do the List!"

One day, Jackie and my VP Malini sat down and started the List, which they update every Friday, and it has changed our lives. I never have to say, "Wait a second, whatever happened to that jacket we returned last month? Did we get the credit?" It's an ongoing life list of nonsense minutiae but it saves time like nothing else. Whenever I'm off to do something, I glance over it. Just the other day, I realized that when I went downtown to buy flowers, I would be right by the leather store. I could bring the purse with me and finally get it fixed. Then that item gets checked off the list.

. . . .

NOTES FROM JACKIE

Bethenny is a huge stickler for organization, so I can't drop the ball. One thing that really helps me is FollowUpThen.com. Any time we get an e-mail that needs a follow-up later, whether it's in two weeks or two hours, I just send it to 2weeks@followupthen .com, or 2hours@followupthen.com, or whenever it is I need to remember it, and the app will send me the e-mail right when I need to deal with it. It's saved me a thousand times.

. . . .

Cook Quicker

How long does it take you to make dinner? If it takes you longer than thirty minutes, it should be a special occasion or you could be doing it faster. I usually don't take more than twenty minutes to make a meal because I don't like to make too much mess, and I use what I have. I don't care what the recipe says—I'll substitute to avoid going out to the store for one or two things, which is a waste of time. Almost any recipe ingredient has an acceptable substitute you probably already have in your kitchen, especially if you stock your kitchen well. Use what you have, and have what you like in your refrigerator and pantry at all times.

Other ideas for time-sensitive cooking:

- **Prep.** It seems annoying at the time, but if you chop and measure everything out before you start a recipe, then the actual cooking takes a fraction of the time. In culinary circles, this is called *mise en place.* You've probably seen people do this on TV segments when they are making a recipe and they can't take the time on camera to measure anything out. Try it at home and you'll see how convenient it is. It also makes cleanup easier if you put away each food container after you measure the food out. Just have plenty of small bowls and ramekins available for your ingredients.

- **Consolidate.** Don't use every pot, pan, spoon, spatula, and plate in the house every time you cook. Plan it out and think ahead. Whenever you can, use just one pan to cook. For example, blanch broccoli (dip it in boiling water to brighten it up and tenderize it just a bit without overcooking) in the boiling water that you are using to cook your pasta. When sautéing onions and garlic, reuse the same pan for something else without rinsing—the vegetable residue will add flavor and nutrients. Mash potatoes right in the pot. Use your immersion blender to puree vegetables or soup right in the pot. I'll serve a frittata in a large frying pan, which I take right to the table and put on a trivet.

- **Freeze.** When you take the time to cook, make extra and assemble high-end homemade TV dinners to keep in your freezer. Put a protein, vegetable, and starch together in a container, like chicken, green beans, and rice, or salmon, asparagus, and mashed potatoes. Label it, date it, and stack it in the freezer. (I don't date mine because I use them quickly, but do it if you know you will forget.) You can also freeze individual pieces of salmon or chicken. Put parchment paper between them in a container, or seal them individually. Portion out things like pasta, risotto, and casserole-type foods and restaurant leftovers. If everything is clearly labeled and dated, you'll never have to wonder what anything is or how long it's been in there.

- **Stretch.** Use leftovers wisely by making meals that can go from one day to the next. A burger can become pasta Bolognese. A steak can be sliced over baby spinach and sprinkled with cheese to become a beautiful steak salad. Roast chicken can become curried chicken salad or chicken chili. Roasted veggies can go into a frittata or an omelet. Leftover fruit, including peeled frozen brown bananas, can go into smoothies or frozen cocktails. Stop wasting food and you'll save time and money. For more ideas about how to repurpose your leftovers, consult my cookbook, *Skinnygirl Dish.*

- **Stock.** If you have basic staples in your kitchen, you can make dozens of meals without ever going to the store.

- **Stack.** I never use round containers because they waste space. I use rectangular containers from to-go restaurants and stack them in the freezer and refrigerator.

- **Sort.** Your refrigerator is like your closet. You need to know what you have in there and use it, but unlike the clothes in your closet, your food will actually spoil if you leave it sitting in there for too long. I'm always sorting my refrigerator and organizing it, rotating foods so the things we need to eat first are in front. I also sort everything by food type. I use dividers, with labeled sections for Bryn's food, water, and juice, and with all alike things together. I do this with my freezer, too: Waffles and breakfast items in one place, frozen vegetables together, fruits for smoothies together. If your refrigerator and freezer are the Bermuda Triangle, break out the label maker and have at it. You'll waste a lot less food. A good sorting system will help you to actually use your leftovers.

- **Save.** Don't waste food! If vegetables are starting to wilt, I puree them and freeze them in ice cube trays. Then whenever I'm making a soup, smoothie, or sauce, I can add the pureed vegetables for extra nutrition and fiber. I also freeze everything Bryn doesn't finish. Kids don't eat very much—four bites of soup, a little pasta, a tiny bit of rice. They don't like to eat the same thing two days in a row, so just freeze the leftovers and defrost them next week when they will be excited about that food again.

- **Snack.** Have healthy snacks in your kitchen. *Always.* My favorites are a handful of whole cashews, hummus with pretzel crisps, baked chips, crackers and cheese you can slice very thin, yogurt, a peanut butter and jelly sandwich on whole grain bread, and Skinnygirl Daily On-the-Go bars. No more wasting time looking for something good to eat.

- **Store.** Don't waste food by letting it get stale or freezer burned. Wasted food is wasted money and wasted time. Everybody has that bag of peas in the freezer with the top just twisted closed or the frozen waffles with the box that won't ever be airtight. Let that stuff sit too long and it's going to get freezer burned and covered in ice crystals that make it taste stale. Instead, dump the frozen peas, corn, or carrots into a freezer container and label it. Put the waffles into a freezer Ziploc and label it. Do this also for the frozen blueberries and strawberries, veggie or chicken nuggets, frozen bread rolls, and anything else you don't use up the first time you open the bag. Do the same with your pantry items. If you opened the cereal bag, oatmeal box, pretzel bag, candy, flour, sugar, cornmeal, or anything else in a bag or box, put the rest into a clear canister with an airtight lid and label it. No more stale cereal, stale pretzels, or flour with those disgusting weevils that somehow appear.

· ·

TIME-SAVING PANTRY LIST

A well-stocked pantry allows you to make a quick, healthy meal at a moment's notice. Make a list of everything you would normally eat or want to eat, and keep it in your smartphone so you can keep track of what needs restocking. This is what I have in my pantry right now:

GRAINS AND PASTA

- Brown rice
- Quinoa
- Couscous
- Wheat pilaf
- Oat flour
- Whole wheat pasta/spaghetti
- Whole wheat shells
- Plain bread crumbs

BEANS

- Dried lima beans
- Dried white beans
- Dried chickpeas
- Canned cannellini beans

VEGETABLES

- Jarred sun-dried tomatoes in oil
- Jarred tomato sauce
- Olives
- Salsa
- Canned tomatoes

NUTS AND SEEDS

- Cashews
- Almonds
- Pine nuts
- Peanut butter

DRIED FRUIT

- Dried blueberries
- Dried cranberries
- Raisins

OILS

- Extra-virgin olive oil
- Canola oil
- Sesame oil
- Truffle oil

SOUP

- Boxes of pureed soup (Imagine and Pacific brands)
- Variety of organic soups
- Vegetable broth

CEREAL (All in large plastic or glass containers)

- Rolled oats
- Cascadian Farm Multi-Grain Squares
- Kashi Autumn Wheat cereal
- Trail mix

BAKED GOODS

- Organic brownie mix
- Tate's chocolate chip cookies

PACKAGED SNACKS (All in large plastic containers)

- Pretzels
- Kind bars
- Dried edamame
- Multigrain Tostitos
- Baked chips
- Rosemary Italian-style crackers
- Kit's Organic bars

SWEETS

- Licorice
- Dark chocolate nonpareils
- Jellybeans in assorted flavors
- Assorted candies from trip to Australia
- Sprinkles
- Mini chocolate chips
- Ice cream cones

SWEETENERS

- Real maple syrup
- Brown rice syrup
- Stevia packets
- Honey

CONDIMENTS AND SEASONINGS

- Low-sugar ketchup
- Mustard
- Mayonnaise
- Pickle relish
- Soy sauce

- Worcestershire sauce
- Assorted herbs and spices

BEVERAGES

- Club soda

Clean Faster

Most people don't organize, clean, and perfect as they go. They let it all pile up, shove it somewhere for the time being, and say they'll deal with it later. When "later" finally comes, cleaning seems like too much work and too much time.

You don't have to spend hours cleaning your house. Instead, every time you use something, put it away before you even put it down. Do this in every part of your life. When the clutter is gone, it's easier to see the dust and dirt. Then you can concentrate on level 2 cleaning: wipe, sweep, mop, polish, or sponge up dirt and dust right when you notice them and you'll be ahead of the game. Your once-a-week cleaning will go much faster if you're continuously spot-cleaning, and your house will be a healthier environment for everyone who lives there.

You shouldn't be the only one helping. Give your family or roommates incentives to help. Start children early picking up after themselves so they enjoy having an orderly environment instead of learning to live in a mess. Bryn loves to sing the cleanup song: "Clean up, clean up, everybody everywhere, clean up, clean up, everybody do their share!" Wise words. Picking up after herself is a game, not a chore, and I really believe that a clean, orderly house can be addictive and contagious. Put everything in its place, clean as you go, and you'll feel calmer and waste less time. Everything about your house will feel nicer.

HOMEMADE CLEANERS

If you want to be green, thrifty, and never run out of cleaner, use products you already have around the house to clean and deodorize your home:

- Make your own general cleaner by filling a spray bottle with one part white vinegar and one part water, one tablespoon of dish soap, and the juice from one lemon. This will clean all your counters (but don't use it on marble or finished wood counters).
- To make glass cleaner, try this recipe I discovered online: ¼ cup rubbing alcohol, ¼ cup white vinegar, 1 tablespoon cornstarch, and 2 cups warm water. Put it all in a spray bottle, shake, and clean your mirrors and windows. This works surprisingly well.
- To keep your garbage disposal smelling good, put a lemon peel in the disposal and grind it up about once a month.
- Baking soda in the fridge will absorb odors. Ground coffee works, too. Put either one in an open container, in the back so it doesn't spill.

By the way, only make homemade cleaners in unused spray bottles—chemical residue in store-bought-cleaner bottles could react with your home remedy.

I'm finally in a position to hire a once-a-week cleaning person, although I did it myself for years. I still clean up after myself constantly, because one cleaning person isn't going to do it all. If you do have a cleaning person even once a month, give them specific periodic tasks in addition to their regular checklist. For example, one day you might ask them to clean inside the bathroom cabinets or under the couch or on top of the refrigerator. Knock out those spots you don't usually get to, like the windows or the bottoms of the garbage cans, and you'll be getting the most out of your dollar.

If you don't have someone to help you clean, do it yourself, but do it in pieces so it's not overwhelming. It's like going to the gym and doing your abs one day and your arms the next day. If you just do a little at a time whenever you can, it will all get done. Once you've tackled the big things like basic decluttering and cleaning, you can get to those things you would never normally notice until you moved out: dust bunnies under the dresser and bed, the gunk behind the refrigerator, the thin film on the lampshades and cabinet fronts, the dirt on the walls behind the furniture. Be meticulous, and know that no one else will do these things if you don't. You set the tone and the standard, and the level of cleanliness in your house will rise to meet it because your housemates or family will follow your example. It starts with you. Fair or not, this is the reality if you want a clean, organized home.

I get that sometimes, cleaning seems horrible. You're depressed or you're stressed and you can't even imagine doing it. Well, fire up your imagination, because you can do it anyway. In fact, it can actually cheer you up and relieve your stress. Believe it or not, cleaning can be therapeutic and cathartic. Put on some loud music and just dive in and get started. Even doing a little bit will make you feel better.

SPONGE HYGIENE

If you like to use sponges for cleaning, keep them sanitary. They attract bacteria, so at the end of the day, rinse them well and microwave them for thirty seconds, or drop them into the top rack of the dishwasher.

Use different-colored sponges for the kitchen counter, dishes, bathroom, and any other use, so you don't accidentally mix them up. I don't want to know how many people wipe down their counters or windowsills and then do the dishes with the same sponge. It's disgusting.

Replace your sponges often. As soon as they get discolored or start to shred, toss them. I buy big bags of sponges at Costco so that I'm never without a replacement.

. . . .

Look Pretty in Less Time

I know some women who spend two hours getting ready to go any-where, but that's totally unnecessary. A streamlined beauty regimen will save you tons of time. It's all about making a plan. You know what you need to look presentable. Plan it out, have everything you need ready to go, and then don't waste time. I have a daily beauty regimen and a weekly beauty regimen, and they only take a few minutes of my time.

This is what I do every day and every week. I hope you can get some inspiration from it, to streamline your own routine:

Daily Beauty Regimen

1. **Wash your face with a good gentle cleanser.** Any brand will do, as long as it's not harsh enough to strip your skin. Cleansing isn't just about keeping your skin clean. It's about taking care of your skin. Your face goes through a lot with wind, sun, makeup, and daily life. Be good to it. You need something that works but that is gentle.

2. **Use toning spray from a spray bottle.** Save the alcohol for your cocktails. The goal is to hydrate. Like many girls in their twenties, I used to be a stripper. No, not on a pole by the airport. I mean I used to strip my skin with drying masks and astringents and scrubbing, wiping my face with a cotton ball several times until the cotton came clean. This can cause dryness and bumps under the skin. Instead, feed your skin with moisture by using a hydrating toning spray.

3. **Apply serum.** I'm not very picky about my brands of cleanser or toning spray, but I am picky about serum. Serum penetrates deeper into your skin to deliver nutrients and repair wrinkles and sun damage. Serum can also help your skin absorb moisture more effectively. Mine has to be super quenching because I have dry skin.

4. **Apply a day moisturizer.** If you have oily skin, use a light moisturizer. There is a misconception that people with oily or combination skin don't need to moisturize. This isn't true. Get one with SPF for sun protection, unless you use sunscreen separately like I do.

5. **Apply sunscreen.** I use sunscreen over my moisturizer every single day, even in the dead of winter. Even if it's hazy out, my dermatologist says we are all still getting the rays. Some moisturizers contain sunscreen, and so do some foundations. That's fine, but

I use an SPF over my moisturizer because I'm wary of combination products that claim to do it all. If every product on your face has an SPF, the more the merrier. Less sun damage for you. Use at least a 15 in the winter and a 30 in the summer. My dermatologist says anything over 45 is worthless.

6. **Apply a night cream/moisturizer.** A nighttime moisturizer can be even more hydrating and can even be in the form of a mask.

. . . .

HOW MUCH SHOULD YOU PAY FOR GOOD SKIN CARE?

Price is not an indicator of quality in the skin-care industry, and about 99 percent of what you pay for when you buy a skin-care product is the packaging. In this industry, it's buyer beware. Look, I'm a sucker for something that looks nice on the counter, and I have some pretty perfume bottles on my dresser, but the difference between a product from the department store and a product from the drugstore might be nothing. The drugstore product might even be better. I've been in the skin-care business and I know the drill. If you've read about a product and it sounds great, try it if you can afford it. However, you can get great skin-care products in very simple packages if you are on a budget. Try some basic, straightforward products and find the ones you like. What works for you will likely have nothing to do with price.

. . . .

Weekly Beauty Regimen

1. **Use an exfoliating scrub.** Exfoliating removes the dead layers of skin on your face so your skin-care products can penetrate better and your face doesn't get flaky. Not everyone can do it—people with very sensitive skin may need to skip this step—but I've determined that my face can handle it. If you want to exfoliate, look for something with grains in it. There are levels of grain—finer for more sensitive

skin, coarser for skin that isn't easily irritated. I use a coarse grain. When your skin is damp or dry, gently rub the exfoliating scrub over your face. If you are sensitive, even a washcloth can be an exfoliator. Whatever you use, don't scrub too hard, because you can break blood vessels. Some people like those buffing pads, but I'm wary of the ones you don't change after each use because they can build up bacteria. I feel like I would have to clean them with boiling water after each use. I also exfoliate knees and elbows in the shower. A body scrub or an exfoliating glove or mitt will work for this purpose, but if you use the glove or mitt, be sure to rinse it well after every use and hang it to dry so it doesn't grow bacteria.

2. **Apply a moisturizing mask.** Exfoliating removes dead skin and opens your pores so the moisture from the mask can soak in. If you are breaking out and/or have oily skin, try a clay mask, which will pull toxins from your skin. However, these are drying, so they aren't good for dry or combination skin, like I have. I prefer a super-moisturizing cream or gel mask. I leave it on for at least ten minutes, or preferably overnight. (I also leave a deep-conditioning hair mask on overnight once a week.) Wash everything off in the morning.

3. **Dry-brush.** Some people dry-brush their skin every day, but I usually get around to it about once every few weeks. Dry brushing is simply brushing your skin before you shower with a soft, dry brush to remove dead skin, increase your circulation, and distribute your skin oils. You should brush toward your heart (like brushing up your arms, up your legs, and down your chest). A good, thorough dry brushing once or twice a week will improve the health of the skin all over your body. You'll be smoother and softer.

4. **Moisturize your whole body.** I live for lotion. I put it on after every shower, but about once a week, I make sure to fully moisturize everywhere. After you dry-brush and shower, or otherwise exfoliate your body, rub a good gentle body lotion or oil all over you. Some people react to heavy oils like mineral oil and olive oil, so test the oil on a small patch of skin first, to be sure you're not sensitive. Wrap up in a robe or a big towel and relax for thirty minutes in a warm spot. If you're somewhere with a steam room or sauna, even better. Breathe deeply, listen to relaxing music, or just take a nap.

5. Treat your feet. If you have dry heels and feet like I do, rub the rough areas with one of those big, heavy-duty emery boards made for feet while your feet are still dry. Then, in the shower, use a pumice stone on the rough parts. Before bed, put on a heavy-duty thick foot lotion and a pair of thick socks. You can also do this with your hands and a pair of gloves. Hopefully this will be on a day when your husband or boyfriend is out of town. It's definitely a sex wrecker.

CLEANING YOUR BEAUTY TOOLS

All the brushes and other personal tools you use get dirty and need regular cleaning, but a lot of people never think to clean them, especially if they are tools used in the shower. You should regularly clean all your brushes, scrubbers, mitts, and even your toothbrush, because every one of these products can build up bacteria, oil, and dirt. Here's how to keep your beauty tools clean:

- Hairbrush: A clean hairbrush will work so much better on your hair because you won't be redepositing old product and dirt from the last time you brushed your hair. Once a week, pull all the hair out of your hairbrush (slide a pen under the hair and pull up to make it easier to catch it all. Fill the sink with warm water and just about a spoonful of a clarifying shampoo that says it strips product out of your hair. Swish the brush around and work the shampoo into the bristles with your hands. Rinse well in warm water and set the brush out on a towel to dry.
- Dry brush: About once a month, wash your dry brush with a little bit of baby shampoo and warm water, then hang it to dry.
- Exfoliating mitts or brushes: About once a month, wash your exfoliating mitt or shower brush with a little bit of baby shampoo and warm water, then hang it to dry. When any exfoliating tool starts to look worn, replace them.

- **Makeup brushes:** This is a pain in the ass, but even sitting in a drawer, your makeup brushes will attract bacteria, and that can give you acne. Every time you do your makeup, take a baby wipe or a cosmetics pad with makeup remover and wipe off your brushes. About once a month, thoroughly clean them by giving them a "shampoo" the same way you do for your hairbrush (see previous page). Do this right before you clean the bathroom, because you'll get makeup residue all over your sink. Rinse them well and lay them flat on a clean towel. I like to put the brush ends over the edge of the sink so they get more air and dry faster. Never let your makeup brushes dry standing up in a cup. The moisture will eventually rot the wood handles.

- **Razor:** Every time you use your razor, rinse it out really well afterward. Make sure there is no soap or hair in it. An old toothbrush can get out any stuck matter. When your razor starts to drag or pull, or doesn't take off your leg hair in a clean swipe, it's time to replace it. If you see any rust on it, replace it. Razors and refills are cheap. You don't need to scrape old ones over your legs. Also never share a razor with anyone!

- **Nail brushes:** Clean in soap and water after every use. Dry on a towel or hang dry.

- **Toothbrush:** Although some people think they should put their toothbrushes inside cabinets or put toothbrush protectors over them, the American Dental Association says this actually increases bacterial growth. This is what they say to do:

  - *Wash your hands before using your toothbrush.*
  - *Rinse your toothbrush before and after using it, rubbing the bristles hard with your thumb under running water.*
  - *Deep-clean your toothbrush once a week in the top rack of the dishwasher.*
  - *Replace your toothbrush every three to four months.*

Better Hair, Faster

Your hair is an important part of your identity, so treat it well and don't wash it too often. Your own natural hair oil is the best conditioner on the planet, so you want to give it a chance to build up a little. If you have oily hair or work in a smoky or greasy place or work with food, you may need to wash it every day. If you work out intensely and sweat every day, you will probably want to wash your hair after every workout. If you use a lot of product, you may need to wash it more often. Some hairdressers say you should wash your hair every other day if you use product, but for people with dry hair in particular, two to three times a week is probably enough.

I wash my hair about twice a week. I like more body in my hair and I like to be able to run my fingers or a brush through my hair and have it feel natural, so I don't usually use any hair product unless I'm going to a big event. This is my twice-a-week system:

Day one: Wash hair and finish with a jolt of cold water, which will close the hair cuticle and make hair look shinier. Style hair, or get a blow-out. The new craze of blow-out bars makes this easy and inexpensive to do. You can have great-looking straight hair for thirty bucks. If you can afford to do it, a blow-out once a week is an easy, quick way to have good-looking hair all the time. In my opinion, your blow-out will last longer if you don't use any product on your hair.

Day two: Spray hair with a root-volume spray, to revitalize it. Use a flatiron to refresh the blow-out, but heat is damaging, especially to dry hair, so use the minimum temperature that works, and keep an eye out for split ends. That's the sign that you need a trim.

Day three: Spray in a dry shampoo to take care of any grease and use a volumizer. Go for the messy, unkempt look. Sexy. Another option is hot rollers, which can really refresh limp hair. I take hot rollers on vacation with me to use on the third day, especially in humid places like Florida that frizz your hair or make it go out of control. (By the way, don't try to maintain stick-straight hair in a humid climate. It's a losing battle.)

Day four: Wear a headband, or use serum to shellac hair down and wear a ponytail, or go for the messy beachy look. Or just wear a hat.

Day five: Wash hair and start over.

. . . .

ABOUT HAIR COLOR

I get grays along my hairline that show up all at the same time. I've named each one after a different man. I get rid of them with color, about every six weeks. Coloring is time-consuming but necessary unless you're really ready to go with the gray-hair look. Cut the time and expense in half by touching up your own roots at home between professional colorings. They say blondes have more fun, but if you are a brunette who goes blond, you'll need to do your roots more often.

I got caramel highlights once, but I didn't have the patience to maintain them. Coloring can also be harsh on hair, so I deep-condition or use a hot oil treatment on the ends only about once a month.

. . . .

Quicker, Better Nails

In culinary school they told us that nail polish chemicals could get into the food, so for many years after that I rarely wore it. At first when I stopped using polish, my nails were dry and brittle. Before long, however, as I went without polish, they grew healthier and stronger. Now I get a manicure every few weeks, just to nourish and buff my nails so they're shiny. Manicures are about keeping your nails neat. I'm one to lightly bite my cuticles, so manicures help me maintain them. If you are on a budget, you can get away with a manicure every three to four weeks unless you use polish.

Truthfully, I've started getting polish once in a while. I'm starting a new life as a single girl, so I'm busting out a little and putting more color into my life. However, once you put color on your nails, you're going to have to redo them at least once a week. It's like getting blow-outs. Once you decide to go that way, you have to keep going back if you want to maintain the look. Do you have time for weekly manicures and polish? You decide.

By the way, I tried a gel manicure, but that turned out to be a disaster. At first, I thought it would be great before a trip because the polish takes a long time to start chipping, but the problem with the gel or shellac manicures is that they have to file down your nails like they do with acrylic tips, so it destroys your nails. Then taking that stuff off is a nightmare and it weakens your nails significantly. It takes half an hour just to remove the gel, then a few months to grow your nails back out. Never again.

· ·

RAZOR, WAX, OR LASER?

Hair where you don't want it. What do you do about it? If you have thick, dark hair, it's a problem. I started waxing when I was fourteen years old because I heard the hair would grow back lighter and finer. I assumed that eventually, I would be hairless, but it wasn't true. Waxing pulls the hair out at the root, and that's great, but one of the cardinal rules of waxing is to never use a razor. I was always told the razor was the devil, especially as it applies to the bikini line. The problem is, a couple of weeks or a month after a wax, you're a Chia Pet because you have to let it grow a certain amount before you can wax again. I did use a razor on my underarms, but I'd get a five o'clock shadow.

When I finally tried laser hair removal, it changed my life. It is the gift that keeps on giving. Lasering is slightly painful, but so is waxing, and we all know beauty is pain. Lasering is expensive, but the good news is that you can go back whenever you can afford it—in six weeks or six months. (I've waited six months.) With lasering, you can't wax between sessions, but you can shave with a razor, to keep leg and underarm hair at bay until you are ready for another laser treatment. Some places let you buy packages, have layaway plans, or let you make payments. Now my underarms and bikini line are completely smooth, and it's so liberating to never have to wax again. It's the best thing that ever happened to body hair.

. . . .

Prioritize

Finally, time management doesn't matter much if you don't spend your time doing what's most important to you. This requires some soul-searching. What matters to you? Do you love the feeling of fitting a lot into your day and checking off dozens of things? Or do you know you need some downtime? This can change from day to day, so check in with yourself frequently and adjust your schedule so it's the way you need it to be. Using time efficiently is great, but if you do too much, you'll burn out and be worthless. If you know what's important to you and what's not as important, you can better decide where you want to spend the minutes of your life. Know yourself. Your ass can't be in forty-two places at once.

People think I live to work, but work is actually fairly low on my priority list. I believe in doing work thoroughly and doing it well and banging it out so it all gets done, but that doesn't mean it comes ahead of more important things. This is my priority list. What's yours?

1. **Family:** Quality time with Bryn is the most important thing for me. And my dog, Cookie, too! For you, that could mean time with your children, spouse, siblings, or parents.

2. **Sleep:** Quality, uninterrupted sleep is a huge priority for me.

3. Exercise: This is a priority so I can stay in shape and feel good, but when I say "exercise" I don't mean I'm sweating it out at the gym. Basically, as far as I'm concerned, exercise is doing anything that doesn't entail lying on my ass.

4. Recreation: Whether it's hiking, skiing, walking on the beach, or having some other kind of adventure, recreation is important to stay balanced and enjoy life.

5. Vacation: Everybody needs time off from work, even if it's just a few days or you just go to a neighboring city to get away from your regular routine. It's like filling your gas tank back up.

6. Work: Work isn't just about making money. It should be about doing something important to you or that you're truly passionate about.

7. Beauty and relaxation: Massages, manicures, the spa, drinking lots of water—all of these are on my priority list. This also includes getting all dressed up to go out.

8. Sex: With someone else or with yourself, this is important for balance. I realize this is number eight on my list. I wish it was number four.

9. Friends: A small group of friends you can really talk to and trust is more important than a big group of friends who are only casually linked. Friends are really there for you when you need them, even if you only talk on the phone. I'm usually racing around doing a million things, and it feels so good when I can really stop and connect and be fully focused on time with a good friend.

10. Social life: Get out there and do things with people. You're not a hermit. You don't live on an island. I know you have work to do, but interacting with the human race will make you more human. (Am I talking to myself?)

Using time wisely is also about knowing how to say no. Even a night out with friends can be canceled if you've done too much that day and you need a break. If you have a reputation for being dependable and on time, and you respect other peoples' time, friends and colleagues will understand when you have to cancel plans.

I try to give myself one night a week to just lie in bed, watch TV, and drool, but sometimes I beat myself up because I stay up too late staring at the TV. Use your nights off well. Have fun or get sleep. Take a relaxing bath and have some tea and let yourself drift off early. You'll be a new woman in the morning.

I'm also really trying to have fun at this time in my life. When my talk show starts, which will happen right about when this book comes out, my life's going to be on lockdown, so I'm doing things now that I won't be able to do then, like spending long afternoons with Bryn being lazy and traveling for vacation, not just work.

I've learned the hard way that I need some alone time every day and that I also need to take care of myself. Sometimes that means saying no to other things. If I don't do that, I get so much anxiety that I lose it. I'm a nicer, calmer, more tolerant person if I schedule time for exercising or getting out and walking around and doing things just for fun. I let myself spend some time reading the paper, because it's important to know what's going on in the world. Vacations are a necessity, not a luxury. Even a day off work in the middle of the week can make you feel like you've had a two-week vacation if you truly relax and do things you love to do.

Another way I take care of myself and keep my stress level in check is to use weekends wisely. I can go like a madwoman all week long but I can't keep that up constantly, so on the weekends, I give myself purposeful downtime. I also use my vacation time wisely. I'm the queen of the four-day vacation. I think that's plenty of time to feel like you really got away from your normal routine, did something different, and recharged. When I went to Australia for a week, that was almost too long.

The bottom line is that all we really have is time, and every moment is precious, so spend it the way you would want to say you spent it when you look back at the end of your life: with people you love, doing things you enjoy, and being happy. The not-so-fun stuff can be made more efficient through organization and multitasking, leaving more time for living your life the way *you* most like to live it.

Chapter Seven

Homebody

If I had my way, I'd never leave my house or take off my pajamas. Being home feels so comforting and reassuring to me. I don't have to look any particular way, I can be comfortable, and I can truly relax. Put it this way: Thank God I only have women working in the office because I'm always braless and I'm constantly accidentally flashing them and apologizing for my nudity.

But that's the way I roll. I may not be primped and perfect all the time, but I want my home to be the place I most love to be, and that means keeping it organized, clean, and beautiful. It's the place I come back to, no matter what exciting places I've been. It's the place I love to be the most.

To be honest, though, since I'm going through a divorce right now, my home is less of a comfortable, calm oasis than I would like it to be. This too shall pass and I know I'll feel relaxed in my home again someday soon, but for now, it's even more important for me to keep everything organized and nice rather than in disarray. My life is in enough disarray, so my home needs to counteract that.

Most important to me are my personal, private spaces—my bedroom and my closet. I like to keep them full of candles and scents I love and the things that comfort me. I like them to be girly and bubbly, like a bubble bath. If you are going through something in your life, it's really important to find your calm space, your "bubble bath," so you can go there and feel nurtured. Keep it exactly how you want it. No matter where you have stress—whether it's money or relationships or work—your home should be your refuge.

For most people, however, keeping a clean, organized, beautiful home is difficult. Your friends and neighbors and people on television might make it look easy, but it's a challenge for everyone. Polly Perfect is an illusion. Life is messy and every home will tip toward chaos if you don't keep it under control. When your home gets messy, dirty, cluttered, or filled with things you don't love, it won't feel like a refuge. It will feel like something you want to escape from, and that goes against the whole idea of home. When I get home from a trip and my stuff is everywhere, I cannot *wait* to restore order and get back to the feeling that everything is in its place.

So let's get on this. In this chapter, we're going to go room by room, area by area, through your home to declutter, clean, organize, and simplify. If you don't love where you live, I want to help you change that. I want to help you make your home a place you want to be, one that energizes you and makes you feel better about yourself and your life. It's not about square footage or price or opulence. It's about *you*. Home shouldn't be stressful. It should make you feel calm and good and cared for. They say home is where the heart is, so make a suitable space to keep your heart.

Decluttering, Cleaning, and Beautifying, Room by Room

Clutter looks bad, but it's also a huge psychological burden. It keeps you from being able to find things, and it will make you feel anxious just looking around at a cluttered space and trying to find somewhere to sit down or set your drink. You will also buy so much less when you know what you have and you know where it all is. People often keep buying clothes and food and toiletries and tools because they don't know what they already have. It's wasteful and environmentally irresponsible, too. When your home is clutter-free,

you will feel an amazing sense of calm. Your life will run more efficiently.

Cleaning comes next. There is nothing more disgusting or de-
pressing than a filthy home, and even if you are used to living in a
less-than-clean environment and don't even notice anymore, you will
notice a clean house. It just feels different.

You could probably spend eight hours a day cleaning, but nobody has time for that. Instead, focus on the things that matter, that
bother you when you notice them, that make you dislike being in a
room, or that you wouldn't want anyone else to notice. Shockingly,
people do look in your refrigerator and notice if it's disgusting. They
will look in your medicine cabinet, too.

Sometimes, I go to someone's house and I expect it to be spotless
because the person is so well dressed and looks so put together, but
the house turns out to be vile. You might notice things in someone
else's house you wouldn't notice in your own house, so here is a list
of things to keep an eye on:

- Are all your trash cans emptied?
- Do you have a dirty litterbox or wee wee pad in plain view
  (or can you smell it)?
- Is there debris on your carpet? Dust bunnies under the
  furniture?
- Is there visible grime in the corners? What about hair?
- Is your bed made?
- Are there toys or clutter everywhere?
- Is the bathroom mirror clean and free of smudges and
  toothpaste splatters?
- Is there sludge in the bathtub?
- Are your toilet-bowl brush and plunger disgusting?
- Is your shower dingy?
- Is your medicine cabinet neat and organized?
- Is there hair on your bathroom floor?
- Does the toilet paper hang under, not over, the roll? (It
  should go under!)

- Are there dishes in the sink?
- Is your refrigerator clean and tidy?
- Are all the handles on all the appliances and all the cabinets clean and new? (Cabinet hardware is easy and inexpensive to change out regularly and can update the whole look of your kitchen.)
- Are the kitchen cabinet faces clean?
- Is the inside of your microwave clean?
- What about the face of the dishwasher and refrigerator?
- Are there splashes and spots on the faucet spigots and handles?
- Are the hand towels clean and uncrumpled?
- Are glass doors clean and free of fingerprints?
- Have you recently wiped down all the phones and doorknobs?
- Are there fingerprints on the walls?

People do judge you on these things. I was thinking about hiring somebody once, and I just happened to see where this person lived. I said to myself, "I cannot give this person a job." It made a difference to me. It was proof that this person would not be a highly organized and meticulous employee. That being said, I've hired many people without ever seeing their homes. I like to think they were in order, but if they weren't before they started working for me, it probably didn't take long for them to transform their ways!

Of course, even more important than what anyone else thinks about the condition of your home, keeping your living space organized, clean, and beautiful is something you should do for yourself and your family. It's how *you* feel in your own home that really matters. Mess equals anxiety. I know cleaning a messy house can be overwhelming. Just do a little at a time. Cleaning has to become a habit. You have to commit to it, the same way you would commit to a challenging work project or to spending more time with your family. You have to convince yourself how important it is to have a clean house and then make it happen. No procrastination! If Monday is laundry day, you do the laundry. If Tuesday is the day you mop the floors, make it as important as taking a shower or meeting a work deadline. A clean house is your business, and it's also part of your personal hygiene, because your home is an extension of you. Just do it. It's so worth it.

Are you ready to give your home a makeover? First, some general principles:

- **Tackle clutter first.** Do one room, or even just one part of a room, at a time. You can't see the dirt if piles of junk are in the way. Do this in levels. Start by going through all the piles and putting things where they belong or throwing them away. That's the first step. Then always be editing. I'm constantly editing in my home, the same way I edit my wardrobe. If I notice something I don't use, I get rid of it immediately, whether it's a chair or a vase or a spatula or a necklace. If I buy anything new, the rule is that I then have to try to get rid of something old. This goes for furniture, makeup, cooking tools, toys, clothing—everything. If you can't bear to throw away something even though you know you will never use it, consider giving it to someone you know. It makes it easier to part with something if you know where it went. I do this a lot, and I love seeing the girls in my office come in looking cute in something I gave them.
- **Declutter as you go.** Some people think it's easier to just let an area get messy and then clean it all up at once. For example, when you have a baby, it's hard to constantly be putting every single toy away. Find your own balance, but think about how much easier decluttering will be if everything gets put away as you go, especially kid clutter.
- **Organize your cleaning supplies.** Once you can see the floor, your desk, your bed, it's time to start cleaning. Organize your cleaning supplies under your kitchen sink or in your bathroom or wherever you keep them. Scale them down. You don't need five products that do the same thing. Put the things you use the most, like all-purpose cleaner and glass cleaner, in the front where you can easily grab them. Put the things you use less often, like silver polish

and grout cleaner, in the back. Make this area nice. The under-the-sink area is usually gross, so clean it out. Get a plastic mat and some bins and keep everything neat. Yes, even your cleaning supplies should be clean!

- **Organize your cleaning tools.** Your broom, handheld duster, and/or vacuum should also be easy to reach, so you can clean up a mess or a cobweb or pet hair at a moment's notice. If your vacuum cleaner is dusty, that's a bad sign! You aren't using it enough.

. . . .

CLEANING YOUR CLEANING SUPPLIES

You don't want to use dirty cleaning supplies. Doesn't that defeat the purpose? Wipe down the bottles, keep the cleaning-supply areas tidy, and keep your cleaning tools bacteria free by cleaning them about once a month, like this:

- **Mops.** If you have a cotton mop, throw the mop head in the washing machine. If you have a sponge mop, put the mop head in the dishwasher. Or use a mop with disposable cleaning pads, like a Swiffer.
- **Brooms.** Most people never clean their brooms, but brooms get disgusting because they pick up dirt, grime, bugs, dust mites, and old food. First, vacuum the broom, or work out all the loose dirt and hair with your fingers (wear gloves!). Then fill up a bucket with hot water and a squirt of dish soap. If your broom is vinyl, you can also add a cup of bleach. Soak the brush for a few hours, then rinse it out. A garden hose works well for this, if you have one. Let the broom dry completely, without the bristles touching the ground, or they can dry crooked. For that matter, don't ever store your broom with the bristles on the ground. Hang it or invert it.
- **Dusters.** Wash rag dusters in the washing machine. Gently swish feather dusters in warm water with a little baby

shampoo, then clear water, then blot with a clean towel and blow-dry.

- **Sponges.** This includes sponges for your counter, your floor, your dishes, and cleaning your bathroom or yourself (sea sponges and loofahs). Rinse your sponges well, then throw them into the dishwasher and they will get cleaned and sanitized. This also works for dish brushes and scrubbers.
- **Toilet brushes.** About once a month, fill a bucket with two gallons of hot water and two cups of bleach. Put the toilet brush in the bleach water and soak for one to two hours. Rinse with clean water and dry. You can also throw the toilet-brush holder in the bucket, if you use one of those. If your bucket is big enough, throw the plunger in there, too. I guarantee the plunger is vile.

· ·

- **Clean as you go.** Don't just clean once a week. Clean as you go, clean as you notice dust, clean when you see a stain, clean immediately after a spill. Cleaning should be something you do all the time, just a little here, a little there, so it never gets out of control.
- **Create projects.** Every weekend, find a short cleaning project, like cleaning the sliding glass door of dog nose prints and toddler fingerprints, sweeping your porch or deck, scouring the bathtub, or vacuuming under the furniture. Once you get in the habit, it's fun trying to think of new things to clean. Even now, with a housekeeper, I'm always cleaning up something.
- **Everyone should help.** If somebody lives in your house—family members, roommates—that person has to be responsible for his or her own messes. Nobody gets to make a mess and walk away from it. Being a mom means you could clean 24/7, but if you give everyone in the house jobs and put yourself in charge of enforcement, they will eventually follow your lead. Don't wait for everyone else to magically

start cleaning up after themselves. This is learned behavior. Don't tolerate filth and mess. Set a good example.

- **Make sense.** Everything in your home should mean something to you and make sense to you. You should love every room and your whole house should reflect your personality, taste, and preferences. If something doesn't make sense to you, whether it's a piece of furniture or a decorative item or the way things are arranged, get rid of it, move it, change it.
- **Don't forget curb appeal.** The outside of your home is a reflection of you that's shown to the world, and it is also the first thing you see when you get home. Is the lawn mowed? Are the gardens neat, or are the weeds taking over? Are the windows clean? Is the roof covered in debris? Are there dead plants on the porch in last year's mildewed flowerpots? Sometimes even the wealthiest people have neglected home exteriors, and that makes a bad impression. They don't have pride of ownership and it shows. Your home is your haven and your castle, no matter how big or small. It should be clean, neat, and kempt, inside and out.

Every room has its organizational challenges and clutter spots, so I'm going to walk you through your house, room by room, and tell you what I do to keep each room functional, comfortable, and beautiful.

Living Room/Den

The living room or den is usually the center of your home. If it looks like a hurricane struck when you walk in the house, that's the tone you set for everyone, including yourself. Even if you don't have a big house, you can have a living room or den that makes you feel calm and happy, so you actually want to hang out in there. Here's how:

The Declutter
- **Get the entryway in order.** This is your first experience when you walk into the house, and if anyone else comes over,

this will be their first impression. Is it filled with fifty pairs of boots, sports gear, and piles of coats? Put up hooks or get a coatrack and hang coats. Store out-of-season outerwear in boxes somewhere else. Get racks or bins for boots, and store sports gear you don't use more than once a week somewhere else, like in the garage or in a closet. I keep a bin by the front door for shoes because we all take our shoes off in the house, but I don't let them pile up.

- **Eliminate the tchotch.** My closet designer, Andrea, always talks about tchotch, the crappy junk that fills our homes for no good reason—little figurines, potpourri, half-dead houseplants in tacky vases, chipped dishes, coffee-table books you won't read, gnomes, and all the rest of it. Just because you used to like something when you were eighteen and got your first apartment is no reason to keep it on display now that you're a real adult with a real job and a (potentially) nice living space. Get rid of all those things you're so used to seeing that you don't even see them anymore, let alone realize you don't like them or don't care about them. That stuff has to go! Better to have a few quality things than a bunch of cheap junk everywhere.
- **Quit the magazine habit.** Cut out what you like and make an inspiration or recipe book, then recycle the rest. If you haven't read them within two months, cancel your subscription. Aren't we all supposed to be reading magazines on our electronic devices now anyway? It's greener.
- **Toss extra clickers.** One universal remote can control everything.
- **Get the board games and toys out of sight.** Find a closet shelf for those. If your child plays with toys in the living room, keep them in one out-of-the-way area. After playtime, everything can go into a nice toy box or covered bin.
- **Donate dated DVDs and CDs.** If you haven't watched it in a year or two, are you really going to watch that DVD again? Besides, everything is on demand now, or you can DVR it when it comes on TV. If you still use CDs, get rid of the

ones you don't listen to anymore, and take the ones you still use out of their plastic cases and put them in a binder. Or just rip them onto your computer.

- **Throw out ratty throw pillows.** If your pillows look old and worn, toss them and buy fresh new ones in colors and fabrics that make you feel good. I buy new ones about once a year. They aren't expensive and they have a lot of impact in a room. Check places like T.J.Maxx, HomeGoods, Target, and Pier 1 for inexpensive pillows.
- **Donate or consign books.** If you have a library of beautiful books because you like the ambience they give your home, that's great, even if you never read them all. If you have piles of paperbacks on the floor, that's just messy, even if you *have* read them all. Are you really going to read them again? Every time I finish a good book, I give it to a friend or coworker.

The Clean

Your living room/den probably gets the most traffic, and the one place most likely to collect dirt is the carpet. Vacuum your carpet and upholstery about once a week, and clean your carpet about every six months. Clean up stains immediately. If you have kids and pets, there will be stains on your carpet and upholstery. Someone once told me that I shouldn't be scrubbing stains on my wool carpet because I was ruining it. Just blot. Find out how to take care of your carpet, and if you really can't get a stain out, call one of those once-a-year steam-cleaner companies. They will do a consultation for free and quote you a ridiculous price, but offer them half and let them walk out the door. They'll usually turn around and give you your price and it's a great feeling seeing them suck dirt out of your carpets.

One way to prevent a lot of dirt from getting on your carpet is to take your shoes off by the door. It's the place where carpets will show dirt first. In my house, all shoes go off at the front door. Some people provide slippers for guests, which is a nice touch. We hang out in our socks. I've heard Bryn telling her dollies, "No shoes in the house!"

I don't do this in every situation. If I'm having a party, I'm not going to make people take off the nice shoes that go with their outfits, but I do clean the carpets after a party. Shoes track in all kinds of disgusting things from the street. Think about what's out there. Do you want it on your carpet, where you might like to sit or exercise and where your kids play? After a party, vacuum no later than the next day.

· ·

YOUR INSPIRATION BOOK

Keep an inspiration book so you always have ideas for how to decorate the rooms in your home (or a future home!). Whenever you see a picture of a great room you really love, cut it out and put it in a clear plastic sleeve in a binder. Don't just stick it in a folder. You'll never look at it. Organize the binder by room, and look at it often.

No matter how financially tight things are right now, and even if you don't own your own home, your inspiration book will help you refine your vision for your living space. You can often get good ideas for small, inexpensive changes just from a picture that inspires you. And who knows? One day, you may have a beach house you need to decorate, or you'll be ready to buy your own home or remodel.

Years ago when I was broke, I started an inspiration book. I would rip out pictures and think, *I'll never be able to afford this*, but when I finally bought my apartment, I used the entire book.

· ·

The Makeover

When I renovated my current apartment, my designers wanted me to buy a lot of fancy new items. They wanted me to pull up my blond wood floors and basically buy all new ones. I wanted to stay true to myself and remember where I came from, so I said no when an expense seemed ridiculously extravagant to me. I chose to stain them so they would be less costly. They are also more interesting because they have a distressed look. I paid a fraction of the price, and my approach was much greener.

I don't think a home has to be expensive to be beautiful. I kept many of my original items, like my Ikea mirrors and my Crate & Barrel chairs, because I really like them, even better than I liked a lot of things people tried to get me to buy, which cost thousands more.

One of my favorite things to do in the living room (or any room, really) is to mix highs and lows. A lamp from Walmart can go next to a custom couch and table. An expensive dining table can have Ikea coasters and candles from Target. I have a lot of things in my home from Ikea, HomeGoods, Crate & Barrel, and Target. I like them and they are functional and look fine in my home. Use what you already have and then accent with new pieces. You won't end up recognizing the original pieces because in a new environment and accessorized differently, they come alive in a new way. Who would know my Ikea mirrors cost $99 each unless I confessed?

When you're buying items that need to hold up, like couches, it's important to save for and purchase quality items that will last forever. Just like with clothing, save your money for quality classics, but if you buy something trendy, then buy the inexpensive version. When it goes out of style, you won't be out much and you'll easily be able to switch up the whole tone of your room whenever you need a change with things like lamps, throw pillows, and candles.

Overall, my guiding principle for my living room (and my whole living space) is: Less is more. Clutter is stressful. Keep it minimal, elegant, and calming, but creative and original. For example, once when Target had a sale I found a really colorful decorative bicycle that I nailed to the floor. I bought three inexpensive picture frames and some street art, and I created a "moment" in a corner of the living room. Original, but not cluttered.

Another idea I saw at Andy Cohen's house: He had taken a picture while he was in France of unfocused neon lights. It was blurry but beautiful and it looked like art. He had it blown up and framed, and it looked great in his home. A truly original piece.

· ·

CREATING A WORKOUT SPACE

At this point in my life, I prefer to work out at home most of the time, but I don't want unsightly workout equipment in my living room. Instead, I made a corner in the den for exercise. I put an elliptical trainer in there along with my yoga mat and some hand weights. Even if you don't have a den, think about where you could create a little workout corner for yourself, out of the way of the main room. An office, larger bedroom, family room, even attic or basement are all possibilities, as long as you make it comfortable and inviting so you want to go there. A television can also help you get through your workout. Walk on the treadmill or ride your stationary bike while you watch talk shows or old movies.

· ·

Kitchen

Kitchens get messy fast, but your kitchen should be clean, organized, and easy to use, so you want to go in there and make dinner instead of ordering takeout. Here's what to tackle.

The Declutter

- **Refrigerator:** Get rid of everything in your refrigerator that is no longer edible or that you realistically are never going to eat or serve: flat soda, browning produce, old condiments. If you haven't used the black bean paste in a year, toss it.
- **Pantry:** Toss pantry items you won't use, and store everything so it will stay good longer. Group like items together: pasta, beans, canned soups, etc. Store everything so it's airtight and label everything. If it has dust on it, toss it.
- **Freezer:** This is where food goes to die. Toss anything with freezer burn or that's been there for a year. Start fresh. I'm

a huge proponent of using the freezer to store leftovers and extra food for future meals, but by "future" I mean next week or next month, not January 2020. Label everything so it's not a mystery, and fill up smaller freezer containers all the way instead of filling large containers halfway, to prevent freezer burn.

- **Spice rack:** Have your basic spices but don't clutter your cabinets with every spice in the store. Never buy those prefilled spice-jar racks from department or discount stores, and avoid those big bottles at the ninety-nine-cent store. Who knows how long those herbs and spices have been sitting there? Pick your ten most used herbs and spices and replenish them often. Only buy unusual spices if you need them for a specific recipe and only in small amounts— because are you really going to use the rest of those cardamom pods any time in the next eighteen months? I doubt it. Most herbs and spices last for about a year or maybe two, so if you've had a jar of coriander seeds or dried mustard for five years, throw it out.

    Another option is to buy fresh herbs and whole spices more often. Buy a ten-dollar coffee grinder just for spices (don't use the one you use for coffee). Pull fresh herbs off the stem and chop them with your chef's knife. Freeze extras in small Ziploc bags or mix with olive oil and freeze in ice cube trays. Freshly grind whole spices like peppercorns, mustard seeds, cumin seeds, coriander seeds, celery seeds, fennel, and cinnamon sticks as you need them.

. . . .

PAN SAVER

I went through thirty-two years of life on this planet without ever figuring out that a sheet of tinfoil or parchment could save my baking pans from ever getting stained. I learned this in culinary school, and now it seems so obvious. Use foil on all your sheet pans and bakers for things like roasted vegetables and potatoes.

For things that stick, like crab cakes or cookies, use a sheet of parchment (you can buy this in the kitchen aisle of the grocery store or in baking stores).

- **Cookware:** The pots and pans you use shouldn't be scratched, dented, or have loose handles. You don't have to buy what Bobby Flay uses. Look for a good-quality set of pans and a good sharp knife at Costco. Inexpensive nonstick pans work just fine for most purposes, and when they get scratched, you can afford to replace them. I see so many totally thrashed nonstick pans in people's homes. The scratches make the nonstick chemicals come out into your food. Your nonstick cookware will last longer if you never use metal utensils on it, but eventually, they all go. When it's time, face it and replace it. Also replace it if the handle is getting wobbly and you can't tighten it, or the pan is so badly stained or burned that it's unsightly and you can't get it clean. If it's your grandma's perfectly seasoned cast-iron pan, that's worth keeping, but the cheap stuff is meant to be replaced frequently. If you're really thrifty, there are cleaners you can buy that make stained or burned pans come clean. Look for special cleaners for your type of pan—stainless steel, enamel-coated cast iron, or uncoated cast iron. It's worth a try, especially if it was a nice pan in its heyday.

. . . .

KEEP YOUR KNIVES SHARP

A dull knife is a dangerous knife. If you try to cut a tomato and the knife slides off, you're going to cut yourself. That long rod thing that comes with your knife set is a honing device or honing steel. It realigns the knife edge so it is centered, but it doesn't actually sharpen the knife. To use the honing device, run the knife along it the same number of times on both sides. Ideally, you should use a honing device every time you use your knife.

A knife sharpener is different. It actually removes some of

the metal from the edge. It has to be a material harder than the knife itself. There are many types of knife sharpeners. Follow the instructions on the type you have, or take your knives to be sharpened professionally.

- **Bakeware:** Just as with your pots and pans, your bakeware should be in good condition. Pull it all out and go through it. Just keep the items you really use. Toss the stained and warped sheet pans. New ones are cheap at Ikea, Target, Walmart, or Kmart. Toss the dented cake pans and chipped casserole dishes. All that stuff is just wasting space and making it difficult to get to the cupcake pan (which is a necessity).

- **Utensils:** Store all your bowls, measuring cups, wooden spoons, spatulas, strainers, and other cooking tools together, organized by function, so you know what you actually have. Do you really need more than one nutmeg grater? Do you really need twelve wooden spoons? Get rid of burned or splintered spoons, melted spatulas, and anything chipped (like glasses and glass bowls), bent, broken, or stained. Pick out what you really use and toss or donate the rest. Organize small items in plastic boxes with labels, like cookie cutters, baking cups, and birthday candles. I use square flowerpots to store my cooking utensils. They stack against the wall, which saves space. I got them at Ikea.

- **Placement:** Put the things you use next to the place where you use them. Everything should be conveniently located. Store coffee mugs by the coffeemaker, spices and pans by the stove, dish soap by the sink. I know this sounds stupid, but if you look in your kitchen, you may realize you're not doing this.

  Also think about what's on your countertop. If you use the toaster or the blender or the rice maker every day or two, that's fine, but if you use it less than once a week, store it. Sometimes a really nice appliance, like a red stand mixer, can actually be both décor and functional, but if it's purely utilitarian and doesn't add anything to the ambience you want in your kitchen, put it in a cabinet.

Put your most used appliances toward the front and the less used items in the back of the cabinets. For example, if you use your food processor and immersion blender frequently, like I do, keep them accessible. You don't want to have to pull everything out of your cabinet to get to those useful appliances.

If you haven't used an appliance in a few years, like a bread maker or juicer or pasta maker or yogurt maker, you're not going to use it, so don't even waste storage space. Just get rid of it. Give it to your mother-in-law. In fact, when you buy a specialty appliance or get one as a gift, keep the box, because you're not going to use it. Life is too busy. I recently gave away my brand-new juicer that never even saw the light of day because I can buy a freshly squeezed juice for $5, and I'd rather do that than wreck my kitchen trying to make one glass of green juice.

- **Dishes and glasses:** If you don't have a complete set of dishes or glasses or coffee cups, give away what you have and start over, or complete the set. Get rid of the rest. You don't need thirty "Good Golfer Dad" mugs and Heineken pint glasses, or even one chipped coffee mug, plate, or bowl. Get rid of everything with a chip, crack, label, or advertisement and anything promotional. Get rid of the shot glasses. You don't need shot glasses. College is over. And nobody needs five sets of champagne glasses. Put them all in a box and donate them.

You don't have to be too rash. Don't get rid of stuff you really will use that is in good condition. If you plan to have a second home someday, or you want to save things for when your kids move out, then go ahead and box up and store them. Or give items you aren't using as gifts or to someone who can use them. But the crap? Be ruthless. You're moving on.

THE ONLY DISHES AND
GLASSES YOU REALLY NEED

You don't need as much dishware and glassware as you might think. You can find good quality without spending a lot. All you really need is:

- A good set of everyday drinking glasses.
- A good set of acrylic or plastic drinking tumblers for your kids to use and for you to use in places like on your bedside table, where you wouldn't want to risk knocking over something made of glass.
- A good set of all-purpose cocktail glasses.
- A good set of champagne glasses.
- A good set of wineglasses. If you have limited space, get dual-purpose glasses that will work for white and red wine. If you have eight and four get chipped, toss the chipped ones and say you have a set of four, or buy four more.
- One good set of dishes for daily use. Optional: Another set for special occasions, but this is totally not necessary because you can use a nice set every day.
- One good set of flatware.

Toss all the randoms and maintain what you have. If you're missing something or you need more of something, go straight to Ikea. Buy eight champagne glasses for eight dollars and be a real big shot.

The Clean

Your kitchen shouldn't just be clean for looks. You're making food here, so this should be one of the most hygienic areas in the house. Instead, it can be one of the dirtiest because grime, grease, and old food can build up in the cracks and drains. Instead of cleaning once a week, do it as you go. Every time you cook, sweep the floor and run the mop over it. It will take you three minutes. Wipe down the counters and cabinet fronts and rinse down the sink. If you stay on top of the grease, you'll never have to waste a whole weekend on your knees scrubbing a greasy kitchen floor. There are better things to do on your knees.

- **Refrigerator:** The cold, hard truth is that people *will* judge you on your disgusting refrigerator. I was once at the home of a very successful television actress, and I just happened to get a look inside her refrigerator. I was horrified that it was filled with slimy rotting vegetables. Just because you have money doesn't mean you have your act together, and by the same token, anyone of any income level can have a clean, neat refrigerator. Every day, wipe down the front and handles. About once a month, clean out the entire refrigerator and scrub it down. Take all the condiments out—I guarantee there are rings under them. If you have a stainless steel refrigerator, you have to get the grease off or it will look smudged. Try wiping it down with bleach wipes or baby wipes, then, once it's completely grease free, polish it with a few drops of olive oil or mineral oil.
- **Floors:** Try to sweep and damp-mop every time you cook, but at least once a week get into the corners. Grease and grime collect and you won't notice it until you look. A scrubber with a sharp edge or even an old toothbrush will do the trick. Between more serious floor-cleaning sessions, clean up any spills or stains on your floor with a rag or bleach wipe as soon as you notice them. If you keep wipes under your sink, they will always be accessible.

- **Pantry:** Take everything out of your cabinets and wipe down the shelves. Rings and debris can collect under the jars, things might have spilled that you didn't notice, and it gets dusty in there.
- **Dishwasher:** It might seem counterintuitive to clean an appliance that cleans your dishes, but dishwashers can collect dirt, old food, and bacteria if they aren't regularly cleaned. About once every two to three months, put in a cup of white vinegar and run it while it's empty.
- **Stove:** Wipe it down after every use. It's disgusting after cooking just one thing. Trust me. Even if you don't see the grease and food residue, it's there. Don't forget the splash guards and knobs. If you wipe it down every time, it won't build up and make your friends raise their eyebrows or throw up in their mouths when they come into your kitchen.
- **Cabinets and walls:** People sometimes forget the walls, but somehow, food gets on them. I don't remember flinging wine or coffee or applesauce around the kitchen, but the little splatters prove somebody did it, and hardened applesauce is not easy to remove from a wall. Every single time you see anything splattered on any wall in your home, stop whatever you are doing and go wipe it off. Food will get on your walls, but food should not be permitted to hang out on your walls. Make it a point to step back and really look around with an eye for where the dirt is.

The Makeover

It's easy to make your kitchen look brand-new and grown-up without spending a lot. Some economical makeover ideas:

- **Put new hardware on your cabinets.** Your kitchen will look refreshed for a few bucks. In my old apartment, I had ratty cabinets, but changing the knobs made them look a million times better.

- **Change your cabinet fronts.** If you want to spend a little more, change out the cabinet fronts, without putting in whole new cabinets. It's a cheaper option for a whole new look.

- **Upgrade your appliances a little at a time.** In my previous apartment, my appliances were old and I couldn't afford to upgrade them all at once, so I replaced my dishwasher one year for $250. The next year, I replaced my microwave for $100. These things look expensive but they aren't so bad if you do them in pieces. Even higher-end appliances may not be out of reach if you only do one per year, rather than replacing all your appliances at the same time.

- **Change your faucets and/or handles.** This is another quick fix for an updated look.

- **Less is more.** A cluttered kitchen doesn't invite you to cook. I don't like the hanging pots and the glass-front cabinets, because then you see everything, and you notice if things don't match or aren't lined up perfectly, and it's annoying. Instead, put most things away. Your kitchen will look brand-new if you take everything off the counters.

- **Organize your knives.** A beautiful set of good knives in a butcher block or on a wall magnet can add to the ambience of your kitchen. (If you have kids, keep knives neatly organized in an out-of-reach drawer.)

- **Mix highs and lows.** Put place mats from Target under your grandmother's heirloom China. Serve wine in your wedding crystal but serve hors d'oeuvres from the fun colorful platters you found online. The nice things elevate the quality of the less expensive things for a greater total impact.

. . . .

EVERY DAY IS A SPECIAL OCCASION

Life isn't a dress rehearsal. If you save your nice things for special occasions, how often will you get to use the beautiful China, light the expensive candles, pour from the antique coffee service, or put out the good towels? Use them or lose them. You should get to enjoy the nice things you have. Make every event in your life special, even lunch with your family, even a snack. Light the candles, play music, decorate the table, arrange the food so it's beautiful, then sit down and really soak it all in. If you're having a snack, put out a platter of cheese or guacamole and chips arranged nicely, rather than eating out of the bag. If you're enjoying a cocktail, use your wedding crystal. Use the fancy truffle oil or the expensive balsamic vinegar you received as a gift. Wear the good dress, the expensive suit, the fancy shoes. Why not? I used to save my best things for some undefined "special day" in the future. Now I'm proud to have people over, light a nice candle, and serve a cocktail in a nice glass. Today is the day to live your life. You never know about tomorrow.

. . . .

Bedroom

This is your oasis. It should make you feel calm and nurtured and comfortable. You know what they say: Only use the bedroom for sleep and sex. I wish I could say I use other areas for sex, but that would imply I was actually having sex. I hope you're getting more than I am. Either way, make the bedroom good and ready for both sleeping and sex—just in case.

The Declutter

Clutter can actually keep you awake, and if you have issues sleeping, like I do, clutter in the bedroom can make it worse. A lot of people stash junk in the bedroom, especially when company comes over, because they think this is the one place no one will look, but what if your new business partner decides to put her coat on your bed and has to drape it over a huge pile of your unfolded laundry?

I'm still working on my bedroom. It's my calm project. Here are some things I think really help make the bedroom into an oasis:

- **Make your bed every day.** Do it as soon as you get out of it, not later, not after you have coffee. It will take you twenty seconds. If you're not the last one out, it's the job of the person who's out last. Your sheets will stay cleaner because they'll be covered, and your bedroom will look more inviting.
- **Get rid of anything stressful.** Look around your room. What stresses you when you look at it? It doesn't matter why. You don't have to justify it. Just get it out of the room. It could be photos of an ex-boyfriend or stressful people, a wedding album if you're divorced, a pile of work, or anything else individual to you.
- **Go through your drawers.** Toss dingy T-shirts and tank tops. Throw away socks with holes or no mates. You're not going to find that other sock. It's been a year. If you do find it, make a sock puppet for your child. Get rid of all the underwear with stains and holes. You only need a couple of pairs of PMS underwear. If every pair is trashed, go to Target, Gap, or H&M and buy a package of new underwear. Get underwear that makes you feel pretty. Panties are not expensive. And do you need all those ugly bras? I don't know how many times I've gotten into a situation where I lamented wearing a sex-wrecker bra and big-girl panties and wished I had a pretty bra I felt proud of. Then I figured out I could just go get pretty bras instead of granny bras. Go to Victoria's Secret and go crazy. I'm forty-two and I'm finally actually wearing lacy bras (not *every* day . . .).
- **Clean your closet.** A cluttered, crowded closet will stress you out every single time you get dressed. Do you ever say to yourself that you have nothing to wear? There is a reason for that. You can't get a grip. You're overwhelmed by too much stuff, most of which you don't like or can't wear. It's time to clean out your closet. Ironically, having less means

having more, because when you only have good-quality pieces that you know how to put together, you will always have something to wear.

I finally have my dream closet, but for years, I got by with a very small closet by being extremely organized. Like, each pair of shoes in a plastic box with a Polaroid on the front, and everything in Ziplocs, including my lingerie.

Even today, now that I have plenty of space, I am constantly editing my closet. Get this idea into your head: If you don't wear it, it shouldn't be in your closet. I don't care if you think you're going to "paint in that someday." You're not going to paint. When was the last time you painted? And even if you do, is that really what you're going to wear? If it's too small, get rid of it. If it's too big, get rid of it. Don't save your fat clothes or your skinny clothes for "someday." Fill your closet with clothes you love to wear, that are flattering and fit you right now.

- Start by taking everything out of your closet. Make three piles: keep, donate/give away, and trash. Go through every single item. Be honest with yourself. If you haven't worn it since last year, there is just something about it you don't like, it never really looked good on you or made you feel good, if it has a stain or a tear, if it's stretched out or the sleeves are wrong, if it doesn't fit you the right way, or if you just don't feel like it's your style, get rid of it. Be choosy about what gets to go back in. What's really worth valuable closet real estate? Either you wear it, it fits you, and you love it, or not. Period. Your closet should only contain things that you absolutely love.

. . . .

JEAN INTERVENTION

Do you need a jean intervention? Are you still wearing acid wash? Do you have ten pairs of skinny jeans and no straight-leg or wide-leg jeans? Get a girlfriend, try on your jeans, and get rid of what doesn't fit, flatter, or excite you. You really only need a few pairs.

. . . .

- Now look at everything you're going to keep, and sort it by style and/or color. Put all the similar colors and items together: black shirts, cardigans, jeans. Go through your bags and all your jewelry. Make a plan for how to put like items together in the space you have. Put the things you wear the most in the front—no gowns or rhinestone-studded shoes. Sometimes adding another rod will give you more space to see your clothes.

- Get rid of all your junky hangers and buy the hangers that will give you 30 percent more room in your closet. Huggable Hangers is the original brand, but then Bed Bath & Beyond and everyone else knocked them off, so just look for the space-saving flocked hangers.

- People waste so much space in their closets. I guarantee you have more space than you think. Organize vertically and add rods or shelves according to what kind of clothes you have. I waited twenty years to hire a closet organizer, and I'm so glad I finally did it. This doesn't have to be expensive. Even a friend in construction might be able to do some simple things to help you use your closet space more efficiently.

- Items that are out of season should be nowhere in sight because they take up unnecessary space. If you pack them away, you always have a reason to do another editing session when you unpack your clothes for the new season. Store seasonal clothes in plastic boxes, label them, and don't just dump everything in there. Put things together nicely, using packing cubes or separators, or just Ziploc bags. You can even get lifters on your bed to make room for your storage boxes.

- Jewelry and items like belts should have their own home and be organized and visible for you to use to accessorize. I bought a jewelry chest at Pier 1 for about a hundred dollars, but you could get something pretty like lacquered trays from the Container Store. You can buy ring holders, bracelet holders, necklace holders. Whatever organizational method you choose, the goal is to be able to see everything so you know what you have.

- Sort and stack your shoes by similar style and color, and edit those, too. If you haven't worn those shoes in a year, you won't. Get rid of them and make room for another pair you will love and wear. If you don't have much space for a shoe rack or shoe shelves, do what I used to do. Buy a plastic box for every pair of shoes and keep a Polaroid of the shoes taped to the front so you can quickly grab the pair you need. Over-the-door shoe racks can also be useful, because you can see everything.

USE WHAT YOU HAVE

You don't always have to default to getting rid of things. If you really love something even though it doesn't fit right, have it tailored. Tailoring can save you a ton of money and make your clothes fit perfectly. Change sleeves, waistlines, hemlines, even buttons, and make old items new again. You can revitalize old shoes by replacing or removing a bow, fixing a strap, having them reheeled or resoled, or even dying them a new color. And use a lint brush. A clean, lint-free, pressed item can look brand-new, even if you've had it for years, especially if you combine it with something new, like a new scarf, bag, or piece of jewelry.

Now, whenever you need something to wear, shop your own closet before you shop the stores, so you always remember what's in there. You don't need to buy another black skirt or another pair of red heels. You already have those. See? Something flattering you've worn for years can have a whole new life if you jazz it up with a new belt or shoes or costume jewelry. Every single outfit you've ever seen me wear anywhere—on a date, on my show, making an appearance—is a mix of something old and something new. I'm rarely if ever in something brand-new from head to toe. I'll talk more about how to shop your closet and find things to wear in chapter 10.

· ·

CLOSET-DESIGN TIPS FROM A PRO

Andrea Gary, my closet designer, designed and organized the closets in my home and is a miracle worker with closets of all sizes. These are her tips (find out more about her at www.andrea gary.com):

- **Use multiple levels.** If you have just one rod, add another one below it. If this is all you do, you've doubled your hanging space.
- **Use your space better.** Think about how you use your closet—do you have more hanging things or folding/ stacking things? What do you use the most? A trip to the Container Store can help you make use of every inch if you add shelves, shoe racks, scarf racks, hooks for jewelry, and sweater shelves. Better yet, hire a closet designer to come and assess your particular closet and how you use it to help you maximize the space you have.
- **Stow bulky items.** Big sweaters take up a lot of room and might fit somewhere else. Can you keep them in plastic boxes in the hall closet or under your bed, or up high in the closet, at least in the off-season? Put coats by the front door, not in your closet.
- **Fold your lingerie.** Don't just stuff it in a drawer. Fold panties in thirds and then in half like T-shirts, and stagger bras, cups inside cups, the way they do in Victoria's Secret. Bethenny never folds her bras.
- **Divide your drawers.** If you have the space, reserve a drawer for panties and bras, another for socks and tights, and another for lingerie. Drawer dividers or specialty inserts (why we love the Container Store!) can also help separate these things. If you arrange your lingerie by color using drawer dividers, it's easier to match the underlayer with the outer layer.

- **No-junk zone.** You don't have to keep every single thing you own in your bedroom closet! I've seen people with poker tables, camera equipment, scrapbooks, photo albums, framed artwork, even shotguns in their closets. Put all that stuff somewhere else, like in the hall closet, the home office, the attic, the basement, or storage.

. . . .

The Clean

You spend a third of your life in your bedroom, so it should be impeccably clean. Once it's decluttered, you'll be able to see the dirt. When you see it, clean it.

- **Your bedside table is not a trash can.** Clean it off. How many books can you read at once? How many glasses of water can you drink at once? Is there an inch of dust on your alarm clock? Toss the Kleenexes, catalogs, and dead flowers. Wash the water glass, and put away earrings you took out at the last minute and the bra you tossed over the lampshade. Put the vibrator back in the goody drawer. Nobody needs to see that.
- **Hunt down the dust bunnies.** They are there, I guarantee it. Under your bed, under your dresser, behind your mirror, on the tops of the doors and moldings. Once a week, wipe down every surface, catch all the cobwebs, and vacuum.
- **Change your sheets.** How long has it been? Every night you're shedding skin cells and sweat into your sheets. Change the damn sheets. Do it weekly. You will love climbing into bed. Clean sheets feel so much better.
- **Improve your air quality.** Make the air you breathe when you sleep as clean as possible. Keep your bedroom dusted and vacuum at least weekly. A humidifier will help keep your skin moist. You might also consider installing a high-quality air purifier. This can really help with allergies. If you paint, use the nontoxic, fume-free paint in your bedroom,

if not everywhere, and use natural fabrics and materials for bedding, curtains, furniture, and carpets, like cotton, wool, bamboo, and hardwood, so they don't off-gas and fill your room with fumes. (This is also crucial for your child's room.)

The Makeover

A few easy shifts will make your bedroom look brand-new.

- If your sheets are shot, buy new ones. You shouldn't have to use torn or stained sheets. Nice ones aren't expensive at Kmart, Target, Walmart, or T.J.Maxx. Buy a higher thread count and enjoy. You should love your linens, too, and they should always feel fresh and clean.

- To preserve your nice duvet, throw a regular cotton blanket on top of the duvet so your pet can lie on it. Take the blanket off when showing people around.

- Candles are cozy, but don't go so crazy that your bedroom looks like a bordello. Peel the labels off. No brand names, no bright colors, no cheap fragrance. Just simple, nice, white candles will add elegance. High-quality candles burn longer and don't have that headachey smell.

- I personally opt for blackout shades because sleep has always been an issue for me. If the sun wakes you up prematurely, invest in these. They can make a huge difference in your sleep quality, which will make a huge difference in your life quality. I also use an eye mask, which can make up for even the flimsiest curtains.

- Choose a color scheme and style you love that calms you but that you can change easily. Your duvet, sheets, window treatments, seating, lamps, any decorative items, and paint or wallpaper can all establish your style but can be switched out when you want to go with a new color or look.

• •

CLEANING THE LAUNDRY ROOM

Ironically, your laundry room can get pretty dirty. Dust and lint collect everywhere, and the tops of your washer and dryer can get not just dusty but covered in detergent spills that get sticky and dirty. About once a week, give your laundry a thorough dusting and sweeping or vacuuming, wipe off the washer and dryer tops, clean the lint traps, throw away empty detergent and stain-remover bottles, and take out the laundry trash. To spruce it up, you might add a table for folding laundry and/or shelves and baskets for keeping dirty laundry sorted and clean laundry folded and ready for people to collect and put away.

• •

Bathroom

Your bathroom can feel like a spa, or it can feel like a disaster. Which do you want? It's up to you. Here's how to err on the side of "spa."

The Declutter

The bathroom is a clutter haven and probably the number one source of overbuying, because you forget what you have in there. Before you know it, you've amassed three tubes of antibiotic cream, four boxes of Band-Aids, and seven bottles of body lotion. Here's how to get control.

- **Eliminate and consolidate.** Most people have closets and medicine cabinets full of duplicate beauty products, all scattered in different places around the bathroom: multiple bottles of shampoo and lotion or boxes of tampons; old makeup; brushes. You don't need fifty brushes. Who are you, Rapunzel? You just need one of everything, and everything together. Vow not to buy *one more personal product* until you have definitively determined you don't already have it. If you do have it, use what you have and don't replenish until it's actually gone. In the meantime, you can have a backup toiletries box, so you can work your way systematically through those seven bottles of lotion before you move on to something else. If it's easier, get smaller bins and sort everything by product type. It's economical, and once you've worked through all your multiples, you'll probably have triple the space in your bathroom cabinets.

- **Eliminate or repurpose products that don't work for you.** If you don't love a product, toss it or repurpose it. If it's body or face soap that just doesn't work for you, put it in a dispenser and use it as hand soap, or put it in the guest bathroom. If it's old, discolored, or smells funny, it's probably going bad and/or is full of bacteria. Throw it away!

. . . .

IF IT LOOKS LIKE HALLOWEEN . . .

You might love that glittery, sparkly makeup, the colored false eyelashes, the black nail polish, and the bloodred lipstick, but if you know you will only wear them on Halloween, get them out of the bathroom and put them in your Halloween storage box with the rest of the costumes.

. . . .

- **Outfit your guest bathroom.** You can also use extra products like soap, lotion, hairspray, shampoo, and conditioner in a guest bathroom. It's nice to have your guest bathroom fully outfitted. You can even put extra perfume in there on a tray, although make sure it's a nice one. I was at my friend Kyle's house recently and she had a pretty bottle of French perfume in the bathroom. I sprayed it on, and then I wanted to kill myself and her because the smell was horrible! I couldn't get the smell off. She was laughing so hard she was crying. If it's a product you hate, just get rid of it. Don't inflict it on your guests.

- **Ditch the product placement.** Don't use soap dispensers with the name brands on them. Buy nice refillable ones, and after that initial expense, you will save money because you can just buy the refill jugs and keep them under the sink. The same goes for any lotions or other products you keep out on the sink.
- **Check under your sink.** Is the area under your sink a disaster? It always is. Clean it up and organize it vertically. I guarantee you have more room under there than you think. Bins or trays that slide out can hold toilet paper, tampons and panty liners, extra soap, razor refills, and Kleenex boxes.
- **Be discerning.** For products where quality really matters, like under-eye or face cream, get rid of the ones that don't do what they're supposed to or that you are just "meh" about. Your face is worth it. Only use the ones that make you feel the best and youngest.
- **Organize medications.** Throw anything away that is expired. Put only the things you use every day in your medicine cabinet or somewhere easily accessible to you but not to kids: Advil, prescriptions, etc. Have one box for medicines you don't use that often, like for ear infections, yeast infections, and motion sickness.

· ·

CHANGE YOUR RAZORS

Just like dull kitchen knives, dull razors are a hazard and you will cut yourself with them. The old razor you throw in your gym bag is the worst. This is how you give yourself a scar for life. Use a good razor and replace the blade when it starts to feel like it is pulling or you notice it is leaving hair behind or about once every six to eight weeks. If you see any rust, replace it immediately.

· ·

The Clean

The room where you get clean can be the dirtiest room in your home. Like the kitchen, you have to stay on this or it will be disgusting, and just as people will judge you on the cleanliness of your refrigerator, they will definitely judge you on the cleanliness of your bathroom.

- **Line your bathroom trash can.** This will get disgusting if you throw the trash right into it. A simple trash liner will keep it clean and make it easy to empty. Always keep a spare under the liner you are using.
- **Wipe down your sink.** Every time you use the sink, wipe it down afterward. This will make a huge difference in how often you actually need to scour it. Nobody wants to see blobs of toothpaste in a sink. Wipe it up!
- **Clean the hair.** If you do your hair in the bathroom, you're going to get hair on the floor, and it will probably collect in the corners. It also collects in the drains and if you don't clean it out, eventually you'll have to call a plumber to snake your drain. At least once a week, do a hair check. Use a bleach wipe and wipe out all the corners in the bathroom.
- **Clean the floor.** About once a week, sweep the bathroom and run a mop over it, to keep hair, dirt, and product residue from building up.
- **Clean the toilet.** Clean your toilet once a week, whether it looks like it needs it or not. It needs it.
- **Rinse the tub/shower.** Rinse out the bathtub or shower after every use, so soap scum doesn't build up. Just a quick splash is fine. It takes thirty seconds. Or use one of those shower sprays. Stay on it and you'll still need to scour it out once every week or two, but at least you won't be cursing when you do it.
- **Shelves.** Every few months, pull everything out of the medicine cabinet, from under the sink, and out of the linen closet, and wipe down the shelves. Rings of dirt collect under all those bottles. This is a good time to go through

everything, get rid of expired medication and products, and consolidate doubles and triples again.

- **Baby wipes will save your towels.** Did you ever notice that when you wash your face and dry it, you still get makeup on the towel and the towel becomes stained like a raccoon used your towel? I notice this because I always buy white towels. After I wash my face, I give it one more good swipe with baby wipes or makeup remover. This simple step will save your towels, even if they aren't white, because otherwise eventually they will get dingy. By the way, you don't have to wash your bath towels every single time you use them. You're using them on a clean body. But do wash them at least weekly, and hang them unfolded so they dry well and don't get moldy.

· ·

MAKEUP EXPIRATION DATES

Your makeup doesn't last forever, so toss that pink glittery eye shadow you bought in the eighties. In general, if you haven't used up your makeup, throw it away according to this timetable:

- Four months for mascara and liquid eyeliner.
- One year for water-based or cream-based products like water-based foundation, concealer, cream eye shadow, and water-based or cream-based cleansers.
- One year for nail polish.
- Eighteen months for oily or waxy products like oil-based foundation, crayon liner, lip liner, and lipstick.
- Two years for powder products like powder eye shadow, powder compacts, and loose powder.
- About two years for perfume in a spray bottle and one year for perfume in a regular bottle. After that, if you still like the fragrance, use it as a sheet spray.

· ·

The Makeover

This is the part where your bathroom can look and feel like a spa. You don't have to go overboard. Just add the spa touches and you'll relax every time you go in there.

- Coordinate your sink accessories. A nice set that includes a soap dispenser, Kleenex box, toothbrush holder, and tray or cup for accessories will make your sink look elegant.
- Put a few candles on the sink.
- Don't use air freshener with a label. Keep it out of sight or use one that has a nice look.
- A basket next to the bathtub can contain clean folded towels that match the bathroom color and a shower cap so you can shower without destroying your blow-out. (Bryn has a Hello Kitty shower cap she puts on when I put on mine.)
- Put pretty bath oils, bath beads, or bubble bath on a shelf by the bathtub.
- Hang a medium-length, inexpensive robe in the bathroom. I prefer the lighter ones that only go to the knee. I don't get the obsession with those big heavy robes. They make me sweat. I also like the strapless robes with the Velcro. They are perfect for blow-drying your hair when you don't want to get dressed yet, and they don't fall down like a regular towel.
- Buy a nice little wastebasket and keep a liner in it.
- Replace all your old, ratty, faded, threadbare towels with new ones. You can get inexpensive towels at all the discount stores. Get thick, soft ones. Avoid the really cheap, thin towels that make the water roll off. They don't feel good and you won't want to get out of the shower.
- If you're a shower person, get the tub really clean and try taking a bath again. Get the accessories: the bath pillow, the iPhone dock for playing music, the candles. Light candles, put some bubbles or lavender oil in the tub, play relaxing music, and just soak. It's good for the soul.

- Be creative. I recently found three little greeting cards I loved. I put them in three small frames and hung them in the master bathroom.

- -

PURSE CONTROL

Why spend money on a nice handbag if you're just going to turn it into a trash can? At the end of every day, or at least once a week, dump everything out of your purse and clean it out. Take out the business cards and receipts and file them. Get rid of the greasy gum, the hair, the debris. It's all gross. No excuses. It's a bad look, to have a purse full of crap. Just keep what you really need in there and nothing else.

- -

Home Office

Your home office is a place where ideas need to flow and people need to be able to think. There is no excuse for disorganization. I am a stickler for this. I've existed in a very small home office where people had to climb under one desk to get to another, but it was always organized.

The Declutter

You can't work if your office is cluttered, so before you buy anything new, you have to figure out exactly what's in there and get everything out that isn't necessary.

- **Paper.** The home office is the place where papers go to die. Although it might sound daunting if you have piles of papers, your only way out of home office hell is to go through it all and get rid of old papers that you really don't need, then *never generate more piles*. It's a paperless world now, so you can almost always do things without ever killing a tree. There are exceptions—certain contracts, for example. Most of the time, however, you can keep documents on your computer. Just be sure you have a regular system for backing everything up in case your computer dies and a way to maintain private information (change your passwords every three months or so—I've had a bad experience with this!). To get rid of all the paper you still have lying around, just plow through it. It might take a whole weekend or two, but crank up the music and just start. Make three piles:

1. If you need it soon, file it neatly in an organized way with a system that makes sense to you, so the next time you need to find your last phone bill, you'll know exactly where it is: under P, for "Phone Bill."
2. If you might need it but not any time soon, put it in a file box you can store somewhere out of the way.
3. If you don't need it (be ruthless), recycle it.

- **Office supplies.** Next, tackle your office supplies. Consolidate everything and put it near the place where you will use it—printer paper and ink cartridges near the printer, stapler and paper clips on your desk, etc. Everything in the office has a spot: trays of pens, paper clips, staples, and envelopes. Have a technology box where you keep backup phone chargers, camera parts, and computer pieces; another box for packing material, like padded envelopes and packing tape; and another box for wrapping supplies, like paper and ribbons.
- **Purge.** Get rid of everything that doesn't work or that you won't use, like supplies for printers you don't have anymore, broken cell phone chargers and mismatched cases, dried-up glue and markers, pens that don't work or are missing caps or leaking, pencils with worn-down erasers, markers that have dried up, stationery you don't really like, and the boxes you've been saving "just in case." Go through

your desk and supplies about once a week so you always have only what you really need.

- **Assemble binders.** For projects that have to be paper based, make a binder for each project. I know we're going paperless, but sometimes it's nice to have a binder with everything in it. Label them. In fact, label everything.

· ·

NOTES FROM JACKIE

Another way we keep track of things is to label our entire office. Honestly, the day we got the label maker, we walked around and labeled everything except the dog. (Bethenny says if we did label Cookie, the label would say "Bitch"!) We have labeled Bethenny's sunglasses (since they are in the case and you can't see them without opening each one), file folders, photo albums, jeans, Bryn's art, personal and work memorabilia—everything! We drew the line at labeling the lipsticks. Bethenny decided that was just a little bit too obsessive.

· ·

The Clean

Your office may not look dirty, but if you spend a lot of time in there, germs will collect. At the end of every day, use bleach or baby wipes to wipe off your desk, keyboard, and phone, and dust your computer screen.

· ·

NOTES FROM JACKIE

Working for Bethenny has taught me that organization is also about communication. Everyone involved in any event or project has to be up to speed so everything runs smoothly. For example, you might not think the drivers care what Bethenny will be wearing or which side of the car she will be getting into and out of, but they do, because depending on the length of her skirt, they might bring a different car that day to avoid paparazzi crotch shots! They have to think of everything.

. . . .

The Makeover

Make a system to keep track of everything crucial to your business, from money to contacts to bills to trip folders where you keep all the information you need every time you have to travel. Your office is information central, so this should be the *most* organized room in your whole house. Make this a priority so your business can thrive and your money can grow instead of fizzling because you're always forgetting to pay bills or losing contracts. Give your home office the respect it deserves.

Your Child's Room

A clean and organized children's room is so much fun to play in, but a messy room full of broken toys and crayon marks and dust isn't just unsightly, it's unhealthy. This is your chance to teach your child organization habits that will last a lifetime.

The Declutter

Every glue stick, marker, crayon, and paper clip should be sorted and should have a place. Get rid of old dried-up glue sticks, broken crayons, pens running out of ink, dried-up markers, and dry paint.

She has hooks for bags and hats, containers for hair accessories, and a trunk for her toys. I keep all Bryn's toys in the trunk and categories of toys in Ziplocs: Barbies and their accessories, play makeup and hair accessories, puzzles, markers, crayons, and toys with small parts like Legos. For toys that are larger, like musical instruments, art supplies, larger blocks, kitchen and cooking toys, and tool sets, I use plastic boxes. Keeping everything organized like this will help you immediately assess whether something is broken or missing pieces. If too many parts end up missing and the toy becomes unusable, I immediately throw it away, but if you stay organized, you won't lose a lot of the pieces, especially with puzzles.

If Bryn hasn't used a toy in three months, I usually donate it. If she's not interested in a book, I donate it. Giving things away lets someone else use them who might really love them, but do not give away children's toys that are missing essential pieces. That's just mean.

· ·

STROLLERS

My stroller journey has been like Goldilocks and the three bears. First I used the mac daddy of strollers. When that got to be too much to transport, I switched to the $15 umbrella stroller from Kmart. This was easy to fold up and carry but it lacked some useful features like a cup holder. Finally I settled on a stroller that was just right: not too big, not too small, with a cup holder and a tray for snacks and it easily collapses for travel. I paid about $50 for it on Amazon.com. Just go on there and look at the reviews to find the one that fits your needs.

· ·

I'm also teaching Bryn to declutter. The rule is that no toy or project comes out until the last toy or project gets put away. I'm not severe about it, but it's a good guideline to keep her room in order. I don't want her ruining her toys or tripping on things. I also limit toys and rotate them so my daughter doesn't get tired of things. I think it's healthier for her to have fewer toys around because too many are overstimulating.

I want her to use her imagination and I also want her to be able to truly appreciate and respect her things. I don't want her to get tired of things and spoiled. I want us to spend time having fun in ways that have nothing to do with material possessions, like having dance parties and bubble baths, reading books, and playing dress-up and using the hallway as a catwalk. I want her to learn to be creative and have fun without constant toy stimulation, and when we do get toys, I want them to be creative, too, like puzzles and finger painting and projects she can do.

I also want her to enjoy playing with things at other people's houses and to know how to respect toys that belong to other children. When she does get to go on a playdate and have fun in someone else's playroom, she gets excited and really appreciates it.

I have friends who are not wealthy but who buy their kids things constantly just to shut them up. I really notice this. Don't get me wrong—Bryn's got plenty of stuff, but I portion it out. Just like I go shopping in my closet, she can go shopping in her toy box to find something fun, and when things get old, we put away the old toys and move to the next rotation. But it's not out of control, like some kids I've seen who don't even know what toys they have. What often happens is that the child doesn't care about the toys because they come so easily, so they get broken or discarded, and that's a wasted toy another child could have enjoyed.

• •

MOM TALK

Bryn comes home with a lot of projects she created, and we paint a lot of things at home, too. There is no way we would be able to keep it all, but we still want to be nostalgic, so while we don't keep every single thing she's touched a Magic Marker to, we do keep the things we really love. File the best kid art in folders or plastic boxes. Someday you'll love to look back at those.

• •

The Clean

Bryn isn't Cinderella—I'm not making her sweep the floors or scrub the bathroom. For now, I just want to teach her to keep her things picked up. However, it is very important to me that her room stays clean. She is learning to make her bed, and her room gets vacuumed, dusted, and polished at least once a week. If your children grow up in a clean and organized environment, they will always want and maintain a clean and organized environment for themselves, and that's what I'm going for. I want my daughter to love being in a clean home.

Another important aspect of cleanliness involving kids is stain control! There are so many opportunities for kids to make a mess that you need systems set up to avoid ruining your house. These are some of the things we do:

- Only eat in the kitchen. The exception: When she is sick, we will occasionally eat in bed, and sometimes we will have breakfast parties in bed with a tray.
- Always take shoes off at the door.
- I usually buy the lemon or clear-colored pink-lemonade Popsicles, so if there is a spill, there won't be a stain. Well, I try. I'm not insane. But she does know not to run around the house holding snacks.
- Messy activities like painting, markers, Play-Doh, and any-thing involving glue happen only on the table covered in newspaper. No messy activities on the carpet or upholstery!

. . . .

PAINTING WITHOUT THE MESS

Bryn likes to paint, but painting is messy and I was always an-noyed by how messy the paint jars got after a few dips with a big brush. The other day, I had an idea. I took one of the plastic tops off a Chinese food take out container. I used it as a palette. I squeezed a little portion of each color onto the lid and filled the bottom of the container with water for rinsing the brushes. It worked great and she loved holding a palette like a real artist.

· ·

The Makeover

Your child's room can be a dream room without your spending a fortune. This is a room where personality can really shine through. You can make a princess room, an ocean room, a jungle room, a sporty room. Paint is cheap, and you can find theme bedding and accessories everywhere. Shop around and don't spend too much, because in another year, your child will be into something else, and it's fun to keep changing it up. Let those rooms be an ever-evolving reflection of your children's passions, so they always love being in places they can call their own. Someday, they'll have their own homes to decorate and manage. Let them exercise their dreams in this one room, and you'll be setting them on the right course.

· ·

DECLUTTER YOUR HOLIDAYS

I'm crazy for the holidays. I love to celebrate, decorate, and change the look of the house for each new holiday and season. That doesn't mean I have huge boxes full of plastic junk. If you keep your holiday decorating classic and minimal, you'll have room to store things and you'll always enjoy seeing your beautiful decorations again.

I have boxes for Halloween, Thanksgiving, Christmas, New Year's, Valentine's Day, Easter, and the Fourth of July. Celebrating is fun, especially if you can just pull out the appropriate box and have everything you need instead of digging through piles of junk to find the skulls and cats or the Easter-egg tree.

It's cost-effective to keep your boxes well packed and organized. Don't just throw everything in. The next year, you'll have a hopeless tangle of lights and broken ornaments. Put it all in nicely. Wrap and tie cords, and cushion ornaments and breakable decorations. Then it's exciting to open, like everything is new. I try to save tissue for wrapping holiday items. Finally, never put anything back into that box if you decide you've outgrown it or you're tired of it. Donate it instead.

. . . .

Your Car

Your car is a reflection of your home, and a filthy car is a big turnoff. You probably spend a lot of time in the car. Make it a nice time.

- Every time you get out of the car, declutter. Take your stuff with you. Don't let your stuff hang out in your car. Also, don't cram things into your glovebox until it barely opens— it should contain your manual, registration, and possibly your service records. Nothing else. Not even gloves.
- Keep the car clean. Get it washed and clean out the inside two to four times a month. This is not too often! Your car seats are no place to hide Cheerios and they shouldn't be decorated in dog hair. Clean out the cup holders that get gross and sticky. Look in the seat-back pockets and get all the wrappers. Clean out the trunk.
- Invest in a DustBuster just for the car. If you can afford it, get your car detailed once a year so it gets new-car clean.

Although you shouldn't keep much in your car, there are some things that do belong there:

- A bag for trash. This will keep coffee cups and food wraps from ending up on the floor. Empty it often. A shopping bag is fine for this purpose.
- Tissues and baby wipes. You never know when you're going to need these.

- A portable vacuum. Tackle spills, crumbs, dirt, and dead leaves ASAP.
- If you have kids, keep a Ziploc bag filled with car toys and crayons. At the end of each trip, everything goes back in the bag, and the bag goes back in the pocket behind the front seat.
- A snack bag or box can keep kids (or you) from getting grouchy.
- In the center console, keep a pen and a pad of paper for ideas. Leave room for your coffee cup. I get a lot of creative ideas while in the car. If you are usually the one driving, get a mini tape recorder so you can record your ideas, or use the recorder on your smartphone.
- Lotion, if your hands get dry.
- Hand sanitizer and wipes to clean off the console as well as dirty hands.
- Gym shoes and/or a yoga mat, if you use them regularly. Having your gym bag in the trunk is a good incentive to get out and exercise.
- Keep an extra diaper bag, umbrella stroller, or other kid necessities in the trunk if you know you will frequently use them.

PERIPHERAL SPACES

Whether you have a garage, an unfinished basement, a shed in the backyard, or a storage unit, that space should not be a mess. You should put as much pride and organization into the spots where you store things as you do in the rest of your house.

But wait a minute . . . why are you storing all that stuff? Maybe you have legitimate reasons for keeping all your ski clothes from the eighties, but I bet you could get rid of a lot of that junk you're lugging around every time you move without ever missing it. Dive in or do a little at a time, but go through it all.

Get rid of everything you don't care about or don't use or don't
like, and you'll take a load off your mind. You might even be able
to stop paying rent on that storage unit.

One good reason to keep a storage unit: gifts. When I find
gifts for people beforehand, I store them where they will never
see them, including gifts I find for Bryn. Also, when she has a
birthday, if she has fifty friends bringing her gifts, I don't give
them all to her that day. She would be overwhelmed. Instead,
I store them and ration them out so she appreciates them. Even
if it's weeks or months later, I always tell her whom the gift is
from.

· ·

That's my take on being a homebody: Embrace the power and
pleasure of a decluttered, shiny-clean home decorated in a way that
works for you, your budget, and your aesthetic. Okay, now you know
how crazy and obsessive I am! But this is how I got to be so good
at organizing and cleaning: by doing things one at a time over the
course of years. I wasn't born this way. However, taking responsibility for your environment is necessary. Otherwise, you end up on
Hoarders.

There is nothing stopping you from taking the first step. Clean
out one drawer, one shelf, one closet, then keep going. It doesn't
matter if it takes you a year, as long as you commit to making your
home a place you love. You'll save the money you would have spent
going out all the time and traveling, because you'll actually want to
be home. When your home is your haven, everything in your life will
feel a little bit better.

Chapter Eight

Entertaining

As a former event planner, I love planning and hosting parties, but I also want to enjoy them and I don't want to spend the whole night cleaning up afterward. Anybody can have people over for drinks, but it takes a certain level of attention to detail to throw a really successful party.

The most important thing I learned about parties long ago is that having a theme pulls a party together. It doesn't have to be an obvious theme like Mardi Gras or luau. You don't have to be tacky or kitschy, but do set a tone. It can simply be an idea you have in your own mind that nobody else even knows, but it can help you keep everything—food, cocktails, music, lighting, décor—consistent, and it will give your party a particular ambience and style. Your theme might be romantic, or festive and fun, or vintage, or edgy and modern, or elegant and sophisticated.

The theme should be the first thing you choose when you are planning a party, but it's not the only decision, of course. I worked for years producing events from celebrity weddings to parties for the Emmys and the Grammys, and I've learned a thing or two about entertaining. This chapter is full of my best event-planner insider secrets and party-planning tips.

Get the Music Right

Music sets the whole tone of a party. The right music can make a party and the wrong music can kill it. If the music is too manic, it can make everyone anxious, but if it's too mellow, everyone can get tired. When choosing, consider your guests. If you are thirty but your guests include sixty-five-year-olds, they might not appreciate your favorite kind of music. Personally, if I'm in a nightclub and they play house or techno, I get anxiety because I associate that with every-body doing drugs. Play hip-hop, however, and I can't stop dancing. I used to love disco. It's a personal choice but I'm not going to play hip-hop at every single party. It all depends on the theme or mood I've chosen for the event.

You also need to decide where your music will come from. You don't have to hire a band or a DJ unless your party is a major event. Instead, make playlists on your iPad or iPhone and put it in a dock. You can customize the music for your whole party ahead of time. You can design a playlist to match your theme or the mood you've chosen. If you aren't sure, start with light jazz or classical and then move into dance music, if that's your thing. If you aren't sure what will go over well, have some options and ask the guests if they like the music or if they want to hear something else. Every party has someone who wants to play DJ.

Another option is to use a service like Songza or Pandora. Just put in a song or artist that typifies the mood you like, or a kind of music (like "Top 40" or "adult contemporary" or "disco"), and Pandora will play a custom-made "radio station" for your party. If it plays any songs you don't like, just click the thumbs-down symbol and Pandora will eliminate that song from the station forever. The more you tell it which songs you do and don't like, the more it will refine your station to suit your mood and personality.

Get the Lighting Right

Nobody looks good with bright overhead fluorescent lights, and nothing flattens a party quicker than bright lights. Think about how a club or candlelit room feels when the lights get bright. It destroys the mood. Dim lights make everyone look better and candlelight is sexy. You don't have to rent lighting. Just put your lights on dimmers, add candles, or use lamps instead of overhead lights.

Have Signature Cocktails

Of course, you could invest in a whole bar full of liquor, but when you put a bunch of different bottles out on the table, the table gets sticky, the caps get lost, people spill when they pour, and it's expensive. It's also very collegiate. Instead, a few pitchers of signature cocktails are easier for people to serve themselves, and they will feel like they are participating in the party. Put out appropriate glasses, garnishes, and buckets of ice. Cute cocktail napkins and interesting cocktail stirrers could be fun. Also put out pitchers of water with lemons and limes and water glasses. If the tap water is terrible, buy jugs of spring water.

If you set up your cocktail area on a table, see if you can put it on risers. It's awkward to lean down to make drinks.

Match your signature cocktails to the theme or mood of the party. If you need ideas, flip to the end of this chapter for different party themes and appropriate cocktails and recipes.

· ·

THE PERFECT ICY MARTINI

I used to wonder how the great steakhouses and good martini bars get those little bits of ice floating on the top of their drinks. I tried, but I'd end up with an ice rink on top of the glass. It took me forty-two years to figure this out, but I finally discovered that if you rinse your glasses and put them in the freezer, then when the drink hits the ice on the glass, you get the bits of floating ice on top.

• •

If guests are making their own drinks, keep the selection limited. You don't need every kind of liquor or mixer. You don't need gin if all the party guests are under sixty-five, unless you have a friend who drinks it. You don't need rum unless everybody's from the Caribbean or it fits the party theme. If you have whiskey drinkers at your party, include a bottle of Scotch or bourbon. Otherwise, keep it simple. This is really all you need:

- White Tequila
- Vodka
- Dry vermouth
- Club soda
- Tonic water
- Lemons and limes cut up in a bowl
- Olives in a bowl
- Light-colored juice, like pineapple, grapefruit, and/or orange
- White wine

If it's your house and not mine, you could include cranberry juice, sweet vermouth, grenadine, cherries, and red wine, but I suggest not ruining your party or life by serving drink elements that can stain your carpets and furniture, not to mention someone's clothes. If someone spills, they will want to kill themselves and you will want to kill them. Save the cosmos, manhattans, and red wine for when you are at a restaurant.

Also prevent messes by putting coasters out everywhere. Coasters are a must if you don't want to ruin your furniture.

. . . .

THE BEAUTY OF THE PREMIXED COCKTAIL

One of the reasons why I created the Skinnygirl Margarita and
all the other flavors that came after is because when I serve a
cocktail, I want it to be consistent. When you make your own
pitcher of martinis or margaritas or mojitos or whatever it is, or
go up to a bar and mix your own drink, it's different every time.
It might be too strong, or too sweet, or too tart. If you put out
bottles of Skinnygirl Cocktails, you know exactly what to expect. I find that reassuring. (It's also a lot easier. No mixing, no
mess.)

. . . .

Easy, Impressive Food

Food has a significant influence on the feel of a party, but you don't
have to make all the food you serve from scratch. If you really enjoy
doing it, then go ahead, but you will save a lot of time and trouble if
you mix homemade things with good purchased foods. If you have
a signature recipe you love to make that everyone requests, that's a
great way to personalize your party. Maybe your meatballs are the
best or everyone demands your carrot cake. For me, it's an old-school
Caesar salad that I make tableside. I also think my crab cakes and
sautéed mushrooms can't be beat. But I'm not going to make every
single thing. Instead, I buy reasonably priced items and doctor them
up with added fresh ingredients and a good presentation. Costco and
Trader Joe's have fantastic hors d'oeuvres.

Here are some of the things I do:

- Put premade food on nice platters or in good bowls that fit
  the theme. For example, store-bought sushi arranged on
  black lacquered trays has dramatic impact. Italian salad
  could go in a big rustic wooden bowl, or pasta with colorful

vegetables in a big white bowl with fancy serving utensils. Painted Mexican ceramics or wood trays and bowls dress up quesadillas or make-your-own-taco ingredients. Serve purchased Asian appetizers like egg rolls and wontons on a colorful chinoiserie tray with fancy chopsticks and home-made dipping sauces. Look for sales at import stores or in catalogs and websites for good prices on themed serving pieces. When in doubt, simple white platters with colorful ingredients are elegant and can match any theme or tone.

- Add fresh chopped herbs to premade dips to brighten and doctor them. Serve with fancy chips, like blue corn tortilla chips, multicolored chips, vegetable chips, or whole-grain pita chips.

- For an Asian theme, choose store-bought items that won't get soggy, like egg rolls, wontons, summer rolls, or steamed dumplings. Make your own miso dipping sauce, hot mus-tard sauce, and plum sauce or peanut sauce. Add eda-mame, Japanese rice crackers, and wasabi cheese.

- Doctor a trio of store-bought salsas in nice bowls: Add fresh cilantro to one, fresh sweet corn and black beans to another, and chopped fresh mango or pineapple to a third. Add colored chips in a big bowl. (I'm not a fan of the bowl-shaped chips designed for dipping. It seems cheesy and unnatural, but maybe that's just me.)

- To go with a fiesta theme, store-bought bite-sized tamales and empanadas are a good choice. Serve with homemade red and green salsas and chili-spiked ranch sauce.

- Make an interesting cheese platter. Costco, Sam's Club, and Trader Joe's have a great selection of cheeses. There are a lot of fun cheese accessories, like cheese labels, or get a small chalkboard and write the cheese selections on it. Add different colored grapes, crackers, apples, and breadsticks for a rustic, "medieval-meets-Tuscan" presentation.

- Create an antipasto by filling ramekins with olives, feta cheese, pitted olives, Parmesan, dried Italian meats, sun-dried tomatoes, and Marcona almonds. Add a variety of sliced toasted bread. Add herbed dipping oil and herbed butter you make yourself. You can find all these things at Whole Foods, Trader Joe's, or Costco.

- A new trend is inexpensive but tasty American caviar. You can buy some varieties in the supermarket and they are much less expensive than other kinds of caviar. Serve it over a dollop of sour cream or crème fraîche on baby potato halves or blini (a thin pancake). This is inexpensive but still feels lavish.

- People love pigs in a blanket. You can buy these, but make them upscale by serving them with different flavors of gourmet mustards.

- For a fancy dessert presentation, put bakery cookies on a platter, or put out fancy little plates with individual items, like gourmet chocolates, petits fours, or little brownies.

- For a fancy dessert, cut lemons in half, slice off the nub on the end so they sit on a flat surface, hollow them, fill them with vanilla ice cream or lemon sorbet, and freeze them in egg cups.

Easy, Budget-Friendly Food Ideas

Always remember your theme or tone when you choose your food. Don't mix it up. A table with hummus and pita chips next to spinach dip next to salsa and guacamole is all over the place. Choose a lane, or at least put like foods together and separate them from other types of food. A Middle Eastern–style cluster could include hummus, feta, baba ghanoush, cucumber-yogurt dip, and skewers of chicken or lamb. On a different table or in a different room, an Italian spread could include antipasti, mini mozzarellas, olives, and rosemary crackers. An Asian mix could include Japanese rice crackers, wasabi peas, edamame, and tamari almonds. This doesn't mean the whole party has to be about one type of food, but don't have a mishmosh all clumped together.

Here are some more easy and inexpensive food and presentation ideas:

- Any kind of make-your-own bar is fun. Try a burger, taco, pizza, or ice cream bar.
- Pesto lasagna and baked ziti are easy to make and inexpensive.
- Do a few things well. You don't need forty-two bowls of pretzels and tortilla chips and potato chips. If you have fewer, higher-quality foods, your party will feel more designed and elegant, and it will cost less.
- Pasta is an inexpensive way to feed a crowd and it feels fancy if you serve different shapes and colors. Try whole wheat, spinach, and beet pastas. Fresh seasonal ingredients combined with olive oil, lemon, garlic, and fresh herbs make it more upscale. Try shredding fresh basil over pasta. In the summer, add tomato, cucumber, and corn, or some feta cheese, fresh parsley, and pine nuts. Choose toppings that are good hot but won't be terrible when they get cold.

Inexpensive presentation ideas:

- For a big dinner party, use a kid's chalkboard and write the menu on it, so guests feel like they are in a restaurant. Or buy cheap frames and print the menu on your computer. You can also put out these frames at the bar, naming the signature cocktails and explaining what is in them. Little details like this make a big impact.
- Even for a sit-down dinner, everything doesn't have to be white-glove fancy. Mix your nice crystal glasses with fun colorful plates or serving platters.
- Never serve chips or dips in the bags or jars. It costs nothing to put them into nice bowls you already have.
- Keep your food looking good. Always be busing, wiping up, and replenishing. To me, nothing is worse than dirty glasses

and plates sitting around. I've been to very fancy parties and seen bowls with guacamole and ranch dressing dripping over the sides and a bunch of crappy crumbled chip pieces in them: Don't let your food table get ratty and disgusting. A clean, attractive spread of inexpensive food is much more inviting than a messy, gross presentation of expensive food.

- Consider how your food will look after an hour and choose foods that won't get disgusting. Dip in a bowl gets disgusting. It's very 1982. Baked brie looks great for five seconds, but then it sits out and gets gelatinous and sloppy.
- If you live in or near the country, collect wildflowers or natural greenery instead of buying flowers, for a rustic feel. Sunflowers are a great choice. Big bowls of lemons and limes also add rustic ambience, especially to an outdoor party.
- You can find super-inexpensive party décor and supplies at dollar stores.

· ·

GET INSPIRED

Every time you go to a catered event, notice how they present the food. Caterers know how to take a plain white platter of food and make it look special. They might have a bed of black beans or baby greens or red cabbage to hold a particular appetizer. They might use hollowed-out vegetables as serving bowls or combine particular surprising flavors into a lettuce wrap or on bruschetta. How do they arrange the cheese and fruit for the most impact? You can also get ideas from pictures in magazines. How do food stylists combine colors and textures to make food as appealing as possible? How do they stack or arrange food to make it look dramatic? You can borrow any of these ideas for your own parties. They are everywhere, but people are often blind to them.

· ·

Easy Party Cleanup

I hate cleaning up after a party, but there are a lot of ways to minimize the work. Here are some of the things I do:

- Cook and serve in one vessel. Many Crock-Pots look really nice and you can make chili or cheese dip in them.
- Make a big pan of beautiful pasta with sauce and fresh herbs, bake it in a nice glass baking dish, then serve it on a trivet. Manage it so it doesn't get sloppy. Baked ziti can stick together but manicotti is good because it comes out in individual pieces. This also works for enchiladas.
- You don't need so many plates. Give people one plate and one fork for food. Design appetizers and desserts so people can eat them off a napkin without needing any utensils.
- Cocktail markers for glasses will help everyone keep track of their own glass, and save you from having to wash every glass you own after it's all over. It's also less wasteful.
- Serve water and drinks in pitchers. It's cheaper and greener than putting out and then having to throw away a bunch of plastic water, beer, and wine bottles. Add sliced lemons, limes, or cucumbers for flavors. It's a lot less expensive to buy a cucumber than a bunch of water bottles, and its greener.

. . . .

THE BEST KID PARTIES

I recently went to a party for a child, and all the parents were standing around staring at the kids like they were in a zoo. Every good children's party should have something fun for the kids to do, and something fun for the adults to do, too. Some of those can cross over. Everyone can have fun decorating cookies or playing certain games or getting manicures, but when the kid fun is strictly fun for kids, I like to plan a little adult fun, too. None of it has to be expensive. Here are some party ideas for your child's next soiree:

- Play music everyone will like—fun, easy pop music, with a mix of children's songs and adult music that is child-friendly, like Katy Perry's "California Gurls" and Rihanna's "Umbrella."
- Sing-alongs and story time are fun for everyone.
- Both kids and adults could have fun with stations for fake tattoos or henna designs, face painting, and cookie decorating. What about limbo?
- Instead of one birthday cake, make cupcakes and let everyone decorate their own batch with icing and edible toppings. This is fun and creative, and each child gets to take home cupcakes, which will prolong the good memories. Provide cute to-go boxes.
- Parties at children's museums provide interactive fun for everyone. Some have science-experiment rooms, art rooms, and dress-up rooms with stages for impromptu performances. See what's available in your area.
- If you have a little girl, a mani-pedi or hairstyle party at a local salon is a fun option. Some have kid-sized pedicure chairs. The parents can choose to get their own pedicures, too.
- Pottery stores sometimes have painting parties. Everyone can paint something and take it home. Or have everyone paint or decorate their own picture frame. Activities like this can make adults feel like kids again.
- Kids' gyms can be fun. Even the grown-ups can jump on the trampoline. These events often come with pizza and cake in a party room, and they do all the cleanup.
- Ice-skating rinks might also offer kid-party packages.
- Older children can do jewelry-making projects. Some bead stores have organized events like this.

- I recently went to a party at a dance studio. The kids got to go off and dance on their own, which they loved.
- Another recent party we attended had kids painting giant sheets of paper. Everyone got to bring home their own artwork.
- Serve light cocktails for the parents to put them at ease. I call this Mommy Juice. Just keep it light—don't get people drunk if they are driving!
- Have a friend dress up as a princess. Pay her—it will be worth it! Teens or twenty-year-olds who work with kids can be great party helpers, and much less expensive than hiring a professional company.
- Along with the kid food, offer some nicer adult food. If the kids get pizza, order a gourmet pizza for the adults, such as a goat cheese and spinach pizza, and a salad. A fruit platter, nice crudité, and some good chips and dips would be nice. You don't have to go crazy, but a little something for the adults is a welcome touch. I think most moms would much rather have a small square of an interesting pizza and a salad than kid-centered junk food.

Party Troubleshooting

Parties don't always turn out the way you envision. When things go wrong, it doesn't have to spoil all the fun. Here's my party troubleshooting guide:

Somebody got too drunk: It's happened to all of us. When this happens at your party, the best thing to do is pull the person aside in another room where you won't embarrass them, look them dead in the face, and say, "I don't want you to regret anything tomorrow. You're probably stressed or you didn't realize how strong the drinks were, but you are out of control and either you need to go lie down or I will call you a taxi. Your choice." If they get belligerent, get your partner or a friend to help, because something bad will happen and you could be liable. You need to get them out of your house, and not behind the wheel of a car.

You got too drunk: Been there, done that. I'm the type of person who can usually tell when a drink is going to be the straw that breaks the camel's back and I know when I need to remove myself from a potentially embarrassing situation. If you can tell you've had one (or two) too many, tell the hostess you aren't feeling well, and go in a back room to pass out. Or have a trusted friend get you a taxi. You should always have "your person" at a party, someone you can call on if you need help. Be there for each other, just in case.

This didn't happen at one of my parties, but recently I was at a big Hollywood party with the most famous people in Hollywood. George Clooney was there, and Brad Pitt, and Bradley Cooper, and Ellen DeGeneres. Madonna was there. This party was huge. The size of a football field. I drank a martini before I went, then had two martinis the size of Pittsburgh at the party. I was talking to the supermodel Amber Valletta, who I knew was also an actress, and I said, "So, do you consider yourself more of an actor or an actress?" I meant to say "model." She just looked at me. Suddenly I was a deer losing its footing. I realized that I was about to fall off my five-inch heels and I was being a complete idiot. My friend Sarah was there, and she was "my person." I waved her over. "I'm saying stupid things," I whispered. "I'm the most stupid person in the world. Take me right now and sit me down in a corner and let's ride this out." She got me to a chair without disaster and gave me some water. She tried to make me feel better. Fifteen minutes later I was fine—still drunk, but I had regained my composure. The next day, I called the host and apologized. I told him I had never been that drunk in my life. Fortunately, he hadn't even noticed. (By the way, I wasn't driving that night.)

If you end up in this situation and you realize you need to get yourself out of there, you really need your person. If your friends are leaving, go with them. Don't stay at a party alone. You never know what can happen. Someone could slip something into your drink. Sometimes, you need someone else to help you get a grip. If you do ever end up in this situation without your person and you know you can't walk, don't walk. Stand still. Talk to the nearest person and hope you can trust them. Tell them to take you to a chair so you can sit down. Most people are pretty understanding about this kind of thing, if you handle it with some grace.

You burned the main course: No matter how wonderful it was going to be, *don't serve it.* Apologize to everyone, make light of it, make a joke, and call and order takeout or beg a friend to bring something from her house. Worst case scenario, you order pizza and everyone will probably like it more anyway.

The stereo broke: Find a music station on TV, or break out a karaoke machine or alarm clock with a tuner and play the radio. You could also put your iPhone in an empty glass with the speaker facing down, which amplifies it. Just keep some kind of music going or the party can die. Incidentally, I think all parties should end up with people dancing. If you can feel people are ready but nobody is doing it, just start. Usually when I start dancing, everybody else joins in.

Nobody is talking: Take your top off. No, I'm kidding. But if the party is dying a slow death, you have to switch it up. Change the music, dim the lights more, show a funny video, or for a smaller party, break out one of those games with conversation-starter cards that get everyone talking. Suggest a game of spin the bottle or truth or dare. Tell somebody to write something on your forehead and then tell everyone you have to guess what it is. Anything to shake people out of their stupor. Or just say it out loud: "This is the most boring party I've ever been to! Who do I have to sleep with to get this party started?" (Tip: Do not do this at someone else's party. Or, maybe do.)

Nobody will leave the kitchen: I hate this. People always want to cluster into the least convenient, smallest space. The kitchen is bright and homey and it's okay for a few minutes at the beginning of the party, but you don't want people to stay there all night. Frankly, it annoys hosts because they can't focus on what needs to be done in there. To keep this from happening, block the kitchen off or turn the lights off and don't have any plates of food or drinks in there. I often physically lead people into another room. Keep the bar and the food in the room where you want people to congregate. If you are the guest, get a clue and don't hover in there!

It's late and you need to get everybody out of your house: If it's before midnight and you're just in a mood, put someone else in charge of your party and go lie down in the back room. If it's after midnight, people should be leaving anyway. This is when you say, "Hey, I love you all, but you have to leave because _____." You fill in the blank. You have an early meeting? Your child has a morning activity? Your dog is sick? It doesn't even have to be a good excuse. People should get the hint and move along.

Ten Party Themes

Want to throw a party but can't figure out a good theme? Here are ten ideas, along with my thoughts on décor and music, plus signature cocktails and some light food recipes to inspire your menu planning.

Outdoor Summer Party

On a beautiful sunny day, have a party outside with lots of fresh food and bright colors:

Décor: Bowls of citrus (not to eat), white dishes, seasonal ingredients, and flowers. Keep things fresh, simple, and crisp. Good-quality plastic ware is fine, if it's nice enough that you will wash it and not just throw it away.

Music: Light rock and mellow love songs. Think Billy Joel and Elton John.

Signature cocktail: Skinnygirl Put the Lime in the Coconut.

PUT THE LIME IN THE COCONUT SKINNYGIRL COCKTAIL

Makes 1 drink—multiply as necessary or make to order

2 ounces Skinnygirl Island Coconut Vodka
2 ounces pineapple juice
Juice of ½ lime
Splash of water

1. In a shaker, add ice and all ingredients and shake.
2. Strain over ice in a rocks glass.

Food: Try turkey burgers or wasabi tuna sliders (check out *Skinnygirl Dish* for recipes) and chips with mango salsa. Here's a great salsa recipe:

MANGO SALSA

Makes about 4 cups

2 large mangoes, moderately
    ripe, halved
½ cup red onion, finely
    chopped
½ medium cucumber, peeled
    and seeded

½ cup minced fresh
    cilantro
¼ cup fresh lime juice
Freshly ground salt and black
    pepper, to taste

1. Over a bowl, score flesh of the mango halves on a diagonal, then score the other way, so the mango is in diced pieces and all juices are captured in the bowl.

2. With a spoon, scoop out the diced mango into the bowl.

3. Combine all remaining ingredients in the bowl.

Simple Elegance Party

Keep it simple and clean.

Décor: Lots of white candles, white dishes, silver accents—elegant with a pop of color, like red. This is a good theme for a wedding. Keep it upscale and simple. Some locations are so beautiful that you don't have to schmaltz it up. You don't need Leaning Tower of Pisa topiaries. It doesn't have to look like the Real Housewives of Beverly Hills vomited all over your wedding. Let natural light and architecture speak for themselves. The natural space, whether indoors or out, can be its own décor. This was the case at my wedding.

Music: Medium-tempo classical, string quartet recordings, or old-style jazz like Ella Fitzgerald and Duke Ellington. Later, switch to dance music, hip hop, or Frank Sinatra.

Signature cocktail: Prosecco with Muddled Raspberries.

PROSECCO WITH MUDDLED RASPBERRIES

Makes 1 drink—multiply as necessary or make to order

4 or 5 raspberries, muddled
1 teaspoon raw sugar
¾ cup chilled Skinnygirl Prosecco

Muddle raspberries together with sugar and pour into a champagne glass. Top with champagne.

Food: You might serve classics like sliced filet mignon, crab cakes, or deviled eggs, with arugula, mesclun, or spinach salad. Try my recipe for Crab and Chive Deviled Eggs.

CRAB AND CHIVE DEVILED EGGS

Serves 6

6 large eggs

¼ cup low-fat mayonnaise
(or low-fat plain Greek yogurt or canola mayo)

1 teaspoon fresh lemon juice

1 teaspoon Dijon mustard

½ teaspoon seafood seasoning (such as Old Bay)

¼ teaspoon kosher salt

¼ teaspoon black pepper

¼ cup lump crabmeat (about 2 ounces)

1 tablespoon chopped chives

1. Place the eggs in a large saucepan and add enough cold water to cover by 1 inch. Bring to a boil. Remove from heat, cover, and let stand for 12 minutes. Drain the eggs and run under cold water to cool.

2. Peel the eggs and cut in half lengthwise. Transfer half the yolks to a small bowl and mash with the low-fat mayonnaise, lemon juice, mustard, seafood seasoning, and the salt and pepper. Fold in half the crab.

3. Spoon the crab mixture into the egg whites, top with the remaining crab, and sprinkle with the chives.

Tip: Chop up your leftovers and put them on bread for a delicious and easy meal!

Asian-Inspired Party

Many Asian foods are easy to make and look beautiful in a party setting. You will also be able to create the mood for this theme with just a few inexpensive purchases.

Décor: Focus on black with strong, vibrant colors like reds, greens, purples, and golds. Go to Chinatown if you have one, or look through the Oriental Trading catalog. Pier 1 has black lacquered platters, paper lanterns, and decorated chopsticks. Keep it sleek and simple. If you find one really unique decorative piece, like paper lanterns or a hanging dragon or a really good tray, decorate the rest of the room around that one item. A few beautiful orchids can add to the décor. This is also a good excuse to buy a nice Asian-inspired dress.

Music: Depending on what kind of food you choose, play music from China, Japan, Thailand, etc. You can find international music online, or plug a song you like into Pandora. A little later, switch to something more familiar and danceable.

Signature cocktail: Skinnygirl Lychee Martini.

SKINNYGIRL LYCHEE MARTINI

Makes 1 drink—multiply as necessary or make to order

2 ounces Skinnygirl Bare Naked Vodka
1 ounce lychee juice
1 ounce club soda
2 lychees for garnish

1. Combine the vodka, lychee juice, and club soda in a cocktail shaker filled with ice. Shake well and strain into a chilled martini glass.

2. Garnish with the lychees.

3. Optional garnish: Prior to pouring the drink into the glass, rim the glass with freshly grated ginger mixed with colored sugar.

Food: Edamame, wasabi, Asian crackers, sushi, dumplings, or satay, with custom chocolate-dipped fortune cookies, or store-bought green-tea ice cream. Or try my recipe for Asian Shrimp Salad.

ASIAN SHRIMP SALAD

Serves 8 as an entrée, 12 as a side salad

4 ounces sliced almonds

8 ounce bag prewashed baby
spinach leaves

1 medium head Napa cabbage,
shredded

1 pound sugar snap pea pods,
halved

1 can sliced water chestnuts,
drained

1 4-ounce bag shredded carrots

1 pound chilled cooked
shrimp, split in half
lengthwise (16 to 20 count)

1 bunch chopped scallions,
green parts only

1. Toast the almonds in a skillet over medium heat, stirring constantly, for about 5 minutes.

2. Toss everything together and serve with Asian Dressing.

ASIAN DRESSING

2 teaspoons fresh grated ginger

4 teaspoons dark sesame oil

¼ cup rice vinegar

4 teaspoons soy sauce

2 teaspoons Dijon mustard

2 teaspoons minced garlic

6 tablespoons extra-virgin
olive oil

Whisk all of the ingredients together in a bowl.

Mexican Fiesta

Everybody loves a fiesta. This is a good party to have on Cinco de Mayo or any day during the summer.

Décor: Inexpensive piñatas, Mexican blankets, mortar-and-pestle serving bowls, streamers, and brightly colored dishes all add to the festive mood.

Music: Mariachi music to start, then dance music after the margaritas have kicked in.

Signature cocktail: Put tiny Corona beer bottles (Coronitas) in a galvanized tub and attach a bottle opener to the tub. And of course, serve margaritas. Try my recipe for a Spicy Jalapeño Margarita.

SPICY JALAPEÑO MARGARITA

Makes 1 drink—multiply as necessary or make to order

4 ¼-inch slices jalapeño (seeds removed)
1½ ounces Skinnygirl Margarita
Handful of ice
Chili powder mixed with coarse salt

1. In a cocktail shaker, muddle jalapeño slices.
2. Pour Skinnygirl Margarita over the jalapeños.
3. Add ice and shake.
4. Pour into glass rimmed with the chili powder mixture with ice.

Food: A make-your-own taco bar or homemade quesadillas are great for a fiesta party. Or for something lighter and different, try my recipe for Salsa Verde.

SALSA VERDE

1½ pound green tomatillos
  (husks removed), washed
½ cup chopped onions
½ cup cilantro, chopped

2 tablespoons lime juice
2 jalapeño peppers, seeded and
  chopped
Salt and pepper to taste

1. Cut the tomatillos lengthwise and roast them either on the grill or for about 6 minutes under the broiler until the skin is a little dark.

2. Put the roasted tomatillos, onion, cilantro, lime juice, and jalapeño in a blender or food processor.

3. Blend or process until you obtain a smooth puree.

4. Place in the refrigerator to cool.

All-American Barbecue

This is a good party for Memorial Day, July 4, or Labor Day.

Décor: Everything red, white, and blue.

Music: Classic rock is perfect for a barbecue.

Signature cocktail: This is another good party for putting Coronitas in a galvanized tub. Pitchers with sparkling or white sangria are good, too, with fresh summer fruit. Also be sure to serve something nonalcoholic if children are present. Try this raspberry-mint lemonade, which is great for all ages.

RASPBERRY-MINT LEMONADE

Makes 5 cups

½ cup fresh mint, rinsed
2 cups fresh or frozen
  raspberries

½ cup raw sugar or agave
⅓ cup fresh lemon juice
2 cups water

1. Muddle mint and raspberries together.

2. Place in a pitcher and add remaining ingredients.

3. Stir until well blended.

4. Serve chilled or over ice cubes.

Food: Ribs, barbecue chicken, or anything on the grill. Try my recipe for Barbecue Chicken.

BARBECUE CHICKEN

This recipe reduces the sugar and calories of regular barbecue sauce and gives a fresher flavor.

Serves 4

4 boneless, skinless chicken
    breasts
Salt and pepper, to taste
2 tablespoons barbecue sauce

2 tablespoons low-fat Italian
    dressing
2 tablespoons yellow mustard

1. Poke chicken breast all over with a fork to let the flavors penetrate.

2. Season well with salt and pepper.

3. Combine chicken with remaining ingredients in a Ziploc bag or bowl and let marinate a minimum of 6 to 8 hours (overnight is best).

4. Grill chicken breasts over medium-high heat, or broil, until cooked.

Moroccan Mystique

Think belly dancing, flamenco, Gypsy style, or the movie *Casablanca* as inspiration.

Décor: Lots of black with dramatic red roses, lots of candles, draped fabric, fringe, lanterns.

Music: Classical guitar or any mystical-sounding music. Ramp up to dance music (or even belly-dancing music, depending on the crowd) as the party gains momentum.

Signature cocktail: Try white and red sparkling sangrias or a cocktail with blood oranges. Or, because olives are such a fixture in this region, try my Skinnygirl Dirty Spanish Olive Martini.

SKINNYGIRL DIRTY SPANISH OLIVE MARTINI

Makes 1 drink—multiply as necessary or make to order

3 ounces Skinnygirl Bare Naked Vodka
½ ounce Spanish olive juice
3 Spanish olives for garnish

1. Fill a cocktail shaker with ice.
2. Pour vodka into shaker with olive juice and shake.
3. Strain into a chilled martini glass and garnish with olives.

Food: A big paella is perfect for a party like this, or make things easy on yourself and purchase a selection of bite-sized tapas from Costco, like Marcona almonds, a variety of olives, stuffed grape leaves, hummus, and skewered meat or Moroccan-spiced tofu.

Game Night

Get together all your friends who love to play games—old-school games like Monopoly and Yahtzee, or more contemporary games like trivia and conversation games. Set up a couple of different games in each room and let people rotate.

Décor: Find old games at Goodwill and hang the boards on the wall or use them to decorate food tables. Or design everything around one game, like a Monopoly or Scrabble theme.

Music: Fun pop music that everyone recognizes, or fifties jukebox music.

Signature cocktail: Cherry Berry Splash.

CHERRY BERRY SPLASH

Makes 1 drink—multiply as necessary or make to order

¼ cup blueberries, fresh or frozen
1½ ounces Skinnygirl White Cherry Vodka
4 ounces sparkling water
Splash of cherry juice
Bing cherry or lime wedge, for garnish

Combine blueberries and ice in a glass. Add the vodka, sparkling water, and cherry juice. Garnish with a bing cherry or lime wedge.

Food: Put out old-school candy, popcorn in bags, and foods people can eat easily and still keep their hands free, like hot pretzels with mustard, pigs in a blanket, or little cups of vegetarian chili.

Girls-Only Party—No Boys Allowed!

It might be a wedding shower, a baby shower, a sophisticated tea party, or just happy-hour-starts-at-noon, but a party with girls only can be a lot of fun, and it takes the pressure off when nobody feels like they have to impress the boys.

Décor: Feminine. Lots of flowers, botanical-printed dishes/linens, or pink. Not because girls only like that stuff, but because it's fun. Put colorful candy in bowls and put together gift bags for everyone, or have a giveaway. You could also provide spa gifts and even rent a photo booth. Keep it sassy and cute.

Music: Make an all-girl-singer playlist.

Signature cocktail: Try the Pink Lemonade Mojito, inspired by my novel, *Skinnydipping*.

PINK LEMONADE MOJITO

Makes 1 drink—multiply as necessary or make to order

4 ounces Skinnygirl Mojito
Splash pink lemonade

Combine and serve over ice.

Food: Put together a variety of attractive finger foods made healthy. I make different kinds of crostini, because everything is better on a little crisp slice of bread. Here is my recipe.

CROSTINI

Makes as many servings as you like—
just choose how many slices of bread to use.

1. Place thin bread slices on an ungreased grill or grill pan. Toast each side for 5 minutes over medium heat or broil until golden brown. (Note: Skip steps 2 and 3 if you're using any of the last three topping combinations listed below.)

2. Remove toasts from grill and immediately rub with the cut side of a head of garlic. The warmth of the bread releases the garlic's aroma.

3. Place toasts on a cutting board and drizzle with oil generously. Sprinkle with salt and pepper. Cut slices in half if they are large.

4. Now for the fun part: Add toppings. Here are some ideas. I haven't included amounts here—just estimate and play with amounts to make as much as you need. And be creative, you don't have to stick to the recipe.

- Avocado slices
- Fava beans with pecorino cheese and mint
- Roasted red peppers with capers and goat cheese
- Pesto with arugula
- Prosciutto, melon, and balsamic vinegar
- Ricotta with lemon, basil, and honey

- Melted chocolate with fleur de sel
- Fresh ricotta with Nutella

Sporting Event Party

Superbowl, World Series, World Cup, Tour de France, Olympics, or NASCAR—whatever it is, it's a good excuse for a party.

Décor: Customize to the event. Football-season colors, old baseball memorabilia, anything to do with bicycles, the Olympic rings, or décor from the hosting country, etc.

Music: You won't need music if you are watching the television, but a pregame cocktail hour/tailgate could feature upbeat music like rock, or Euro-pop for international events. Once the game is on, you could play low music in the background.

Signature cocktail: Depending on the crowd, everybody might want beer, or might even want to do shots. For a more refreshing option, try my recipe for the Skinnygirl Arnold Palmer.

SKINNYGIRL ARNOLD PALMER

Makes 1 drink—multiply as necessary or make to order

½ ounce Skinnygirl Bare
Naked Vodka
2 ounces unsweetened tea

Splash of lemonade
Juice of 2 lemon wedges

Mix all ingredients in a shaker with ice and strain over ice into a rocks glass.

Food: Even if you're not tailgating out in a parking lot, tailgating recipes are the perfect food for sporting events. Try my recipe for guilt-free artichoke spinach dip.

GUILT-FREE ARTICHOKE AND SPINACH DIP

Don't worry about exact amounts for this recipe. If you can only find artichokes or spinach in slightly smaller or larger amounts, that's fine. In this recipe, frozen is actually better than fresh because the softer texture works better for dip, so take the easy way.

Makes about 4 cups

1 box or bag frozen artichokes (about 9 ounces)

1 box or bag frozen spinach (about 9 ounces)

¼ cup freshly grated Parmesan cheese

¼ cup shredded Monterey Jack cheese

¼ cup part-skim ricotta cheese

4 ounces reduced-fat cream cheese

2 tablespoons low-fat mayonnaise

½ tablespoon lemon juice

1 garlic clove, minced

¾ teaspoon salt

½ teaspoon pepper

2 dashes Tabasco sauce

1. Defrost the vegetables in the refrigerator overnight, then drain them in a colander in the sink or over a bowl. You can drain them together in the same colander because they'll get mixed together anyway, and that makes fewer things to wash. After they are drained, press on them with paper towels to get rid of any extra moisture that would dilute the dip's flavor.

2. Preheat the oven to 350 degrees. Combine all the ingredients except 2 tablespoons of the Parmesan cheese in a food processor. Blend or pulse until mostly smooth, but leave some artichoke chunks for texture.

3. Pour the mixture into an oven-proof dish or casserole. Sprinkle with the remaining Parmesan. Bake for 20 minutes or until heated through and just starting to bubble.

4. Remove from the oven and let cool for at least 10 minutes. Serve hot or warm with thin slices of a baguette, raw vegetables, baked tortilla chips, or crackers.

. . . .

TAILGATING TIPS

Tailgating can be fun or tacky . . . or both. Here are some ideas to help make your tailgating experience a memorable one (unless you drink too much to remember).

- Instead of just eating out of the bag of chips or pretzels, bring a plastic platter. Place the dip in the center and surround the dip with the chips. This looks nicer, and it'll be less tempting to keep grabbing handfuls from the bag.
- Bring Clorox wipes for quick cleanup and to sanitize.
- Choose whole wheat whenever possible: Whole wheat pretzels and hummus are easy and can be presented in the same fashion as the chips and salsa.
- Be organized and plan ahead. You want to have a good time.
- Bring a Sharpie and mark all plastic cups with names so you keep from throwing away more cups than necessary.
- Use natural food coloring in cookies, ice trays, or dips to bring your team's colors to life.
- Doctor store-made guacamole or hummus with chopped tomato, Tabasco, and cilantro.
- Make sure all knives are covered with a knife guard.
- A cutting board can serve as both a place to cut and a serving platter.
- Plastic utensils are easy to clean up and worry free.
- Make yourself a tailgating checklist; this way you won't be as likely to forget anything (for example, trash bags, napkins, plastic utensils, etc.).
- When at home, prepare as much as possible. For instance, create a chicken or steak quesadilla by topping a single tortilla with cheese and precooked chicken breast or sliced steak pieces. Then bring a small five-inch nonstick pan and place entire tortilla in pan on the grill. Once

everything is warmed and melted, fold quesadilla over on itself. If you are making chili, you can prepare it ahead of time and reheat over the grill in a small nonstick pot. Serve in precut bread bowls, and add cheese and green onion.

- S'mores are fun but eliminate the mess by wrapping the whole thing (graham crackers sandwiching a chocolate bar and a big marshmallow) in foil and putting it on the grill for a few minutes.

. . . .

Oscar, Emmy, Grammy, or Tony Party

Invite your movie, TV, music, or Broadway-obsessed friends; print ballots so everyone can guess the winners; and offer prizes for most correct guesses and best dressed. Encourage people to dress in their finest. Have someone stand at the door and make sure your guests are "on the list."

Décor: Decorate according to the awards show you choose. For example, silver everything and old Hollywood for silver screen, music paraphernalia for the Grammys, or theater décor like the comedy/tragedy masks for the Tonys. Can you create a red carpet for when your guests arrive? You could hire someone to play a paparazzo, snapping pictures of the guests with a flashbulb as they arrive. Another friend might be willing to play cigarette girl with candy cigarettes.

Music: You'll be watching the show, but a preshow cocktail hour could include movie soundtracks, TV theme songs, a playlist of all the Grammy nominees, or a playlist of famous Broadway show tunes, to get everybody in the right mood.

Signature cocktail: Skinnygirl Red-Carpet Showstopper.

SKINNYGIRL RED-CARPET SHOWSTOPPER

Makes 1 drink—multiply as necessary or make to order

2 ounces Skinnygirl Cucumber Vodka
1 ounce club soda
Splash of cranberry juice
Splash of ginger ale
Slice of lime

1. Pour all ingredients except lime over ice.
2. Stir until mixed.
3. Garnish with the lime slice.

Food: Name all your dishes with clever plays on the names of nominated movies, shows, music, or stars. You could even have a potluck where each guest brings a movie-themed, TV-themed, or music-themed dish. Or serve simple but elegant hors d'oeuvres so everyone can have their hands free for cocktails and ballot marking.

I hope this chapter inspires you to start throwing more parties. It's a great way to celebrate or catch up with friends. Parties help keep you connected, and they remind you how much fun life can be. So . . . party on!

Chapter Nine

Traveling Affordably, Enjoyably, and Without Losing Your Mind

Traveling can be fun or it can be stressful. It's up to you. It's been a sometimes bumpy road, but I've learned over the years how to travel lighter and how to find time to unwind, no matter how full my itinerary looks. Here are my best travel tips.

Planning

You may not have any control over what kind of trip you're about to take, but if you do, a little planning can make your whole travel experience easier. Some things to consider:

- **What kind of getaway do you want or need?** A weekend car trip can be inexpensive and you will still feel like you've been somewhere, even if you haven't left your region of the country or even your state. But maybe you hate car trips. Maybe you want to jet to Europe for a long weekend or only a beach will do. Know yourself. If you're not the outdoorsy type, don't let someone talk you into camping. If fancy hotels make you uncomfortable, don't book one just because it went on sale. If you love the sun and the water, don't book a trip in a city center. If boats make you nervous, don't go on a cruise. Your trip should be whatever will make *you* feel excited about going, whether the destination is Hong Kong or Miami Beach or Anchorage, Alaska.

If you're traveling with your partner, you'll have to make a marriage of what you both want. If he likes adventure and you like relaxation, try to find a place where you can go white-water rafting and get a massage afterward, or if you can afford it, split the time: three days skiing and three days in the sun.

- **How long will your trip last?** I'm the queen of the four-day vacation. I think that's plenty of time to truly relax and unwind. Sure, you could live on ramen noodles so you can afford a high-end resort or a European tour or whatever it is, but after a week, you'll probably be sick of it and wish you could go home. If your vacations are shorter, you get to have more of them.

- **Will you fly or drive?** Driving can be less stressful than flying, especially if you have your family along or you have to bring a lot of things. You won't have to go through security holding kids and snacks, take off your shoes, wait in long lines, or risk delays. You can bring as much stuff with you as you want to, and a car trip can be a fun and interesting journey in itself. On the other hand, if you are traveling alone or with one other person, you can pack light, and you just want to get to your destination, flying can be less stressful. Take a carry-on only, wear slip-off shoes, and bring work or a book so you don't waste any time in case of delays. It all depends on what kind of trip you're taking.

- **Never pay retail.** I say this about clothes, but it applies to traveling, too. You can find great deals online if you sign up for travel-alert sites, but comparison-shop, because what you think is a great deal might just get greater at a different site.

Join all the frequent-flyer and hotel clubs. They are free, and you get points based on travel you have to do anyway, for both flying and hotel stays. Stay on top of it and always have your frequent flyer numbers handy (store them in your smartphone). You could end up earning enough for a free trip. Sign up for travel-deal alerts for last-minute travel, if you can take off for a weekend on the spur of the moment. You can save a ton if you can get away and unless it's a very popular travel time, you can always find a great last-minute deal.

As long as you use a credit card, you might as well use one that gets you airline or hotel points. Always ask if the hotel includes free breakfast. They might include it but not tell you.

- **Comparison-shop for spas and yoga retreats.** If you are dying for a spa vacation (who isn't?), definitely shop around, because there is a wide range of spas. A spa used to be a fancy place where wealthy women went to lose weight, but now that everybody wants the experience, many spas have answered the call, broadening their services and lowering their costs. Some are super high-end, but many spas with beautiful surroundings and great services are surprisingly affordable, with yoga classes and fun exercise activities like drum dancing or hip-hop dancing. Some are spiritual, some are hard-core for weight loss or fitness, and some are all about stress relief. They often have stellar menus with healthy, lower-calorie foods and services like saunas and steam rooms for detoxifying, facials and body wraps, and massages. Some are more rustic and eco-chic, with open-air sleeping quarters and yoga on the beach. Some have sweat lodges or native beauty treatments. Some focus on meditation or spiritual exploration or holistic healing, with spa treatments in between.

Yoga retreats can give you the spa experience with a more intensive yoga and meditation schedule, if that's what you like, and they almost always cost even less than a good spa. Decide what you want out of your spa vacation. If you just want to lie around in a robe and get a facial and a massage, you can probably get those services at a less expensive hotel that has a spa in it. If you want more structure, look at a spa or retreat with a theme or purpose, like yoga or cleansing. Costa Rica, Hawaii, Panama, Belize, Jamaica, and Mexico have some very reasonable spas and great yoga retreats. Go with a girlfriend or two and add female bonding, which is also rejuvenating, especially if you spend your days around men. Look at SpaFinder.com for ideas.

DIY SPA WEEKEND

You don't have to go to a spa to have the spa experience. Just go somewhere, anywhere, with a group of girlfriends. Get out of town, preferably to a beach. Bring a juicer, do yoga, walk on the beach, find an inexpensive place nearby for mani-pedis and massages, and cook healthy food together, or go to restaurants with options like fresh seafood and salads that feel like spa food.

An inexpensive trip to Florida could become just as rejuvenating as a week at the Mandarin Oriental. Sometimes, just a dip in the ocean will make you feel like you've been to a spa. Once you get there, the ocean is free (which I can't say about the Mandarin Oriental).

- **What do you need in a hotel room?** Are you traveling to get out and see things or to sit in a hotel room and look around at the art on the walls? For me, if I'm away for fun I don't need a fabulous room. I need a clean room. If you really will be in the hotel a lot and a weekend of luxury matters to you, then spring for it. However, if you have a hotel mostly for somewhere to sleep, you need a clean bed and a clean bathroom. It shouldn't be 90 percent of the cost of your trip.

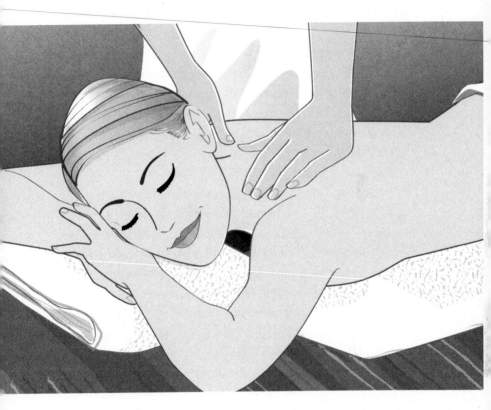

There is a new-agey health spa in upstate New York I've been going to for years. It has clean rooms that feel like cabins, and it just happens to have a steam room, which I love. It has healthy meals and an optional juice-fasting program. It's quiet and peaceful and it has no televisions—it's just the kind of place I like to go for a getaway. It's not exactly barebones, but it's definitely not fancy. Consider what you really want out of your hotel, and spend accordingly.

- **Who's coming?** If you travel with friends, you can split expenses and your trip won't cost a lot. One of you can get airfare, the other the hotel, or however you want to work it out. If you are traveling with your partner and your money is all the same, you can still save money. Look for romantic things to do at low or no cost at your destination. Lying on a beach or going to a park or outdoor concert might be free, but figure out things you both want to do. You might have to spend a day on the golf course, but is that too high a price if it means your partner will spend a day with you at the spa getting couple's massages, then having a candlelit dinner on the beach? Of course, there's also no reason you have to spend every second together. You could get your massage while he's on the golf course, then meet up for a romantic dinner afterward.

- **If you bring kids . . .** If you are traveling with kids, you don't have to get two rooms. A junior suite can be more economical. Some of these rooms have an enclosed bedroom for you and your partner, with a separate space that has a pull-out couch and an extra half bath. If your children are still young, consider hiring a sitter to come on vacation with you. The sitter can stay on the pull-out couch and you can get a crib or roll-away bed for your child. This gives your sitter a free vacation and you get your romantic time with your partner. A young girl in your neighborhood or a relative might like to do this. When traveling with family, it's also more economical to get a room with a kitchenette and go to the store. Do you really want to take your kids to a restaurant three times a day when your young kids really just want peanut butter and jelly or your teenagers are constantly starving and need 24/7 snack food available?

- **Plan your meals.** Unless meals (like breakfast) are included in your package, don't eat at the hotel. This is much more expensive and often not all that good. Instead, look for good restaurants in the area and try new things. You can often eat like the locals for a fraction of the price of a hotel meal and get a more authentic experience at the same time.

. . . .

TRAVELING ALONE

I spent a lot of time traveling alone in my thirties, and I loved it. I've been to yoga retreats, surfing retreats, new-age health spas, and even Europe. I went to Bali by myself and found places to do yoga. As long as you are careful; stay in public, well-lit areas; and especially if you participate in group tours or activities, you shouldn't fear traveling alone. It will make you feel independent and powerful—because you will be.

. . . .

Packing

Packing well can make your trip so much easier, and packing poorly can turn your trip into a disaster. For years, I was the person who never checked a bag. I always figured out the most efficient way to combine clothing for different outfits so I didn't have much to take with me. Most airlines charge you to check a bag, and even if they don't, you risk losing your bag, having your luggage damaged, or having your stuff stolen. Why wait in that long line at the airport? If you only carry on a bag, you will always have everything with you and you can just print your boarding pass online, get to the airport, and go straight to security, which can save valuable minutes, especially if you're running late.

However, full disclosure: Now that I travel so often for work, I check a bag because I need to have the right outfits and I want to be able to use what's in my closet. I don't want to wear a T-shirt and leggings the whole trip. Also, traveling with Bryn always means taking more things because she's still so young. However, when I take off for a long weekend, I still don't check a bag. It's carry-on only.

To do this, you have to be a highly efficient packer. There are a million ways to combine a few basic clothing items in any climate. Here are some ideas I swear by:

- **Have a color theme.** Stick to basic neutrals but add that pop of color and nobody will notice you're wearing the same jeans you wore yesterday. For example, you might decide on black clothes with colorful accessories. Your color can come from jewelry combinations, scarves, and colored tank tops or T-shirts. This allows for infinite possibilities. If black is your theme:

  - *Black jeans with a red tank top, colorful scarf, and black cardigan the first day*
  - *A black dress with a long colorful necklace, earrings, and black jacket the second day*
  - *A black skirt with the red tank top, cardigan, and a different scarf the third day*
  - *Black jeans with the black jacket, a white tank, and the colorful necklace the fourth day, etc.*

  It's just like what I do with food: Today, turkey burgers. Tomorrow, pasta Bolognese. I'm not saying you have to wear black for the entire vacation, but just be sure every item in your suitcase can be worn in more than one way or go from beach to dinner. If it can't, take it back out. This also goes for shoes, bags, sunglasses, and hats.

- **Have a hardware theme.** I also like to pick a hardware theme, especially if I'm only going somewhere for a few days. Is it going to be a silver trip or a gold trip? If your jewelry and handbag hardware all match, you can switch things out endlessly.

- **Go beach-to-dinner.** In warm weather, a sarong or tunic can be a cover-up over a swimsuit on the beach but can morph into a skirt with a nice beaded top or a tunic over white jeans for evening. A sundress during the day can transition to night if you add a scarf and jewelry and a cardigan. Cute shorts during the day can look great at night with heels and a sexy top.

- **Pack light for the mountains.** In cold weather, a pair of black leggings, a black blazer, a turtleneck, and a selection of colored fitted Ts can last for days, in different combinations, if you change out the accessories.
- **Just the basics.** Truthfully, you could probably get through most trips with a pair of jeans, a T-shirt, and a blazer, just by changing out your shoes, scarves, and earrings. Go crazy and pack black jeans, a black skirt, a black dress, and a black blazer with a few tank and T options, and you could head to Europe for the summer. Just remember to bring enough clean underwear.

· ·

NO VALUABLES

Keep stress to a minimum when you travel by bringing costume jewelry only. Fun accessories make basic outfits more interesting and you won't have to stress about your valuables being safe at the beach or back in the room.

· ·

- **Plan for the plane.** Although it won't go into your suitcase, a well-thought-out travel outfit can help your packing effort and your comfort level. On the plane, wear your heaviest pair of shoes (although don't travel with extremely heavy shoes—there is no point) and a cardigan or wrap. Once you're in flight, you can peel off layers if you get hot. Wear the same outfit on your way home, and those items will never have to take up suitcase space. When I travel by plane, my traveling outfit usually consists of:

- *Flats and fuzzy socks. Flats are easy to slip off in security and socks keep my feet from touching the disgusting airport floor.*
- *Really comfy jeans or leggings.*
- *A white tank top I can rinse out so it's ready to wear on the way home (or I bring two).*
- *A comfortable cardigan I can use as a blanket.*

Unless you're going somewhere cold like the mountains, don't even bring your winter coat. Have someone drop you off and pick you up at the door, and keep your coat in the car.

- **Refine your toiletries.** Why bother to pack a bag of all your personal products for every trip? Instead, keep a toiletries bag that is always ready to go. I first started doing this when Sephora came out with a set of empty bottles, jars, and pump tubes for filling with your favorite products, all packaged in a clear zippered pouch with labels so you know what's what. I filled those bottles up with my favorite products and it was my go-to travel bag for years. Eventually I expanded this idea, adding a separate bag for makeup brushes, hair items, a hairbrush, curling iron or straightening iron, a travel toothbrush and paste, a deodorant stick, and everything else I need daily (which isn't really very much). When I go on a trip, all I have to do is grab the bag and throw it in my carry-on. You can also find clear bottles at drugstores. Label everything so you don't wonder whether something is conditioner or hand lotion. I've even gotten a few men into doing this.

If you aren't that particular, you could just go with the shampoo, conditioner, soap, and lotion that hotels provide for free. Just bring your toner, serum, day face lotion with SPF, and heavier lotion for night. I also bring an under-eye cream/concealer. I usually live with the hotel hair products and body lotion.

- **Easier cosmetics.** Make up a cosmetics bag with doubles and extras you have lying around, so you don't have to figure out your makeup for every trip. Just remember to keep any liquids in a separate Ziploc if they are in your carry-on, for when you go through security. This is what I keep in my travel makeup bag:

   ○ *One eye shadow palette in neutral colors, with one dark color that can double as an eyeliner, and makeup brushes for shadow and liner.*
   ○ *Under-eye concealer.*
   ○ *SPF foundation for day or night (I actually use a tinted mois-turizer) and a foundation brush.*
   ○ *Blush and a blush brush.*
   ○ *Mascara and an eyelash curler.*
   ○ *Little sample bottles of perfume.*

- **Easier hair.** I travel with a small set of five Conair curlers (the kind with the clips, not the pins). These are a life-saver. Whether you're in a warm climate where your hair gets frizzy or a cold climate where your hair gets flat, they'll make your hair something you can work with.

My Packing Method

People often ask me what to pack for different kinds of trips. Instead of having a general packing list, I look at each day and think about what I'm going to be doing, then I try to figure out the fewest number of individual items for the maximum number of outfit combinations. It's like putting a puzzle together. Remember to consider both day and night, and how one outfit can transition, instead of packing two outfits for each day. For example, day might be jeans and flats. At night, switch to heels and add a jacket.

Consider how you can layer, reuse, and dress up each item. After I have my outfit plan and my list, I add a few basics:

- Pajamas that can double as loungewear
- Workout clothes, including comfortable but cute light sneakers that work for an elliptical trainer or treadmill but that you can also use for walking around a city
- Sunglasses and a hat for sun or messy hair in the city
- A few scarves, for a pop of color
- Underwear
- A few tank tops
- Jeans
- Leggings
- A cardigan sweater
- A purse that goes from day to night
- Swimsuit, cover-up that can double as dressed-up evening wear, and sandals for the beach
- Jewelry

Make Jet Lag Your Bitch

Jet lag can absolutely destroy the first day of your trip and the first day home again if you aren't careful. On short trips, it can wreck your whole experience. But it doesn't have to! This past year, I traveled to both Hong Kong and Australia, and the jet lag was major, but even going from the East Coast to the West Coast can feel pretty severe. However, you don't have to let jet lag kill your good time. Get control and minimize the damage. Here's how:

- **Try to get at least eight hours of sleep the night before traveling.** Sometimes I find this impossible because I'm thinking about everything I need to do before I leave, but I always try. If you travel when you're already going on just a couple of hours of sleep, you're going to crash and burn when you arrive. Even resting in bed is better than staying up too late.

- **Plan when to sleep.** I always plan what hours during the flight I can sleep. This takes precedence over everything, including work, so I can feel refreshed when I arrive. When I went to Australia, the flight left at midnight. I planned to get some things done and relax until about three A.M., then sleep so I would wake up as close as possible to morning in Australia. To make sleep easier, bring noise-canceling headphones and a sleep mask. Sleep aids can help if you find this hard to do. I may take half of a sleeping pill if I really need to guarantee a good night's sleep. If you're more the natural type, I've heard melatonin can help coordinate your sleep/wake cycle with dark and daylight, but I've never tried it. If your throat is a little scratchy, NyQuil might also knock you out for a few good hours.

- **Stay hydrated.** Drinking a lot of water will help you to de-bloat and avoid dehydration. Air travel is dehydrating, and it also dries out your skin. I once heard that Victoria Beckham travels with a layer of baby oil on her skin. I always bring a hydrating facial toner spray and mist my face while I'm on the plane. Otherwise, I'm coming off that plane like a lizard.

- **Don't booze it up.** Ha-ha. Okay, sometimes I'm so excited to be on the plane that I bring my own olives, but at least go easy, and if you do drink, also have a lot of water. Otherwise you'll be woozy, dehydrated, bloated, and not thinking sharply when you might have to be on guard in a new city or foreign country. Alcohol can also disturb your sleep—even if you think it will help you pass out on the plane, you won't get good-quality sleep and you'll wake up cranky.

- **Skip the salt.** Salt will make you swell like a balloon on a plane. Go low-salt the day of your trip.

- **Manage kid jet lag.** If you are traveling with kids, consider when they should try to sleep on the plane too, so they aren't leaping out of bed at three A.M. in the hotel thinking it should be morning.

· ·

MOM TALK

Kids can be challenging on long flights because they get bored and they want to move around. I don't normally let Bryn watch too much TV, but as far as I'm concerned, she can watch for fifty-five hours in a row if we're on a plane. Get some good DVDs and a small player or laptop computer and let them zombie out. Bring snacks, earplugs for yourself, comfy socks for both of you, and headsets you can both use at the same time if you suddenly realize you're in the mood to watch *Finding Nemo*. Again.

· ·

- **Have what you need.** I always take these things with me on the plane:

  ° *Facial toner spray, like Evian.*
  ° *A mini makeup bag, hair tie, and brush. It feels good to refresh your face and brush your hair and pull it back after a long flight.*
  ° *Hand sanitizer. If you go in that disgusting bathroom or touch anything around you, use it before you touch anything on yourself, especially your face. Planes are germy.*
  ° *Wipes. Use after the hand sanitizer, just in case. These are also good for wiping up smudged eye makeup after sleeping.*
  ° *Under-eye moisturizer. I usually bring a cream, a gel, or the kind with the roller ball that cools and depuffs.*
  ° *Healthy snacks.*
  ° *Moisturizer for face and hands.*
  ° *Lip balm and breath mints.*
  ° *Feminine wipes. Who knows what you're going to do at your destination? Wipe your wazoo.*

- **Stay awake!** When you arrive, don't go straight to your hotel and nap if it's daylight at your destination. Stay awake until nighttime. You might still wake up early the next day, at four or five A.M., but no napping. Just suck it up. This will be easier if you lay off the wine during that first day (you could pass out), and no caffeine anywhere close to bedtime. Instead, keep yourself busy. Walk to lunch so you don't feel gross. Get fresh air. Go dancing. Do something fun and interesting. Don't go to bed until it's actually nighttime. If you act according to your destination's time schedule, you will adjust much quicker.
- **Eat well.** The next morning, have a nice breakfast and try to eat healthfully throughout your trip.

While You're There

Once you're finally at your destination, enjoy it! If you don't enjoy travel, why go through all the trouble to do it? Whether your trip is for work or leisure, don't overschedule yourself. If you're traveling for work, see if you can schedule a few extra days for fun. If you're on vacation, see the things you really want to see, but don't pressure yourself to see every single thing on somebody else's list of "must-sees." It's your trip. Schedule at least one day where you have nothing planned. Walk around, explore, people-watch, or do something that just comes up, that you didn't know existed. Be sure to get regular exercise so you don't feel rundown. It sucks to feel like a sloth on your vacation.

To make packing easier at the end of your trip, put things back in your suitcase after you wear them when you know you won't wear them again. That leaves you more beach time on your last day.

SHIPPING VS. SCHLEPPING

If you travel light, with only a carry-on, consider shipping your shopping purchases home. It's fun to buy new clothes or souvenirs in exotic locations, or even things to decorate your home like rugs and art. If you ship your purchases home, you won't have to worry about how to get them on the airplane. The cost of shipping may actually be less than the checked-bag fee, but even if it's more, you won't have to schlep your purchases to the airport. Then you can look forward to getting that package in the mail.

Ask your hotel about the best way to do this. They may even be able to mail things for you. Just watch out for hidden fees and taxes that make international shipping a rip-off, and always track and insure your package, just in case.

Home Again

The first day back from a trip, it's very important to eat something healthy. You've probably been eating crap on the plane and overdoing it for your whole trip, so it's time to repair. Don't binge or go out to eat. Instead, have some soup, tuna on crackers, or a salad. Reel it in. Eat the minimum and don't give in to the "I'll start tomorrow" mentality. Don't go off the rails.

Then unpack and get organized, rather than heading straight back to work. Do you want to come home Monday night to a full suitcase? I always unpack right when I get home, unless I'm absolutely dead. Get your family together and have everyone unpack their own bags and make laundry piles. This is recovery time. You're not having sex tonight. If you really can't face it, go to bed early, then get a grip on your laundry first thing.

Finally, be prepared for a little bit of a letdown. This doesn't happen to everybody, but even if you couldn't wait to get home, you might feel a little depressed. You're no longer at the beach or in the mountains or in the big city, and all you can think about is wanting to go back. Your everyday routine may seem extra dull when all you're left with is a suitcase full of laundry and fading tan lines.

If it's at all possible, get home on a Friday or Saturday so you have the weekend to decompress and recover. Be with your family, reminisce about the trip, organize your photos. If you can ease back into your normal life, you might feel more appreciative of being back home. A screen saver of your trip pictures on your computer monitor will bring it all back to you.

And you know what they say: 'Tis better to have traveled and come home than never to have traveled at all.

Chapter Ten

. . . .

Do Everything Better

I'm on a permanent quest to be my best. I want my life to be more efficient, more organized, more relaxing, less stressful, and more environmentally responsible. I want to be better than I was born to be, better than I was yesterday. I want to be a good person, a good woman, a good parent. And I want you to be your best, too. This chapter is about all the little ways you can make life better.

Dress Your Best

How well do you put yourself together? Do you throw on whatever, or do you construct an outfit? Don't get me wrong, when I'm working, I'm wearing my pajamas half the time—and probably no underwear. If I go out, however, I like to put together a look. I think it's fun, and it's a way to present myself to the world purposefully. I might dress to fit my mood or to fit the situation or the weather, but every time I decide on an outfit, I see it as an opportunity to be creative and use what I have in my closet. If your closet is organized (see chapter 7), you're on the right path, but dressing well is about more than an organized closet. It's also about knowing how to put things together and not being afraid to think outside the box.

Here are my tips for making the most of the clothes you have and enjoying the creative art of dressing yourself:

- **Know what you have.** I think the most challenging part of dressing is being able to see what you have. If you can't see your stuff, you'll never use it or wear it because you'll forget you have it. Out of sight, out of mind, and if your closet is too stuffed, your clothes can't breathe. Organize your closet so you can easily see everything you have that is in season.

- **Use what you have.** Dressing well on a budget is just like eating well on a budget: Use what you have! A dress you wear all the time can look totally new with a blazer and different shoes or new, inexpensive accessories that are in fashion. Jewelry you never wear might work perfectly with a new blouse. Build a whole outfit around a great hat, or a pair of boots, or a great necklace. Get rid of anything you don't like, but keep everything you love and figure out all the ways you can combine things. Just because you never wore that skirt with those shoes doesn't mean it can't work if you add colored or patterned tights and the right scarf. I have pieces I've owned and worn for ten or fifteen years, and every time I wear them, I try to make them new so I'm excited about what I have instead of constantly wanting to buy more.

- **Build outfits around items you don't wear often.** If you really love a suede skirt but you hardly ever wear it, make it your mission to figure out a good way to put it back into your regular rotation. In the winter, maybe you can pair it with a wool blazer and a silk T-shirt for an interesting mix of textures, or maybe a new bag you just bought matches it perfectly and you wouldn't have noticed unless you pulled out the skirt and looked around to see what would go with it. You could design an entire outfit around a cool vintage purse you usually don't grab because you think it doesn't really match anything. You can even do this with things you don't think you like because you haven't found the right context for them yet. What about the tangerine dress that seems just a little too bright? Find a way to class it up. Pull it out, hang it up on a door frame, and think. What about that flattering beige jacket, gold belt, and flats? Suddenly, it's not so loud. That ill-fitting tank top in the great pattern might be fine under a jacket where you can't tell that it shows your bra straps.

- **Always have outfits on deck.** How many times do you have three minutes to put something on and you can't think straight, so you just grab the same thing you wore yesterday or the same thing you wear on most days? You have tons of clothes, and this is all you could come up with? This will never happen again if you have a cool outfit on deck. I have a part of my closet that I call the staging area. When I create a new outfit idea, I put it all together with the accessories and shoes and bag, and I hang it in the staging area. That outfit is now officially on deck. When I'm in a hurry and I need to look put together, I just grab what's on deck. When I find something I should be wearing, like a purse or a pair of sunglasses, I'll work it into an outfit to go on deck. If you really want to get serious about this, create different on-deck outfits for work, dates, special occasions, hot sexy nights out, and running around during the day. You can do this in your spare time, or do it when you're stressed or bored to make yourself feel better. It's fun and can help get your mind off your troubles.

· ·

THE CLOSET FILES

If you want to get obsessive about it, you could keep track of your outfit ideas on index cards and keep them in a file organized by appropriate event. When you see outfits in magazines, tear them out and keep them in a file, too, then go shopping in your own closet and see if you can put together an outfit that has a similar look. Or put outfits together and take a photo. Sometimes, an idea you thought would work looks horrible in a photo and you get the chance to rethink it before you wear it.

• •

- **Alter it.** Maybe you love something but it has just one thing wrong with it that keeps you from wearing it. Change that one thing. People don't think about tailoring, but I have had pieces I thought I would never wear again, and after I got them tailored, they became favorites. I lost the belt off a black wool winter trench coat I got at a sample sale, but I had the belt loops removed and the waistline taken in, and now it's a coat that doesn't need a belt. I've had it for ten years since then. Change the sleeve length or hemline, or have the tailor take in the waistline to give a baggy piece more shape.

- **DIY.** You can sometimes alter things without going to a tailor. Can you sew on a button? A cool jacket or shirt with tacky buttons can get a whole new life with nicer buttons. Can you wield scissors? Snip out ugly shoulder pads or the tacky fabric flower that ruins the otherwise awesome dress. The other day, I was getting ready for *Ellen* and I wanted to wear an orange skirt I've had for two years. I wear it all the time, so I wanted to make it new. I had this Banana Republic mesh polka-dot blouse with an attached camisole that I liked but never wore. I realized it was the camisole under it that was making me not wear it. The blouse was perfect but the camisole was too big and showed my bra straps. Jackie and I just cut the camisole out. I put one of my own navy tank tops under it, and it worked great. If we hadn't done this, I would have tossed it. Now it's a workable item in my wardrobe.

- **Buy quality classics.** Another way to dress better is to have a few classic pieces. If you are going to shop, invest your money in quality pieces with a classic style and fit, in a neutral color. These will last you for years, so it's worth paying for quality. This goes for black pants, nice jeans, pencil skirts, blazers, cashmere sweaters, black turtlenecks, black and neutral heels and flats, and classic totes. Mix these neutrals with patterns and pops of color.

- **Don't spend on trends.** Here's how it works: When the fancy stores come out with something, all the suckers run out instantly and buy it. Three months later, the same trendy pieces are knocked off in all the inexpensive stores and you can get it for much less. I saw this happen with colored jeans. First they were on the runway. Now they're at Old Navy. This also happened with studded shoes. Don't be impulsive. Just wait three months. You don't want to pay a lot for trendy pieces because you won't wear them for long. Next year, they'll be out.

    If you aren't totally sure whether something is a trend, here's a hint: If it's studded, bell-bottomed, acid washed, blinged-out, or tie-dyed; if it looks like a wild animal; or if it's neon or a very bright color or heavily patterned, it's a trend. If it looks like a trend, it's a trend. If it smells like a trend, it's a trend. I love trendy clothes and I buy them, but I don't spend much on them. Fun, colorful jewelry and scarves, patterned pumps, brightly colored dresses—I love that stuff, but I'm going to buy those things at H&M, Topshop, Express, Gap, Target, and other inexpensive stores. Go to sample sales. Shop online at deep discounts. If you know it's a trend, then spend accordingly. It *will* go on sale.

MOM TALK

I don't know how the children's specialty clothing stores and fancy children's sections in department stores stay open. For kid clothes, I shop at Target, Old Navy, the Children's Place, Gymboree, and Baby Gap. They have the cutest stuff for a reasonable price. The only really fancy clothing items Bryn has were gifts, or things for very special occasions, like holiday dresses.

• •

- **Clean out your closet.** If you don't like it or wear it and you can't tailor it or fix it, get it out of your closet. I have friends who are flat broke but they have $5,000 worth of perfectly resaleable stuff in their closets. Take all that stuff to a consignment store and get cold, hard cash for it. Many nice consignment stores now take all brands, not just designer brands, so you can get cash for your less expensive trendy items, too.

• •

NOTES FROM JACKIE

We use the website ClosetCouture.com to catalog Bethenny's closet. This cool free website allows you to catalog all your items. You can photograph everything you own and upload the photos to the site, then style your own pieces so you have outfit ideas. You can also upload items from other sites that you are thinking of buying and see if they work with what you already own. You can also create packing lists for trips and save them. We do this for Bethenny's trips, checking pieces out when she leaves and back in when she returns. It's a fun site to use if you enjoy playing around with your clothes.

• •

- **Use your dresses.** Skip the jeans and leggings and use your dresses! They are so versatile, but many women hardly ever wear them. A dress you wear to work with a belt and a blazer can turn sexy for night with a dramatic necklace and higher heels. A day dress you wear with flats can be dressed up with jewelry or a scarf and heels for a casual wedding or a christening. A short dress you usually wear in summer can work in winter layered over a long-sleeved T-shirt, leggings, and boots.

- **Mix highs and lows.** I always mix my highs and lows. I'll wear a twenty-dollar pair of pants with an expensive pair of shoes, or a high-quality blazer with a cheap tank top from Gap. It's boring, predictable, and arguably a little pretentious when every single thing you are wearing is an expensive name brand. Mixing highs and lows raises the perceived quality of your less expensive pieces and gives your quality pieces a more casual, approachable vibe. Plus, your outfit will be more intriguing if people can't guess where you bought it all. That cute black T-shirt was five bucks on sale at Target?

- **Mix mediums.** If your entire outfit is conservative or rock and roll or ultrafeminine, it can be too much (or too little). Instead, mix your mediums. If you're wearing a conservative dress, add a rock-and-roll bracelet, necklace, or bag, or fun nail polish. If you are wearing black or navy, add a pop of color in a shoe or a bag. If you are wearing a lacy, delicate dress, add some boots or a leather jacket.

- **Use, but don't overuse, color-blocking.** Color-blocking is in right now—people are pairing pink shirts with purple jeans or green shoes with yellow shorts. Try it, but don't wear a pink shirt, purple jeans, *and* green shoes. Then you're an Easter egg. Two colors max. Keep the rest neutral.

- **Bare one thing only.** If you're showing cleavage, don't also wear a miniskirt. If you're going sleeveless, don't also wear short-shorts. Pick one area to bare and feature it. Two is too many.

- **Accessorize, accessorize, accessorize—then twirl.** Accessories can make your whole outfit, but don't overdo it. My friend Chuck offers this advice: When you think you look perfect, get in front of a full-length mirror, twirl, and look: Whatever accessory you notice first, take it off. Now you're ready to go.

- **Accept that you can't wear everything.** Sometimes people get depressed because they just aren't built to wear something they think looks cute on someone else, but welcome to life. Nobody can wear everything. Curvy girls could rock a dress that would hang like a sack on a thin girl, but a thin girl might look awesome in a straight-cut vintage style that would pull on a girl with hips. Some people have boobs and look great in low-cut tops, but some people have sun damage and want to cover up the chest area. If you're a pear shape, you might look awesome in a fitted skirt but not so much in a pleated skirt. Get real. It doesn't matter what doesn't fit you. Find the things that do fit you and make you feel amazing. If you don't like how you look in a bathing suit, don't let that keep you off the beach. Put on a sexy sarong, big earrings, and a hat, and walk on the beach like Beyoncé or a Kardashian. Own your body and own your style, and you will look hot no matter what shape you are.

EMBRACE THE BUMP

Some people feel and look good from the beginning to the end of a pregnancy. Others feel sick and bloated the whole time. I was coasting through mine until the wheels fell off at eight months and my face exploded, but I always tried to keep some sense of style. I wore belts for as long as I could and then I wore leggings to show off my legs. I wore boots and made sure my hair looked nice. I tried to focus on my arms and accentuate the parts of me that weren't swollen beyond recognition. Pregnancy can be challenging and stressful, but pregnant bodies can be beautiful, too. You should be proud of yours! If you work your new curves into your look and focus on the parts of you that still look familiar, you'll feel a lot better (even when you can't see your feet or no longer have ankles).

- **Stock up on staples.** Just like your pantry should have all the basics for making a good meal anytime, your closet should have all the basics for putting together a good outfit anytime. Everybody wants to know what basic pieces they should have. I'm not Tim Gunn, but I have my own list. First, I would say not to be afraid of color. Black is safe and slimming, so people overdo it. Color wakes up your face and can actually put you in a better mood, but you don't have to wear it from head to toe.

  Here are the basic wardrobe pieces I think every girl should have—you can combine these endlessly and dress them up or down depending on shoes, bags, and accessories:
  - A good blazer that fits you well in a neutral color (black, camel, navy).
  - Five good-quality, well-fitting, nonfaded tank tops in gray, nude, black, and two fun colors. (When they get faded or stretched, throw them out. They are cheap to replace.)
  - Two pairs of good, nonfaded leggings.
  - Two to four pairs of well-fitting jeans in different styles: skinny, straight leg, wide leg, and boyfriend.
  - A wrinkle-free black dress you love.
  - A colorful wrap dress you love.
  - A good-quality wrap cardigan in a neutral color.
  - Two to three cardigans in different colors.
  - A good-quality belt in a neutral color.
  - A good pair of neutral flats.
  - Comfortable heels that make you feel sexy.
  - One really great statement necklace.
  - Silver and gold hoop earrings.
  - Bangles
  - Colorful dangle earrings for summer.
  - Two or three scarves in different colors.
  - A good day purse.
  - A good night clutch.

- Sunglasses that flatter you in two neutral colors that go with many outfits—I suggest black and tortoiseshell.
- A good summer sun hat.
- A good winter hat.

You'll probably have many other things you like and want to own, like sweaters, skirts, dress pants, and sandals, but if you have these basics, you'll be able to get dressed for any occasion.

Celebrate!

I believe in celebrating, not just when you entertain, not just for the big holidays, but for little reasons. Celebrate a good report card, the opening of a school play, a promotion. Make a big deal about St. Patrick's Day, the Superbowl, Valentine's Day. This is especially important if you have kids, but even if you don't, why not be that person who loves to celebrate each new season and every little thing? It's fun to get into the mood of the season. Celebrating is one of those things that makes life sweeter, and celebrating with kids makes this even better.

Whenever there is an event, I like to change up the house with decorations, just to get everyone in the spirit. Here are ideas for how to enliven your home for the holidays and new seasons:

- Glasses and dishes. Do you have special ones for Christmas, Thanksgiving, Halloween, birthdays? Or just themed platters and bowls?
- Bowls of seasonal fruit (pumpkins, apples, lemons, depending on the season).
- Bowls of colorful candies. There's a candy to match any occasion, like jelly beans in seasonal colors or red and green M&M's for Christmas.
- Fresh flowers. Seasonal bouquets are easy to change out, and many places, like grocery stores, and even drugstores, have inexpensive bouquets or potted plants, like amaryllis

in winter, poinsettias at Christmas, roses on Valentine's Day, daffodils and tulips in spring, shamrocks, Easter lilies, patriotic bouquets for July 4, tiger lilies for Halloween, etc. A bouquet of daises in a galvanized bucket only costs a few dollars and can make the whole room feel like spring.

- Homemade decorations. It's fun to make crafts for the season, with or without kids (but having kids is a good excuse to indulge your crafty side). Depending on the quality, you can save these from season to season or just throw them away and do them again next year—as your kids get older, they'll be ready for more advanced projects. Make popcorn strings, ghosts to put in the windows, Easter trees, homemade Valentines, etc.
- Always store your holiday décor neatly and carefully so you can preserve quality items from year to year. Keep everything in clearly labeled plastic boxes in storage.

Present-ation

Giving gifts is a creative act that starts with being prepared and ends with putting the gift together in a thoughtful way, customized for the person who will be receiving it.

The first step is to always have gifts. I rarely run out and buy gifts at the last minute. Instead, when I see something that would make a good hostess gift, gift for a child's birthday party, or thank-you gift, I stock up. When I see good deals on nice candles, gourmet food items, or beauty and bath supplies, I buy them right away. When I see something that would be perfect for someone I know, even if the holidays or her birthday is months away, I'll buy it and save it for the right time. If you see something you know your mother-in-law or sister or best friend would like, buy it now.

I keep everything in a gift closet. If you don't have a spare closet, make a gift shelf or a gift box. Then, when it's time to give a gift, get creative by adding personalized touches to the gift item. This makes a big difference. Make it look nice with contrasting colors and decorative details. The way something looks has a psychological impact, so don't just throw it all together carelessly. The sum is greater than the parts. Here are some ideas:

- For a friend, pair a nice candle with a picture frame holding a picture of the two of you together. Add a box of chocolates or your friend's favorite candy.

- For someone who loves to cook, buy a colander and fill it with a jar of pesto, olive oil, whole wheat pasta, recipe cards, and an apron or a cookbook. For the eco-conscious cook, fill a bamboo salad bowl with a bottle of organic wine, organic chocolate, and organic and/or locally produced salad items like blue cheese, whole-grain croutons, olives, marinated artichoke hearts, and roasted red peppers.

- For a baby shower, fill a cute basket with nice newborn things like bath towels and all-natural lotions. Add a pastel ribbon and a silver rattle, spoon, or tiny picture frame.

- For a guy, put a set of decent beer mugs or pilsner glasses together with a unique bottle opener in a silver or steel ice bucket. Add guy snacks like pretzel nuggets or corn nuts. If he's not a beer drinker, he might like a martini set with a shaker, strainer, and a jar of olives, or a nice wine opener with wine and gourmet flavored nuts.

- For a child, make a book box. A wooden box that can double as a mini bookshelf can hold age-appropriate classic children's favorites (*Goodnight Moon, Curious George, Alice in Wonderland, Where the Wild Things Are*, anything by Dr. Seuss, etc.).

- A cute plastic tub of musical-instrument toys can also be fun for kids. Add a harmonica, recorder, tambourine, slide whistle, toy keyboard or guitar, and little drum, along with a CD of children's music.

- For any woman (and some men), assemble a basket of spa products: Combine bubble bath, bath oil, pretty soap, face scrub, a loofah, a candle, and a CD of relaxing music. You could also add a yoga mat and yoga DVD.

It's so nice to know you'll never have to run out and grab a gift at the last minute because you have what you need in your gift closet, but it's even nicer to know that you've given somebody something that will have meaning for them.

Ultimate Mom

I've only been a parent for a couple of years, so I know I still have much to learn, but there are some things I do that really work. In the past year, I've been lucky enough to spend a lot of one-on-one time with Bryn. Here's what I've learned so far:

- **Don't be a helicopter parent.** Sometimes you have to let kids work out their own issues. If they aren't sharing or they get frustrated, don't jump right in to fix it. They will develop more confidence in their own problem-solving abilities if they get a chance to figure it out themselves. Most of the time, they will.
- **Don't negotiate with terrorists.** I'm definitely the disciplinarian parent. No means no, and once you say no, you can't go back on it. "I told you that you could not have candy if you didn't eat your lunch." "You can't eat all your Easter candy at once." "It's time for bed now." If Bryn cries because she can't have something she wants, I tell her that it's just fine for her to cry. I'm the boss, and that's the end of it. Kids want discipline, even if they don't know it in the moment, but a lot of parents take the path of least resistance. It's okay for a child to be frustrated, but it's not okay for a parent to give in every time a child shows the slightest displeasure about something. That just teaches kids that they can manipulate the world to get whatever they want,

deserved or not. It's your job to parent, not be your child's best friend. Stay firm, do the right thing, and don't negotiate with terrorists.

- **Teach good hygiene.** All children should learn to wash their hands after playing or being out in the world and to touch their own faces as little as possible. Kids get dirty, but some things kids do are particularly germ riddled. A sandbox is a petri dish. So is a water park. If you go somewhere dirty (it might even be someone else's house!), rinse your child off afterward, or use hand sanitizer. You don't have to be psycho about it. I'm not above the ten-second rule. If a jelly bean falls and nobody saw it, did it fall? No. It's fair game. However, viruses are rampant and you can save your whole family misery if your child learns good basic hygiene.

- **Keep a regular schedule.** Kids thrive on regularity, and if the days are usually the same then it's extra fun when something special happens. Bryn gets up, eats, goes to school, snacks, plays, has a bath, and goes to sleep at regular times every day. She also sleeps in her own bed every night, except on rare occasions like if we are traveling or she's not feeling well. This gives her a sense of security.

- **Never obsess about food.** If you have a food obsession, please keep it to yourself. So many parents stress and practically panic about food: Will I get enough? I need my own food! Don't touch my food! It's insane and it teaches kids to overeat and panic and fear sharing and get emotional about food. Just relax and your child will, too. A relaxed attitude toward food will definitely rub off on your child. If someone takes a bite of Bryn's ice cream or asks for some candy, she almost always shares willingly (unless she only has a tiny bit of something she really loves). I think this is because we never make a big deal about food. We love it, but we don't obsess.

Also take it easy on the snacks. I am amazed at how obsessed people are with giving their children snacks. Do kids have to be holding snacks at all times of the day? It's no wonder our country has an obesity issue. If an adult snacked all day, she would have a weight issue, so why teach this to kids? It's not a big deal to hand your child a snack to help her calm down on a road trip or on a plane, but not every day. Regularly placating children with food teaches them to link food to comfort, and that's a very bad habit. Too much snacking also leads to eating less healthy food during regular meals. A scheduled morning snack and afternoon snack are fine, and an evening snack can also be perfectly reasonable, but have them sit down, pay attention to what they're doing, and then move on with the day. There are much more important things for kids to be doing than whining for more Fruit Roll-Ups or Goldfish crackers.

- **Parent on a budget.** You don't have to spend a fortune on your baby. Babies need to be cleaned, fed, kept warm, and loved. Don't waste money on tons of toys, the highest-priced wipes, or fancy designer baby clothes. Your baby doesn't care about that. Your baby just wants you.

When your child is older, you don't have to spend a ton of money on fancy children's museum memberships and pay-to-enter play places. There are so many things for children to do that don't cost anything. Try story time at a bookstore or the library. Go to parks. Read local parenting papers for information on child-friendly events. Have playdates so your child learns to play with other kids and you get time socializing with other moms. If you can't afford a truckload of toys, consider yourself lucky. Too many toys are overstimulating, and kids won't appreciate them. Have tea parties, puppet shows, or paint. Let your child play with things that aren't toys. Bryn likes my velcro rollers and cooking utensils. Even if you do have a lot of toys, put most of them away and rotate them out. Every month or so, bring out new ones, so old toys feel like new toys.

. . . .

WIPE BETTER

Don't use forty wipes when your kid poops. Wipe, fold the wipe, wipe again, fold the wipe again, wipe a third time, and you're done. If it's a real mess, you might need two wipes, maximum. By the way, wipes are cheaper online.

. . . .

- **Schedule activities.** Planning regular activities for kids keeps them busy, stimulated, and interested in the world, instead of staring at a TV screen or a video game. If kids learn to be engaged with the world early, they might be less inclined to turn into couch-potato kids who are addicted to screens and technology (I say as I check my smartphone). Sign them up for activities that interest them or that you think they would like, and get them outside as much as possible. Kids can't get too much fresh air and sunshine.
- **But don't overschedule.** I don't think that kids should be busy all the time. I'm not a fan of people who overly structure their children's lives, putting them into French and Latin and fencing. I think kids should be able to play on their own. Kids need time to be creative and make up their own activities without defaulting to the easy way out, which is staring at an electronic device. If you have time every day where the TV and video games are off-limits, you won't have to micromanage them. They'll find something to do, and they'll learn how to develop their own preferences and make their own decisions. Some days, Bryn and I take whole days off and just veg out. We might color or play dress-up. I think it's good for kids to get days off to do nothing and just hang out at home.

- **Never miss a meaningful moment.** I have a rule for myself: Unless I'm in a serious hurry, like I have to board a plane, I will stop what I am doing and make time for a meaningful moment with Bryn. If she says, "Mommy, I want a hug," or "Mommy, I want to stay in the bathtub," I never say no. I never say, "No, Mommy's busy, we have to get out now." I'm a person who is always in a hurry, so this has been a big change for me, but I recognize how important it is to take those moments and cherish them. I could be on the phone having an important business meeting, but I will hang up the phone if Bryn wants to do something with me. I don't care how rude I am. This is more important. I know these moments with her are fleeting, so I celebrate everything we do together.

  For example, when I take Bryn to ballet class, she gets all dressed up in her pink tutu with her hair in a bun and she feels like a real ballerina. I make a big deal about it because we both enjoy it so much. Things like this create family memories, and so I swear that I will never be too busy for my daughter.

TIME MANAGEMENT
AFTER DIVORCE

If you are divorced, you will probably need to split your time with your child with another person. This can be painful, but you have to suck it up and put on your best face so your child doesn't suffer or feel the negative energy.

Sleep Better

Sleep is a constant challenge for me. I lie awake unable to get my brain off the express and relax. However, I know how crucial sleep is, so I have learned some strategies that really do work to help me get to sleep. If they can help me, they can help anyone.

- **Calm down.** It's really true that if you go straight from one hundred miles an hour to trying to lie down and sleep, you're still going to be wired. Relax gradually. Take a bath. Dim the lights. I have a neck warmer with chamomile in it that I put in the microwave and then wear when I need to settle down. Turn off all electronics, including the television. Read a book or write in your journal, or just meditate and calm your mind. A white noise machine can drown out distracting sounds.
- **Get off.** Masturbating can relax you, or at least help you feel a little less uptight. Or it could wind you up. Not that I would know or anything. This is purely a theory.
- **Get herbed.** Chamomile, mint, or other herbal teas can help calm you down, especially if you get in the regular habit of having a hot cup of tea before bed. Lavender sheet spray can also help you feel more relaxed and trigger your brain to think about sleep.
- **Give yourself a break.** If you really can't sleep, don't torture yourself. Get up and do something. Read something. Or just rest. Resting is almost as good as sleeping, but tossing and turning and beating yourself up because you're not sleeping will just make the next day a thousand times worse.
- **Medicate.** If sleep is really important, it's okay to occasionally take a sleeping pill. It won't make you a bad person. I don't do this very often, but when it really matters, I'm glad I have this option.

Be a Better Woman

You are already a great woman. I don't even have to know you to say that. However, we all have room for improvement, and being a woman has unique challenges that we all have to deal with every day.

Many of them are hormone ruled, and you may not be able to control your estrogen levels (without some pharmaceutical assistance), but here's my advice for handling the ages and stages of being a woman.

Your Period

It tricks me every month. I get irritable, I start eating like a wolverine, and I wonder what the hell is happening to me. Then I get my period. Oh, right. That. I'm forty-two and it's like a bad surprise party every month I had no idea was coming.

My period and I have an uneasy alliance at this point. I used to have endometriosis and every month I was in the hospital, gushing blood like a murder scene and screaming. I got laparoscopic surgery and it's better than it was, but I'm definitely a stage 5 bleeder. I've definitely been the woman with the maxi-pad bulge.

What do you do about it? The best you can do is to keep track of when it's coming, so at least you know why you have suddenly transformed from a rational person into a raving lunatic. There are good smartphone apps for this, like Period Tracker.

Also, if your bleeding is really heavy, your pain is particularly bad, or your PMS causes you to do things that actually affect your life in a negative way (like break up with a perfectly nice guy or succumb to road rage), talk to your doctor. There are definitely things they can do to make it a little bit better.

Here are my other period tips:

- **Debloat.** If you get bloated, drink green juices and eat debloating foods like celery, asparagus, and cucumber.
- **Soothe your skin.** If your skin breaks out, that's totally normal because of your fluctuating hormones, which make your skin swell just enough to close your pores and clog them. Some women get better skin during that time of the month, but for most of us, it's the opposite. Supposedly, some birth control pills can help your menstrual acne, but be extra careful not to pick your face during this time of the month, and never go to bed without washing the makeup off your face.

Use a gentle cleanser and a hydrating light moisturizer. If the problem is severe, a doctor can likely give you a prescription to get it under control. I've researched this a little and I didn't see one shred of proof that chocolate will make you break out more when you have PMS, so if you need some, have some. Just don't eat a pound of it. Savor an ounce or two of dark chocolate, then move on to something else.

- **Dress for PMS.** You might feel like a bloated mess and you might want to prove you can fit into your jeans, but don't torture yourself. This is a time to be comfortable. Wear a cute loose-fitting dress or leggings and a tunic, but don't use that as an excuse to eat like a pig or hate your life. Stay calm and carry on with your life and your meals the way you would normally do.

- **Accept a little crazy.** A gang of feminists led by Hillary Clinton might come to my front door and beat me up, but there probably hasn't been a female president yet because no matter how together we are, we all get a little crazy during that one week. (Or maybe we could use some of that in a president!) If you know you're going to be more emotional or volatile or irritable than usual, just be aware of it and take precautions. Give yourself more space, more time, and less socializing. Warn your family members, and apologize ahead of time. PMS may be the reason you're feeling bitchy, but it's not an excuse to be unkind, so if you slip and say out loud what you only meant to think to yourself, it's not going to kill you to say you're sorry or that you didn't mean it (even if what you're thinking is that you *do* mean it; next week, you probably won't mean it anymore).

- **Stock up.** Don't be like me and forget that you are actually a woman who needs tampons every month. I don't know why I never remember to do this. I'm always raiding my travel bag hoping I've got an extra tampon around somewhere. Get the industrial-sized box of generics at the drug or discount store so you never run out. While you're there, get the industrial-sized box of panty liners too, so you don't keep ruining all your new underwear. Personally, I think these things should be government issued, but until that happens, just get the generic brand. You don't need Rolls Royce tampons.

• •

SHOULD YOU FREEZE YOUR EGGS?

Many women these days are considering that they might not be ready to have children until they are older and are wondering if they should freeze their eggs, so they don't have to hurry or obsess about who to marry before it's too late. It's a cool way to stall the biological clock, but I wasn't sure what was involved, so I asked my friend Stacey Weinstein, who is also my personal hairstylist. Stacey is an entrepreneur and career woman who owns a salon and a bridal beauty agency. Stacey froze her eggs, and this is what she has to say about the experience:

I'm very career driven and although I've had some amazing long-term relationships, I never really thought about having a family. Then I turned forty and I thought, Did I not have a family because I never met the right guy? Did I make a mistake? Although I still didn't exactly feel like it was time, I started worrying that I might someday regret that I didn't have a child. Instead of regretting, I decided to give myself an option and freeze my eggs.

I researched the subject for a full year, then did the procedure when I was forty-one. It was really an easy experience. First you take fertility drugs to prime your eggs. They make some people very emotional, but not everyone, and it's only for a week or two. I took them for ten days, and a nurse in my building helped me with the shots because there was no way I was giving myself a shot. I know some women give themselves the shots, but that wasn't me. When a blood test shows that the eggs are ready, you go in for about three hours. They give you a local anesthetic, they take out your eggs and freeze them, and then you leave and go about your day. I did have a mild complication called hyperstimulation syndrome, which involved some swelling, but it went away on its own.

When I had this done, the waiting room was filled with women from all walks of life. The $10,000 price tag will deter some people, but for others, no matter what their income, it's a no-brainer. For women who really want to do it, there are ways, like payment plans.

I'm still not sure I will ever decide to have children, but now I can relax. I refuse to wake up one day and have regrets about how I've lived my life. Now if I really want a child, at least I can try. There is no guarantee and although there are healthy babies out there that came from frozen eggs, there aren't yet enough statistics to really know the odds. But that's okay. Nobody has a guarantee. The peace of mind this procedure gave me is totally worth the whole experience. I consider it an investment in myself.

· ·

Pregnancy

Pregnancy wasn't kind to me. At first, I thought it was easy. I was thrilled and exercising and feeling great, although my boobs hurt like they were in a vise. Then one day I woke up swollen like a watermelon. My toes were pigs in a blanket. My ankles were cantaloupes. My eyes were slits, and I thought something was wrong with my eyelashes because they were curling into each other, but it was just the swelling. I was looking up online how to remove my jawbone because it was so gigantic. I was literally deformed. Swollen and deformed. I was boiling asparagus and drinking the water in a desperate attempt to debloat, but this was bloating beyond remedy. It happens to some people. Just go easy on the salt, drink as much water as you can (you're going to be peeing every five minutes anyway), and don't skip your doctor visits so they can make sure your blood pressure and everything else are normal.

Other than that, do what your doctor says. Take your prenatal vitamins—they will make your hair, skin, and nails better than they've ever been before. (I still take them sometimes for that reason.) And then relax. Try to enjoy yourself and take it easy. Women have been having babies for millions of years, blah blah blah. It's the hardest thing you will ever do, but you're a woman and you're strong, so you can handle it. Especially with an epidural and plenty of pain meds.

Be a Better Person

You know yourself better than anyone else could ever know you. You know your strengths and your weaknesses, your skills and your areas of ignorance, and you (and only you, when it comes right down to it) know what you like. You are also the boss of you and the manager of yourself. That means nobody else is responsible for your behavior, your actions, or how you react to what happens to you. If you go through life acting as your own manager instead of acting like a child who must have a parent around somewhere to tell you to stop eating that, or saying those things, or acting that way, you'll go far in life. You'll reach a level of maturity some people never achieve.

You can grow up. It's not a bad thing and it doesn't mean you still can't have your lighthearted, free-spirited side. Just take responsibility for yourself. In the end, that's how you'll end up doing *everything* better.

Part Three

Skinnygirl on the Job

- ✦ How did you know what jobs were right for you?

- ✦ When is the right time to quit my job?

- ✦ How do I get my dream job?

- ✦ What is the best way and best time to ask for a promotion?

- ✦ I have a great idea—now what do I do?

- ✦ I want to strike it rich. What's the best method?

- ✦ I love my job but I don't make enough money. Can I work on the side?

- ✦ I hate my job, so I slack off. Am I wrong?

- ✦ Should I start my own business?

- ✦ How do I know my idea for a business is a good one?

- ✦ How do I balance my work life and my personal life?

Chapter Eleven

Career Planning

You have dreams. You have plans. You have an idea of where you want to go . . . or do you? If you don't, you should. Women have always had difficult lives, whether we work or stay home with our kids or try to do both. When we try to do both, life gets even more complicated because we're always pulled in two directions. Do we dedicate our lives to our families or to our careers? Can you do both? It's confusing and it requires some serious thought and planning to toe that line.

A girlfriend of mine got married when we were both in our early twenties, and she was constantly trying to set me up with someone, telling me I needed to get married, too. Now many of my friends who got married young are getting divorced and wishing they had committed more to a career, or at least developed their own interests so they would have had something to pursue when their marriages ended. Others whose children are just starting school are suddenly left alone for hours at a time and have no idea what to do with themselves. They didn't have a plan. Others are facing empty-nest syndrome. Their kids are graduating and moving out, and they are stuck wondering, *What do I do now?* They forgot to plan for that time when they would be out of a "job."

If you go against the grain, the culture, or popular opinion, you can feel like there is something wrong with you, but no path is right for everyone. Some women really do want to get married and have children and let that be their purpose. They don't want to be career women, so that is the right path for them, but that's not everyone. Recognizing what you really want to do and preparing so you can actually do it, soon or in the future, is essential. People around you will always try to make themselves feel better about their own lives by trying to convince you that you should do what they are doing. It's a crowd mentality and it's just human nature. People want to stay in their comfort zone by reassuring themselves that everyone should get married, or have children, or have a career, or whatever it is that "everyone" around you seems to be doing.

I bet if you look more closely, you'll see that not *everyone* is following the social norm, and you don't have to, either. If you go along a path that is right for someone else but not you, and you never get the courage or the will to stop and turn around and go another way, then days and months and years could pass and you won't ever make the most of your potential.

I don't want to see that happen to anyone, so in this next part of the book, I want to call you to action. It's time to start planning and moving forward in your life on the path you choose. It's time to become the person you want to be. It's time to get a career path, even if it involves something that isn't necessarily a career but is more a passion or an interest. It could be making some kind of art or getting involved in charity or playing a sport. It's finding "your thing." Even if you don't "have to" work, you should have something that's just for you, that gives you energy and makes you feel like a human being who can stand on her own two feet. Work is more than earning money, although that's empowering, too. Work, whether paid or volunteer or a serious hobby, is about self-esteem and contributing to the world. It's about standing up and saying, "I am here, and I made a mark."

Maybe you want "mother and wife" to be your thing, and I'm not saying that's a bad thing at all. For some people, it's everything. But I also want you to know and believe this: Your life doesn't have to be only about supporting someone else or raising children. You can do those things, and do them well, while also benefiting from the confidence, security, and power that comes from having a passion and a personal direction for your life. No matter who depends on you, you can still make your own dreams come true in some form or another.

Also, I want you to be honest with yourself. If marriage and motherhood are your passion, ask yourself why. Is it because you believe you will be great at it and you have a true passion for it? Will you feel unfulfilled if you don't do it? Then great. Or is it because you want the easy way out and you think (mistakenly!) that it will be easier to be financially and emotionally dependent on someone else, and raising kids will be "fun?" The sooner you get over the idea that someone on a white horse is going to whisk you away so you can enjoy easy days of leisure, tons of money, and mind-blowing sex while your perfect children bring you breakfast in bed, the sooner you'll start enjoying life in the real world.

Hey, everybody loves the idea of Prince Charming. We all dream about it, but in many cases, that horse turns out to be a horse of a different color. Family life can be a beautiful, challenging, and ultimately uplifting part of your life, but bottom line, you exist as an autonomous individual in addition to your roles that have to do with other people, and I hope you won't ever forget that. I understand not wanting to miss a moment with your children, but what happens when they don't want you around so much anymore, and eventually don't need you at all? Will you still know who you are? I believe you have to find a balance—and so should everyone else in your family. Be there for them, let them be there for you, but also be there for yourself, and encourage each of them to be there for themselves, too. If you live only for others, you might forget that nothing is permanent. People grow up, move out, leave, pass away. Be there for yourself so that even when your whole family is lovingly gathered around you, part of you knows that no matter what happens, you are also lovingly gathered around yourself. It will give you strength and courage and the power to love other people better.

So let's make a plan. Let's look closely at you and start thinking about how to find your thing and how to get from here to the place where your passion and path are clearly laid out before you.

Know Yourself

To understand your calling, you really have to assess who you are and be honest with yourself. What are your passions? What are your strengths? Where is your experience? Dreams are great, but they should be based in something you actually know how to do, or can learn how to do, as well as what you love to do.

If you can't carry a tune, you're probably not going to make it as a professional singer. If you can't do math and you weren't good at science, medical school probably isn't in your future. But if you've always been good with money and have ambition and good ideas, you might be a great entrepreneur. If you love food and you know all about it, you might be a good chef, caterer, food critic, or food blogger. If you have a flair for fashion and everybody comments on your excellent taste, you might be a great clothing designer, owner of a clothing store, stylist, or buyer. If you have the right body type and you are photogenic, you might love being a model. If you can't imagine a day without exercising, maybe you would be a great fitness class instructor or personal trainer. If you've always been good at drawing or you love painting, you could be an artist or you might be great at designing websites. Any of these things might become a career, or possibly something you do on the side to keep you engaged in your life while you make money at another job.

I've done a lot of soul-searching and I've learned a lot about who I am and what I need. I'm a person who really likes structure but needs flexibility. I need to live in a world where no two days are the same, and I need action, but I also need time off. I need extremes. I'm very creative, yet I need to be organized. I have to be in a place where I'm in charge, and I can't solely work for someone else, although I can work with people. There are a lot of careers I would have enjoyed, and plenty I would have hated, based on these qualities. I would have been a great copywriter or someone who designs advertising campaigns. I would have been a great restaurant owner or manager because I love food and I'm detail oriented, but I wouldn't be happy as a restaurant chef because even though I love to cook, it drives me bananas when my hair and hands smell like food and I'm really more of a business person than a food person. I would not have been good at any job where I had to sit in an office all day. I would have been a terrible, dreadful accountant, and I would have been horrible at any job having to do with computers. I would have thrived in a job with action and a lot of balls in the air, like a floor trader.

In order to do this for yourself, it can help to ask yourself some questions and really think about the answers so you are being honest with yourself. These thirty questions relate to all fields and work environments and help get at your compatibility with other people as well as the level to which you will depend on other people and the kinds of skills you have:

1. Do you consider yourself independent?
2. Do you work better alone or in a group?
3. Do you need to be in charge? Are you a leader?
4. Are you energized by hearing other people's ideas?
5. Do you need to be alone to process your ideas?
6. Do you dream of working at home, or do you fear you wouldn't be able to get work done without some oversight?
7. Do you like to leave your work at the office?
8. Do you consider yourself a creative person?
9. Do you consider yourself an analytical person?
10. Are you a neat, even a fastidious person? Does a messy desk make you crazy?
11. Does your office look messy to others, but you know exactly where everything is?
12. Do you believe that there is a place for everything and everything should be in its place?
13. Does someone else's mess annoy you?
14. Do you love creating organizational systems?
15. Do you prefer to follow someone else's organizational system?
16. How do you feel about authority?
17. Do you prefer somebody else to be in charge?
18. Do you work best with guidance or independently?

19. Do you get impatient following the timetables of other people or do you prefer an imposed structure for how and when things happen?

20. Would you be comfortable with all the responsibility and all the liability of running your own business?

21. Do you prefer having assigned tasks, doing them, getting paid, and then going home and enjoying your personal life unrelated to work?

22. Do you need to be able to use your imagination in your work to feel fulfilled?

23. What are the things you know you aren't very good at doing, even if you don't mind doing them?

24. What kinds of tasks really annoy you? Math? Writing? Contracts? Public speaking? Having to come up with new ideas?

25. What would you never do at a job?

26. What are you best at? What are your talents?

27. What do other people always say you are good at?

28. What do you love doing more than anything else?

29. If you could have any career in the world, what would it be?

30. Can you imagine yourself actually having your dream job, or does it seem impossible?

These questions should start to give you direction or clarity about your career path. Maybe you will realize you are already in the perfect job. If not, this might help you start to think about how you could make changes so your career path is headed in the approximate right direction.

Where Are You Now?

Do you feel stuck in a job because you know it's a "good job" with good benefits and a decent salary but no upward mobility, or it's not really focused on what interests you or on where your talents are? This can be okay when you're twenty-six and still finding your way, but if you're thirty-six, it's time to rethink your position. Are you going to be unhappy when you're forty-six or fifty-six if you can't progress except maybe in small increments? Or are you happy where you are and you really enjoy the security?

Every stage of life is different, and a lot depends on what you want. If you're a flight attendant and you love the benefits and the flexibility and you're in a two-income family, you might be fine even if you won't ever progress to a much higher position or make six figures. On the other hand, if you have a job that doesn't challenge you, don't get stuck. More important, know when you're stuck. Two people could have the same job, and one would feel stuck because it wasn't right for her, while the other would feel blessed and be happy to keep that great job forever. It's time to think about which one you are.

Age has a lot to do with it, too. Although these ages are just random, this is a map of how you might want to be thinking about your career at different stages in your life:

- When you're twenty-one, you just want to be independent and pay your bills; you may not care so much what the job actually is. That's fine. Get out on your own and start taking responsibility for your life by making enough money to pay your own rent and bills, buy food, start saving a little, and have fun. If you know what field you want to go into and you can get a job in that field, great, but for many people, twenty-one is still an age of experimentation with career possibilities, not to mention life.
- When you're nearing thirty, you may feel more pressure to be on some path toward the future or doing some meaningful job. Even if you aren't on a clear path to your ultimate dream job, that's okay, but you at least want to be learning and growing and gaining great experience. This is the time to be sure you are moving forward toward something, even if you aren't sure exactly what it is yet.
- At thirty-five, you hit a more critical time where you need to evaluate your situation. Is this where you want to be?

Are you in the right field, even if you don't yet have the job you want? Is it time to go full speed ahead, or is it time to change directions and start moving toward where you really want to be?

- At forty, ask yourself if you are satisfied with what you are doing. Are you fulfilled? Are you moving the needle? Are you inspired, or do you need to make a life change?

Think about the present and the future, and assess your past. Are you happy? What would make you happy? Are you locked in the golden handcuffs? This is what they call a job with good benefits and good money but no upward mobility. If you have children or you are thinking about starting a family, then you might need those benefits right now, especially the medical benefits. Or maybe you love having a regular job that isn't going to change. That might give you a great feeling of security. It all depends on you.

If you are at a stage where you just want to make a bunch of cash for a few years so you can do something you want, like move to Europe or buy a house or make a major life change, then long-term career goals are less important. You could bartend or cocktail-waitress intensely for a few years, make your money, and move on. When I was in college, I wanted to go to Europe for a semester, so I cocktail-waitressed from nine P.M. to two A.M. every night and made wads and wads of cash while other college students were probably interning at banks for low pay but great job potential. I wasn't planning on cocktail-waitressing for life. I had a short-term goal and that worked for me at the time. There are also times in life when you just need to hustle to make cash. Christmas is coming, or you've got a major household expense, or your child is about to go to college, so you sell a few things or you work extra hours. It is what it is and you do what you need to do. That could be a part of where you are right now.

Maybe money right now isn't as important to you as growth potential. You might have a long-term goal to do something with no limit for growth. I've always said I don't like jobs with caps. I want a job where there is no limit to how far I can go. If you know who you are, you won't waste your time in a position with little money now even if it has potential, or good money now but with no upward mobility.

Also assess how happy you are with the work you do, even if the money is right. Is your job okay? If you can deal with the politics because you know you'll get promoted if you do it well, then suck it up. If you are absolutely miserable and depressed at your job, then maybe you need to make a change, even if it's a lateral move or a step down. A lesser job with more upward mobility is more promising than a golden-handcuffs job that makes you despise waking up in the morning.

Also consider whether you can evolve in your job. Are you working for people who want you to move on or who might be keeping you down? I've talked to people who have assistants and say they don't want their assistants to move up. They want them to stay exactly as they are forever, but why shouldn't assistants move up, if they are good? I understand that you want to keep a good assistant, but if you aren't going to provide any opportunities for advancement, you're not going to get the best people—or you'll get people who aren't truly honest about their dreams. People like to keep moving, and your employer should understand that.

If you love waking up every day and you can't wait to get to work because it excites you and makes you feel good about your life, then that's a pretty good sign that you're in the right place, at least right now.

Where Do You Want to Go?

Now that you've taken an honest look at yourself, it's time to start dreaming. Think about your life now, and think about where you want to go. Even if you are fifty-five years old, you can still ask yourself, "What do I want to be when I grow up?" You can narrow it down to a particular job or just a particular field. Or maybe you are already in the right field or job, but you want to advance to a higher position.

Maybe you haven't quite decided and you have several options. It's time to nail them down. Entertainment industry? Law? Education? Culinary? Technology? Engineering? Computers? Maybe you are devoted to helping children or animals or working for world peace or maybe you want to do charity work. Maybe you love the company you work for, but you would really like to be a vice president or a partner. Maybe you want to be the editor instead of the assistant editor, or you want to be the principal instead of the social studies teacher.

. . . .

MO' MONEY, MO' PROBLEMS?

For some people, the answer to "What do you want out of a career?" is "I want to make money," and I get that. However, the notion of being "rich" is a little bit like the notion of Prince Charming—it's never as easy as you think it will be. Nobody is crying for me financially right now, and it's true that it's a huge relief not to worry about meeting basic living expenses anymore. However, having more money costs more money, and the more you have, the more you're going to have to spend. I have a lot more expenses than I ever had before, and suddenly, unlike when I had less money, things like gambling or shopping for no reason seem frivolous and irresponsible to me. I have to pay for multiple employees, both on staff and contracted. I've got accounting fees, management fees, legal fees, tax expenses, the many seemingly unending costs of running multiple businesses, and personal expenses, too—right now, those include a child and a divorce.

Now that I have more money, I also want to use money to help other people. It's all a lot of responsibility and it's a lot more complex than it was in my cocktail-waitressing days. I still have to hustle sometimes when a big expense is coming, but most of all, I have a lot more worries about handling my money the right way. There is a high price tag to running a lucrative business, and although most people say they wish they had more money, some people ultimately realize they really don't want that kind of stress and constant pressure to keep an eye on everything. It's my personality to do that anyway, but it's not for everyone. Some people realize they just want to make enough to be comfortable. Add that into your equation as you think about where you want to go.

Honestly, I think finding a job you are really passionate about is a lot more important than choosing a career path only based on how much money you will make. If your job fires you up because you love it, you'll be more likely to be successful at it anyway.

· ·

Whatever it is, take a frank look at yourself. What do you want? Where do you want to go? What job would be truly fulfilling for you? What pursuit fuels your passion? Is it something you could turn into a career? There are so many options and paths for channeling passions into professions. When you do something really well, when you nail it and you love it, ride the wave of that success. Could you turn it into a business? Whether it's planning a child's birthday party or the homecoming dance or writing a short story or baking an amazing cake or cooking a fabulous dinner or helping a friend with her taxes or sewing the most amazing Halloween costume, think about how you might turn it into a business. There is a potent psychological component to career success, and this is how you get it—you let yourself feel how good it is to be good at something, and you take that energy and leverage it. Once you've launched your new career direction, all you have to do is hang on.

I'm not saying that just because you're good at something, it will be easy. In fact, I can guarantee it will not be easy. There is no easy way to get to the top and stay there, and when successful people make it to the top, they are there for a reason. Your father could hand over the most successful business in the world to you, and you could run it into the ground if you didn't care about it or didn't know what you were doing. You have to believe in yourself even when it's hard and scary, and you need to really know your industry. Using the energy from your successes, no matter how small, can help to push you in the right direction. You also have to read the signs. If the world is saying, "Hey, you're great at that," then believe it. By the same token, if the world seems to be saying, "This isn't going to work," it might be time to reassess, or at least come at your goal from a different angle.

I didn't always know where I wanted to go, but I was passionate about certain things. I wanted to make my mark in the world, and I knew that I could, although I wasn't always sure that I would. I knew I wanted to help people solve problems because I was good at problem-solving, but I wasn't completely sure how to do it. I wanted to be successful, and I wanted to be able to be myself, working in an environment where my personality was a strength rather than a liability. I never said, "I want to be on reality TV." Until I got the idea for my first book, I never said, "I want to write a series of bestselling books." Until I was already on TV, I never said, "I want to have my own talk show." These specific ideas grew out of what I was already doing, but everything I was doing was moving me toward those goals.

This is what I mean in my book *A Place of Yes* when I say, "All roads lead to Rome." You don't necessarily have to know exactly where you are going, but if you know who you are and you have a general idea of the kind of life you want, then as long as you keep moving in that general direction, you will make progress and you will get to a good place. Just keep moving forward. Don't stagnate unless it's temporary and you have a good reason. You might get derailed along the way. You might hit roadblocks. That's life. Just keep your eyes open and look for other options. Sometimes, what seems like a setback is actually a new and better opportunity that will introduce you to something totally different—something that you love even more than the goal you thought you had. Sometimes a job you thought was just to pay the bills until you could fulfill your dream turns out to lay the groundwork for a new dream.

My assistant Jackie went to school for engineering, but now that she's taken a job with me, she is realizing she has skills and interests she never knew she had. She's learning a lot about digital technology and marketing. She might go in a completely new direction that's more suited to her personality and aptitude. We don't always know in college what we're best at, and although Jackie would probably make an excellent engineer, she might be even better at something else, and she might enjoy it more. You have to remember your goal, but it's also good to stay flexible and remember that you are a complex person who could probably go in several different directions successfully. You may change course a few times before you nail it down, and that's all part of the excitement.

Should You Quit Your Job?

People often ask me if they should quit their jobs to fulfill their dreams. There is no easy answer, but if you look honestly at your own situation, you'll probably know the answer. Of course you have to think about things like paying your rent, keeping your health insurance, and supporting your family. How much are those things worth? What if your child needs to go to the doctor?

Also consider your personal situation at the moment. Do you have a lot going on in your personal life? Did you just meet someone and you're feeling uncharacteristically optimistic? Did you just break up with someone or get divorced, and you think you have to change everything about your life right now, even though you might regret it later? Are you pregnant? Are you in a stressful relationship? Is a parent having health issues? Are you having a problem with one of your children? Is there something unsettling or unhappy about your living situation? You might not be in a position to make a sound decision right now, or you might be in the perfect place to make a change, but really consider both sides so you don't do something rash. You have to be realistic about when to sit still and when to make a move.

Being realistic also means looking at the big picture. Ask yourself what your goals were when you first took the job. What did you set out to do? My friend Molly knew that she wanted to work in music, but she needed to pay her rent, so she took a job as my assistant a few years ago. She was a great assistant and she learned a lot about the entertainment industry, but after a couple of years, she started to get moody and grouchy, as did I. She didn't enjoy the job as much as she used to. She felt like she wasn't doing what she was supposed to be doing, and she had some personal things going on, so she decided it was time to leave. It was probably a scary decision, and she had to take on freelance work, but that was the right decision for her because she eventually got back on the path toward where she wanted to go.

My assistant was young and single at the time she quit, but you might have a family depending on your income and benefits, and it may be selfish or stupid to chuck it all for your dream, at least until you've got something else lined up to pay the bills. I would rather you lose your dream than lose your house. Not every idea is a great one and not every great idea will actually translate into a successful business. Maybe you can quit and be okay cutting out the lattes and gym memberships and skipping the yearly vacation and bartending on the side, or maybe you can't. Don't just walk out of the office saying, "Fuck you, boss, I'm out of here, I'm going to go be a *magician!*" But if you can do it, you have the freedom to do it, you have some kind of financial support, and you have a plan, then maybe it's right to quit, now or sometime in the near future.

If you can possibly manage it, start looking for a job while you still have a job, but manage the risk. Subtly and quietly start networking before you turn in your resignation. Your ability to do this depends on the size of your industry. If you're a great teller at a bank, the other banks in town probably won't know about it, and if you apply elsewhere, your bank probably won't hear about it, but in smaller industries, people will talk and your company could find out you're looking. Be smart about it, but know that the best time to find a job is when you still have a job. People who are employed have more confidence. They have a lot going on, especially if they are good at their jobs, and people are attracted to that. If you've quit and you're freaking out, it's a lot harder to score a better job. Scared money never wins and desperate energy is a turnoff.

You might get offered a job when you didn't even think you were looking, and you will have to decide whether to quit a job you had no intention of leaving. This happened to my VP of Marketing and Strategy, Malini Patel, who quit a corporate job where she was successful to come work for me when she wasn't even sure she was looking for another job. She had worked at Unilever for many years, working on brands like Axe, Dove, and Degree, as a brand manager.

Malini went from working in a big office to working in my apartment. I can't imagine what she thinks of this environment change. Half the time, I'm walking around in my pajamas with no bra and doing things like pulling out a big box of vibrators I got from a talk show and yelling, "Does anybody want a vibrator? Who wants a vibrator?" Last week, our primary topic of office conversation was "Do you have a bald eagle or a landing strip?" I bet nobody ever asked her that at Unilever.

This was a major change for her, but she did exactly what I would have done: She took the meeting, and she took a risk because she decided it was worth the potential payoff. This is her story about how she made her decision.

. . . .

NOTES FROM THE SKINNYGIRL TEAM
Malini Patel, VP of Marketing and Strategy

How did I get a job with Bethenny Frankel? A former boss and mentor inquired if I would be interested in exploring a unique opportunity: working for Bethenny Frankel, helping her with her brand strategy for Skinnygirl. I thought about it for a moment, then responded that of course I would take the meeting. I always like to know what's out there and am open to opportunities. If nothing else, I figured I would have an interesting experience—an interview with Bethenny Frankel! I didn't know what to expect but I prepared for the interview and learned about the company, the products, and Bethenny. I prepared to try to get the job, and then I could figure out if I was going to take it or not.

This was tricky for me, of course. I had a steady and successful career with a major company. I loved my job, and it was secure. I weighed the pros and cons:

PROS

- This was a unique opportunity. I knew I couldn't pass this up now and hope it would be there next year when/if I was "ready to leave." I am a firm believer that life is all about experiences and the more diverse you can make your experiences, the more interesting and therefore marketable you are.
- After meeting Bethenny, it was clear that she was looking for someone to really dig in and help her run this company. She had a ton going on and there was no sign of her stopping, so it was clear that she was looking for someone to help her manage the amazing brands and business she had built. It was also clear to me that if I did my job well, she would allow me to grow. In other words, there was upside. I used the interview process to find out what she was really looking for to see if it matched what I was interested in and capable of doing.
- I had always toyed with the idea of starting my own business or working for a start-up. I knew this opportunity and experience would let me really experience what it is like to move out of a massive organization like Unilever.
- Bethenny and her company span a lot of industries. She is in entertainment; publishing; licensing in apparel, foods, fitness equipment, etc. I knew I had enough of the skills she required of me, but I still had a lot of room to learn about new industries and meet all kinds of people.
- I didn't have children and I was also fortunate enough to have a spouse who had a stable income, so it was definitely easier to take a risk.

CONS

- Job insecurity—she could have fired me on day six if she wanted. However, because I had worked hard, taken on interesting roles, and built and maintained a good network of people, I was pretty sure I could get another job quickly if I needed to. In fact, I left my old job with my boss and colleague saying that if things didn't work out, I could always come back. I maintained good relationships, even on my way out.

- There was no clear career path. At larger companies there are general career paths. You know if you do well, you will get a promotion, and that path is carved out. Here I was unsure of what exactly would happen if I was successful. In the end it didn't matter, because I was taking this job for the experience, not the title, and because I knew if I was successful, there would be opportunities for me. Part of this was believing in myself but also believing in defining my own path to a certain extent. It sounds cliché, but no one great ever became great by following a path that was carved out for them.

I was excited about the opportunity, I mitigated the risks I was concerned about so I didn't have to stress about making the move, and bottom line, I knew that I wouldn't regret taking this chance, even if I ended up failing. You have to make the choice based on your goals and personal situation and priorities. Because I knew where I wanted my career to go (eventually I want to run a company) and I knew the things I valued (interesting experiences), I could evaluate the opportunity through my personal lens and decide if it was right for me.

I had a series of three interviews, and when she offered me the job, I accepted. Now that I've worked here for a while, it's been a lot of things: surprising, challenging, fun, and stressful at times. I realize in retrospect I did a good job asking a lot of questions and being honest about what I wanted. Bethenny was honest about what the job involved so I was prepared for the drastic environment change, a whole new level of accountability, wearing a bajillion hats, and an up-close-and-personal view of what it's like to run a company—it takes guts, commitment, and drive! This is the exact learning experience I need for my own career trajectory, and I'm loving it. It has definitely paid off.

• •

Only you can know if quitting is right for you, but if you weigh every option and consider both sides, you will probably know inside yourself what the right move is for you right now. Even if you can't quit today, you can start making plans to make a change and move toward your goal. Lay the groundwork. If you feel like you've been derailed and gone in the wrong direction, then you can start going in a different direction, but get something solid going before you say good-bye to that all-important paycheck. Set yourself up so you have an escape route to a better life, and the days at the job you dislike won't seem so painful.

How Do You Get There?

You won't always know the shortest route from point A to point B, but you can definitely start making plans. After you've done your dreaming, it's time to get real. To help you decide what to do next, consider a few important things:

- **How's the market?** Think about the job market right now and the climate in your industry or field. You don't dump stock when everybody is dumping stock, and you don't jump onto the end of a trend after it's already peaked. Is it a bad time to get a PhD or open a restaurant? Is it a good time to get into the medical profession or to write your own series of e-books? Do some research, and ask people who are already doing what you want to do.

- **Know what you need to do.** Does what you want to do require special training or skills? For example, if you want to be an actor, you don't just show up in Hollywood expecting to make it big without any preparation. (Trust me.) In your desired field, make a list of the skills you need, including any degrees or certifications required, to do the job you want to do. Start working on those things. Go back to school, or go to night school or Internet school. Start researching your field and reading trade journals. Find out what really needs to happen to get yourself started. Even if the steps will take time, at least you will be moving toward your goal.

· ·

NOTES FROM THE SKINNYGIRL TEAM
Malini Patel, VP of Marketing and Strategy

How do you get from point A to point B? In other words, how do you get from where you are now to a job or industry you really want to be in?

- Knowing where you want to go is more than half the battle. Most people stay where they are, even if they hate it, because they don't know what else they would do. Meet people in your industry. The days of sitting behind a computer and submitting your résumé are over. There was an article recently about how over 45 percent of jobs in companies are being filled by referrals, so get out there.
- If you really want the job, join a professional organization in your industry, use your network of friends and colleagues, and talk to strangers. You never know who you could end up meeting, and an opportunity could be right in front of you. Most people are willing to help and love to talk about what they do. Just ordering drinks, I've met a

designer for Tiffany jewelry, a fabric coordinator for Diane von Furstenberg, managers of top hedge funds, CEOs of banks, and many more interesting people in dynamic fields.

- Although it sounds counterintuitive, you might get great advice from coworkers or previous bosses about how to progress. They could give you honest feedback and help you navigate the best ways to make a move. In my own experience, every job I have gotten was through a recommendation from a previous boss.

- If you get an opportunity, explore it. You don't need to take any job that comes along, but by taking the meeting or learning more about a potential position, you will better define what you want and don't want.

- Do every job well. Bethenny always says, "Everything's your business," and I agree. Be a rock star at everything you do and people will seek you out for the job you want. Whether you are making coffee or making a major business decision, give it your all. If you are committed, hardworking, and passionate, someone will notice.

· ·

- **Follow your interests.** When I was in event production, I met all kinds of people and was responsible for a million things at once, but one thing I really enjoyed was hiring the restaurants to do the food. I wanted to know about their menus, what kitchen rentals they needed, and how they ran their businesses. That started me down a path of being interested in food, which led to several different businesses later, and the relationships I formed with chefs and restaurant managers helped facilitate those businesses, even though I hadn't planned to go in that direction at the time.

- **Keep learning.** If you never stop learning, you'll open doors for yourself. Ask people about what they do. Be curious and interested. Read the newspaper and trade journals in your industry. Try new things, and always be open to new ways of thinking.

- **Commit to your goals.** If you decide you want to do something or be something, don't give up the second it gets hard. You have to commit to moving in the right direction, even if it's difficult, even if the end goal is far off.

- **Change your approach.** Always be willing to come at things from a new angle if they aren't working. Sometimes the goal is right, but the approach is wrong. When I first wrote *Naturally Thin*, it was called *The Thin Book*, and everyone said it would never happen, but I kept going back and doing it again and again and trying different approaches, and that book became my first *New York Times* bestseller. People kept telling me the talk show wouldn't happen, but I kept saying it would. I approached it from a lot of different ways, and finally I found a way to make it work. Now the talk show is happening. When you're not getting what you want, take a breath, step back, then find another way in.

- **Dive in.** When I became an event planner, I took jobs producing events even though I didn't know how, because I knew I had the energy and will to learn fast. It doesn't matter what your résumé says. A résumé is a phone number on a piece of paper. Be smart and willing to do things the next person won't do and think fast on your feet, and you'll be more valuable than the next guy with the fancy résumé who doesn't want to get his hands dirty.

- **Adapt to opportunities.** Be open and meet people. Talk to people you don't know. Mention what you do and where you are headed, even if you don't know how you're going to get there yet. You never know when you could meet just the right person or run into just the right opportunity. One day, when I went to a polo event in the Hamptons where people go to socialize, I just happened to meet the producers for the show that would become *The Real Housewives of New*

York City. I didn't want to do it at first because I had just been getting some press for my natural-food chef business and I was finally making a little money after being broke for so long. I didn't want to blow it and make a fool of myself (arguably, at that moment, I did), especially after just coming off not winning *The Apprentice: Martha Stewart.* Then I decided that maybe I could adapt my strategy because this was such a rare opportunity. It took me months to accept, but eventually, I did. If I hadn't been adaptable to doing something that seemed completely out of my wheelhouse as a not-married, not-wealthy non-housewife who was trying to be a natural foods chef, I might not be where I am today. You never know when your next great opportunity might arise at a dinner party, over cocktails at a bar, or when a friend just happens to introduce you to a friend.

- **Be courageous.** Sometimes, forging the path to a new life is scary, and you might have to take a leap of faith. There is a difference between courage and stupidity, so listen to your inner voice. If you are waking up in the middle of the night thinking, *This is a huge mistake*, then maybe you need to rethink your move. However, if your inner voice says, "Jump," then jump! It's like skydiving. It should be a healthy, thrilling fear but not a crippling, nauseating fear. Don't jump out of a (metaphorical) airplane with your kids strapped to your back and don't throw away your 401(k) and your insurance if your family needs those things, but if you have the freedom and the financial cushion to do it, then do it, even if it involves scary things like moving or adjusting your family to a new situation. The greatest things that ever happened to me were the things I was a little bit afraid to do but that I felt, in my gut, were going to be life changing. In the talk-show industry, I've been told that the shows that are the hardest to sell end up doing the best. Sometimes you have to push through fear and resistance to get where you want to be.

- **Map it out.** You don't have to make an official one-year plan, five-year plan, ten-year plan. I never did that. But you should at least be thinking about the future. Where do you want to be in one year? Working on your move? Making money so you can afford to make a move? Shifting to a position with more upward mobility while you pay your rent? Think about where you want to be in five years. By then, you should have made great strides toward your goal, even if you aren't there yet. Will you be there in ten years? Will you be living your dream? Will you be doing something you love and have a nice savings account and feel secure?

Planning a career is exciting, but not as exciting as making it happen. When you've got a plan, it's time to move forward, and once you're moving, never stop. There is always somewhere even better to go.

Chapter Twelve

Managing Your Career

No one will ever manage your career with your true interests in mind like you will. In the same way that you have to manage your diet, exercise, stress, sleep, and relationships, you also have to manage your career if you want your work life to progress and satisfy you. It's your job to take ownership.

I haven't made all the right choices in my personal life, and I've definitely made some mistakes in my professional life, but a girl-friend once told me, "You make all the right moves." There are exceptions, but I generally take pride in the fact that I have good instincts and I do make the right moves most of the time. Life is a chess game, and the moves you make now will affect your future moves and decisions.

I've learned a lot in my career, even since I wrote my book *A Place of Yes*, which contains many stories about my work life over the years. Since that book, I have sold my Skinnygirl cocktail business to Beam, I have moved on from reality television into the talk-show world, and I've created a host of new Skinnygirl products under the part of the business that I still own and control. I'm always look-ing forward, and this is what managing your career is all about. You won't always make the right decisions, but you have to keep moving forward and growing and developing and changing with the times, the market, and your customers, clients, or audience.

. . . .

Be constantly thinking ahead. Develop and monitor short-, medium-, and long-term plans. Very often, people expand before they are ready and end up falling short of expectations. Consider the restaurant that is always crowded and makes you think, *Hey, they should take over the space next door. They would do so much more business.* When they do, if the chef and the kitchen cannot handle the increase in business and they don't have enough or appropriate servers, bartenders, and hostesses, the whole operation can fail.

. . . .

Here are some basic principles that I believe will carry you forward and help you manage your career to the best possible effect. These are the principles I follow in my business life, so I know they work.

Act On It

When you have a good idea, act on it, *if* you believe you can actually execute it. Don't wait around for someone else to provide you with an opportunity. Go out and find an opportunity for something you know will work.

The Skinnygirl Margarita is the perfect example. When I first got the idea to do the Skinnygirl Margarita, I shopped the idea around, but nobody was interested, so I got a business partner and we produced the product ourselves. Ironically, shortly after I came up with the idea of the Skinnygirl Margarita, Beam, the fourth largest liquor company in the world, asked me if I wanted to be a spokesperson for one of their tequila brands. I decided not to do this because I wanted to build my own brand. This was early on, and it was tempting to take the low-hanging fruit, but I decided that Beam obviously smelled something about what I was doing, so I wanted to spend more time developing it myself. I wanted it to be my own achievement, not someone else's.

Years later, after the Skinnygirl Margarita was a success and I had just come out with my second flavor, Skinnygirl Sangria, my partner told me we had been approached by Beam to sell the brand. I said no several times, but then I thought about how I had kept saying no when I was asked to be on *The Real Housewives of New York City*, and how finally saying yes turned out to be one of the best decisions I ever made. I decided maybe we should sit down and talk to them.

I remember that day clearly. There I was at a table with six liquor-business men, and they were telling me that summer was coming and this was the big season for cocktails, so we needed to do the deal right now, or the deal wouldn't happen. They would come out with their own "skinny" cocktail brand and they would never offer to buy mine again. I didn't really believe it. I had an instinct that they would still want to buy it after the summer because it was just going to get bigger, but I decided to think seriously about it.

These are the things I thought about:

1. I wanted the street cred. If you have a heavy deal under your belt, people will want to get into business with you. I've seen this happen to many people in the music business, like when Jay-Z sold his apparel company for $204 million. I wanted that first deal under my belt. I also knew it would provide me with the money to be fine and secure running my other businesses, but although I could have hammered it out and tried to get a little more, it was less about the actual dollar amount than getting that security and being able to say I did this one great thing. I had a feeling this could be my one big thing, my ace in the hole.

2. Bigger companies were copying me. I know every great deal is only as good as its execution, and now that I'd done it, now that

I had effectively invented the skinny cocktail category, everyone was going to copy me. People bigger than me with more money (cheater brands) were coming after my idea. The competitors were gearing up. Restaurants were already knocking off my idea, with "Skinny Margaritas" on their menu. Nobody had been doing that before. I knew that was coming from me, but because I couldn't trademark the word "skinny," they could do it. I've always said you have to know when to hold 'em and know when to fold 'em, and I knew I wasn't in a position to compete at that level. I thought, *What if I'm the little guy and the big guys swallow me?* I kept thinking of David and Goliath.

3. Demand was much greater than supply. I was having a hard time keeping up with the demand. I had a small distribution partner and I knew my cocktails should have been everywhere in the country. I knew I needed more muscle in my distribution, and Beam is the fourth-largest liquor brand.

4. I was liable. The company was growing fast and it was just little old me. I owned it, so I was totally liable. If anybody sued me, it was all on me, and that was scary.

5. I liked Beam. Although they are corporate, they are the least corporate of all the big liquor brands. They are the only major liquor company that still operates like a small business, and that made me comfortable.

6. Beam wanted me to be involved at every level and with a few exceptions, allowed me creative control. They said they needed me to be involved and would only do the deal if I was involved. They wanted to lock me in, and although some people might prefer to sell a brand and leave it behind, I liked this aspect. I wanted to be involved at every level. I told them, "This company is my baby. This is a 'fuck you' brand; when nobody would buy it, I made it happen out of nothing. Whatever price you pay for this company, it will be the biggest bargain you will ever get in your life."

After thinking seriously, weighing my options, and feeling confident I was doing the right thing, I acted on it: I sold Skinnygirl

Cocktails to Beam. That was two years ago, and now we have eighteen different varieties, if you include the mini margaritas in the four-pack and the limited-edition prosecco coming out in the fall. It's unheard of to have that many flavors in such a short time.

· ·

NUMBER GAME

People always ask me about the number: how much I made in my cocktail deal with Beam. It's been in the media all over the place, from $8 to $120 million, even though I have never once revealed the actual number. I never said I made a dollar and I never said I made a billion dollars. I don't ask people how much money they make, and I don't think people should ask me. I'm not mad at people for asking. I know people are curious, but this is all I will ever say: I did very well, I did have a partner who exited after the deal, and I stayed in business with Beam and continue to do well with that brand. However, the deal also involved taxes and lawyers and agents and a lot of expenses. Nothing is ever as simple as people think it is, and in any case, the least interesting thing about me is how much money I have or make.

· ·

Think of Everything

Skinnygirl®

Every time I make a business deal, I never just accept the terms as is. Try to think of every bizarre thing that can happen. I think of every possible scenario and I make sure those are covered in the contract.

When I signed the deal with Bravo to do *The Real Housewives of New York City*, one of the smartest things I did was put a clause in the contract saying that any of my preexisting, current, and future business ventures belonged to me and me alone. If I created it, it was mine. After I sold Skinnygirl Cocktails—and Bravo didn't get any of that—networks started pushing to include what they unofficially call the "Bethenny clause" in their talent contracts, which says they have a stake in any business ventures related to or created because of the person's stint on their show. That's because of me. (Agents everywhere curse me for this.)

With the Skinnygirl Cocktails sale, I obsessed over every possible scenario. For example, I never want the Skinnygirl logo to be compromised, so I put it into the deal that they can never use "Skinny" and "Girl" separately. It always has to be one word, and now it's a brand name, where the individual words aren't as meaningful as the whole name. The sum is greater than its parts. Think of brands like Banana Republic, whose name is a phrase that used to be associated with safaris. Now it's associated with the clothing brand. Nobody thinks of the fruit when they talk about Apple computers. I'm building that for Skinnygirl.

I also added clauses saying that the colors of the Skinnygirl logo could never change, and although I change what she's wearing or doing for different products, I would not allow them to ever put her in a bikini, like some bimbo selling beer, or degrade her in any way.

Then there was my biggest success and the best thing I ever did in terms of deal making. When I was selling Skinnygirl Cocktails to Beam, they wanted everything. They wanted to buy the Skinnygirl brand, across the board. I said, "Slow down, buddy. You can have Skinnygirl Cocktails. I keep her for everything else."

I had a good argument. I told them that everything I did with Skinnygirl would build on their brand, and everything they did with Skinnygirl Cocktails would build on my brand, so one hand was washing the other. I said, "The better my other brands do, the better it is for Beam." I explained that this extended to everything I did—

the talk show would help the cocktails, the cocktails would help the talk show. This has built my other Skinnygirl products in a big way. Now I'm the number-one-selling liquor brand in Target, and when you have all that real estate in Target, they want your other products, too.

They agreed, and this turned out to be huge for me. When Grey Goose sold for $2 billion, that was it. It sold. The person who sold it can't go make Grey Goose dressing or Grey Goose soda, but I can make Skinnygirl coffee, Skinnygirl snacks, Skinnygirl anything. Most people think I sold the entire brand. I sold one piece of the pizza . . . not the whole pie. It was the smartest and most important decision in this deal, and probably the most crucial and intelligent business decision I've made to date. Thus proving my point: think about every little detail!

MY SKINNYGIRL PIZZA

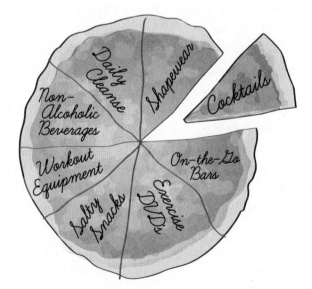

Keep Your Hand in It

No matter what kind of career you have or deal you make, don't be blind to what's going on. You have to keep a hand in it. You can delegate and you can hand over the things you're not as good at to professionals, but never let anyone think you aren't keeping an eye on them.

I do this at every level, from basic accounting to the sale of Skinnygirl Cocktails. Even though I sold this one part of Skinnygirl, I'm beyond connected. Every tagline is created by me. Every single flavor is created and approved by me. Every bottle, every commercial, every publicity party. Everything is me, and I love that.

I also built into the contract that I would promote everything, as long as I believed in it. If they want to do a flavor or a style or something I don't like, they can still do it because they own it, but I won't promote it. Early on in our dealings, Beam wanted to change the flavor of the Skinnygirl Margarita, and I was beyond psychotic. I said, "The Skinnygirl Margarita will not change. People love it." I told them that per the contract, they were not permitted to change the flavor for a period of time. People didn't want it to change, and they realized this, so the Skinnygirl Margarita remains true. They stuck with what works—if it ain't broke, don't fix it!

My hand is in every aspect of my talk show, too. I am a thousand percent involved. Every idea, every guest, every piece of furniture on the set, every piece of music that plays, the décor of all the rooms, every piece of food in the dressing rooms, every outfit—it all goes through me, and that's just the way I like it. It's the best way to ensure quality control.

Foster Trust

The concessions Beam made in our contract proved that they trusted me, and selling Skinnygirl Cocktails to Beam was a leap of faith for me, too. It was a great decision for both of us, that has resulted in a great partnership. Generally, brands are reluctant to get involved with celebrities. What if the celebrity gets hit by a bus or has a serious image issue that reflects on the brand? They were very trusting of me and the fact that I would not do something deceitful with the other Skinnygirl products or screw up the brand.

· ·

THE NEW FACE OF LIQUOR

Back in the day, celebrities weren't supposed to associate themselves with liquor. Publicists were always telling their clients, "Put your drink down!" especially in front of cameras. Until Sean Combs (P. Diddy) became a spokesperson for and part owner of a liquor brand, such a thing was unheard of. Now it's the new thing to do. Dozens of celebs, many far more famous than I am, have signed on to represent wine and liquor, but most of them have failed because the deals were not true to who they are. Now people say to their agents, "Get me a Bethenny deal," but so far, Sean Combs and I are the only ones to do deals at this level. Coincidentally, we have the same birthday.

· ·

Learn to Listen

I haven't always been the best at listening to other people's advice, especially about business. A lot of advice I've gotten in the past was bad advice, and I'm glad I didn't take it. You want to listen to people who know what they are talking about, but if I had listened to people who supposedly knew what they were talking about, I never would have done a lot of great things. Intelligent and accomplished professionals as well as friends advised me not to do *Housewives*. If I had listened to the big companies with their market-research numbers, or even walked into a few liquor stores and looked at the competition, I never would have launched my own cocktail line. However, there is a fine line. You should let the experts help you, but there is a point when you need to ignore what the experts say and go with your gut. In my case, ignorance was beneficial.

However, now that I've become even more experienced in business, I'm refining my sense of when it's appropriate to listen to the experts, and I've realized that some of my partners and colleagues really do have smart ideas. When I sat down with Beam, I was only interested in the bottled cocktail market. Nobody was buying those when I got into the category, and I broadened that business across the board, but Beam explained to me that despite the growth, ready-to-drink is still a small percentage of all liquor sold. They said, "Bethenny, what you don't realize is that 90 percent of the liquor business is wine and vodka. That's what women drink the most."

I didn't realize this because I was still caught up in what I like and want, and that is a good cocktail. However, they said that the bottled cocktail market, although growing steadily, was still a very small percentage of the market, and that wine and vodka were huge opportunities for the Skinnygirl brand. I decided to listen because they are a big company with focused research numbers and what they said made sense to me. You need to find a balance between your gut and research.

I realized maybe Beam was right and I was missing a big opportunity by ignoring 90 percent of the liquor market. I thought about it, and then I said, "Fine, I'll do it, as long as you let me decide what kinds of wine and vodka to make. I choose the flavors, names, and concepts, you make it work." Without listening, I would have missed this opportunity, but I listen to them, they listen to me, and it's all good.

Reinvent Yourself

If you don't like the way your career is going, or if you are ready for a change, you can switch directions and reinvent yourself. This is different from being a jumper. There is a fine line between changing directions and jumping. Some people give up and change to a new one every time a job or career direction gets hard, thinking it will be easier or their ticket to fame and fortune.

I've done some job jumping, but most of my moves have been legitimate changes in direction when my direction wasn't working out as well as I wanted it to. I've gone from actress to chef to reality TV personality to talk show host. I've told you many of these stories in my other books, but I haven't told you about my talk show.

When I was on *Housewives*, I just had a feeling I was going to get a spin-off, even though what I really wanted was a talk show. All along, I was talking to agents and different companies that produce talk shows, and a lot of people were interested. Then I met Hilary Estey McLoughlin, who was president of Telepictures, which produced *The Tyra Banks Show*, *Ellen*, *TMZ*, and *Extra*, and who had done *Rosie*. We were friendly and had meet-and-greet meetings about once a year. When *Bethenny Ever After* aired, one day Ellen DeGeneres tweeted, "Have you seen the show *Bethenny Ever After*? I love her." That's when Hilary called me to be on Ellen's show.

I came out to L.A. to meet with Ellen and Hilary. That morning, before my meetings, I was with an agent, and I was feeling ballsy and I said, "If Ellen is smart, she'll 'Oprah' me," meaning she'll want to produce my show and put her stamp on me, do what Oprah did for Dr. Phil and Dr. Oz. A few minutes later, I was sitting at the table with Hilary, and she said, "What are we going to do with you?"

I said, "If you want to fuck me, you're going to have to put a ring on my finger."

That day, I went on *Ellen,* and we really connected. We've since become great friends. At that point, however, we barely knew each other. During the break, she said, "I hear you're talking to Telepictures. I would love to produce a talk show with you." I died. I went home and I kept saying to myself, "What just happened?" I'd said it. I'd believed it. But somehow, the reality of it stunned me. I had a plan, and I had an instinct, and it was dead-on. Ellen has great instincts, too, and I think this is one reason why we connected so well.

The first step was to shoot a pilot, which is like a sample of the show that the producers sell to the network. I came out to L.A. to do this for two days, and it was the greatest experience of my life. My guests were Jennifer Love Hewitt, Kevin Nealon, and Michael Strahan. I couldn't believe real celebrities were right there on my talk show. The producers said I was born to do it.

Then Telepictures had to go out and sell the show. That season, we were going up against a handful of other talk-show pilots: Katie Couric, Ricki Lake, Jeff Probst, and Steve Harvey. We were all trying to sell our shows to the same person. A network's schedule is like a parking lot. There are only so many spaces. Fast-forward: All those shows got approved . . . except mine. I was disappointed but the shows came out and Ricki Lake and Jeff Probst were subsequently canceled. Steve Harvey did well, and word on the street was that Katie Couric did fine considering the expensive cost of producing her show. Fox came to us and said, "Okay, we'd like you to do a test run."

My initial reaction was no. I was angry. Why do I always have to prove myself? I had the highest-rated series premiere in Bravo history. I had three *New York Times* bestselling books. I had one of the fastest-selling liquor brands in the world. Wasn't that enough? I didn't want to be tested. I was sick of being tested.

Then I sat back and said to myself, "Okay, listen. Maybe I'm not even meant to do a talk show. Maybe I should go test this for the summer, not just to see if they want me, but to see if I want them and if I really want to do this. Do I really want to suffer through what Ricki Lake, Jeff Probst, and Anderson Cooper had to endure, being on a show that gets canceled?" I decided to see if I liked it and see if it was something I felt I could do for the next ten years. I wanted to know whether audiences would respond to me the way I thought they would, and whether the network would respond to me the way I thought they should. I needed to know they really wanted me, and that I really wanted them.

I did the test, and it was the highest-rated test in Fox history, in the middle of the summer when everyone should have been out at the beach and nobody is watching TV. You all showed up and watched, so thank you! This is why I love you. (And you're better for it—you have less sun damage than your friends!)

The next step was to sell to good stations with good time slots. Then it got exciting, like the buildup to a book launch. We got ready, and now, here we go! *Bethenny* airs in the fall of 2013. It's the reinvention of a lifetime. Let's hope for a long ride!

Everything's Your Business

Every problem I encounter in my life becomes an opportunity for a business move. I carefully separate my work life from my personal life. I protect my family's, friends', and partners' privacy. However, when it's just about me, I use my own problems and dilemmas in my business because this is how I come up with new products. How do I solve it for myself, and then how can I solve it for someone else?

If, in my personal life, I can't find shapewear that looks good under my clothes and is actually comfortable, then I want to solve that problem. If I can't find a healthy snack or I want to work out at home to a good DVD or I want to cleanse or I want to make better coffee at home or I want something refreshing to drink that doesn't contain alcohol, then I make a product that will provide what I need.

Expanding the Skinnygirl product line has been an exciting and challenging road. When I first came into the spotlight, I had a lot of people coming to me who wanted to get into business with me, but they weren't all capable of producing the level of product I wanted, so I had to be careful. I did some things then that I wouldn't do now—put out products that were good but that might not be what I would choose today. I also brought out products in an order I wouldn't have necessarily chosen, because at first, you don't have every option open to you. You just have the opportunities that come.

For example, I think that coming out with salty snacks to go with my cocktails would have been a natural early business, but I couldn't find a good partner to work with until recently (salty, healthful snacks coming out soon!). Instead, a great company that made shapewear came to me early in the game, so I went with that, and it was one of the first post-cocktail Skinnygirl products.

I'm still doing this, with a lot of new healthful products in development, including ice cream and other frozen treats; nonalcoholic beverages, like tea and juice spritzers; barista drinks you can make at home, like lattes, hot chocolate, and chai; and maybe longer-term, a line of Skinnygirl cooking tools and appliances, like blenders and coffeemakers, as well as more Skinnygirl food products, like salad dressing and frozen meals. Everything has clean ingredients with no artificial colors or flavors, and everything is lower in calories than the standard alternatives. They all solve problems. You also won't find boring flavors, because that doesn't go with the Skinnygirl brand. Everything is something a little different, gourmet, or indulgent, like snacks flavored with sea salt and cracked pepper or pink-peppercorn ranch, or ice cream flavors like red velvet cupcake.

We've also got new Skinnygirl Cocktail flavors: the Sweet & Tart Margarita, which is flavored with grapefruit; the White Cranberry Cosmo; White Cherry Vodka; Moscato; and the Mojito.

• •

NOTES FROM THE SKINNYGIRL TEAM
Kevin George, Global Chief Marketing Officer at Beam Inc.

Do you have what it takes? Successful people have certain qualities in common. Bethenny is a brilliant, intuitive marketer who understands her consumer very well. She has a terrific gut for what will work and I respect that immensely. She also is someone who will listen and take other people's opinions into account (although the perception may be the opposite). She is also what I call an "idea hamster." Her brain is always going, like a hamster on a wheel, coming up with new things. You can't teach that.

. . . .

Stay in Motion

Never stop moving, changing, evolving, and getting things done. There is always something to do. You should never be sitting around on your ass doing nothing. Write about something. Start a blog about your business. Read the newspaper, because something in it will apply to you. Work on your website. Start writing a book. Get into social networking. Make your master list of everything you need to do on a daily, weekly, and monthly basis. Start a list of everything you want to accomplish this year. Organize your office. Go through your e-mails and file them into folders. Go through your phone list, get rid of old contacts, and update new ones. Clean out your wallet. Organize your receipts. Set up a better accounting system. Connect with people. Send thank-you notes. Get out there and network and say hello and shake hands. On those days when the work is piling up and you can't get it all done, you'll be so grateful you got these little things in place that will save you time and nourish your connections and reputation later.

That's not to say you can't take breaks or go on vacation. You have to do this so your brain can rest, but don't waste your actual work time. Move quickly and make the most of it, so when it's time to relax you can actually truly relax.

I'm known for adhering to deadlines and when I get a quick task, I do it immediately if it's at all possible. If someone wants an article for a magazine, I'll write it without agonizing over it. When my partners say they want new flavor ideas, I'm on it. I'll do it in less than five minutes. If my partner at Skinnygirl wants new ideas for the

Skinnygirl Daily bars, I come up with them instantaneously. When Skinnygirl Cocktails wants a new tagline for a campaign, I think of it on the spot. Procrastination is the thief of time, and time is the greatest commodity we have, so bang it out.

Your career is in your hands, so manage it like you would manage your very best, most influential, most powerful client. Because that's exactly what you are.

Chapter Thirteen
· · · · · · · · · · · ·

Should You Start Your Own Business?

Should I start my own business?"

It's a pivotal question and something people often ask, as I've started so many businesses myself. Some worked, and some didn't. I love making a great idea become a reality, but it doesn't always happen. Even now, some of my business ventures struggle to succeed, and if they do survive, it's only because I revive them from the dead using the resources I now have and by being a dog on a bone. I've always been tenacious, but I only recently acquired those resources. In the past, when a business died, it was my funeral.

If all businesses were successful, I would say yes, jump on every business idea you think of. Unfortunately, there are no guarantees. Not every good idea makes it, and some bad ideas do pretty damn well, considering. It's not all about money, or even knowledge of your field. What decides whether your idea will take off is a little mysterious, but the more you know about what you're actually getting into, the smarter you are about the moves you make, and the closer you monitor the climate of your business and public opinion, the better your chances.

The most important thing to realize is that starting your own business is a huge, sometimes overwhelming, and sometimes painful experience. Having a good idea doesn't even remotely qualify anyone to start a business. People think if they have a good idea, they can just run out and tell someone with a lot of money and that person will buy it or fund the whole thing. Don't we all wish! The fact is that great ideas are cheap. If you don't have the knowledge, skill, and resources (your own or a willing partner's) to make an idea become an actual, profitable business, then you're probably not going to get very far.

In this chapter, I want to prepare you for what starting your own business is really like so you don't jump in without knowing what you are doing, or torture yourself unnecessarily, or lose everything.

WHAT MAKES A SUCCESSFUL BUSINESS?

Think about the businesses that work. What sets them apart? Why did Starbucks succeed when there are delis and diners all over the country where you can get coffee? They created a culture and a consistency that they could duplicate, store after store. Successful companies have a good system, good employees, and smart managers. They educate their employees, like McDonald's does, sending their managers to Hamburger University, where they learn the McDonald's procedures that work and how to maintain that consistency people rely on.

The Entrepreneur Checklist #1:
Do You Have the Right Personality?

Business is hard, and being an entrepreneur is even harder. Having the right personality helps. Nobody can have every quality on this list, but this is a hell of a good start, and successful entrepreneurs have a lot of them. Are you:

- ☐ Accurate
- ☐ Analytical
- ☐ Attentive to detail
- ☐ Certain
- ☐ Compassionate
- ☐ Competitive
- ☐ Conscientious
- ☐ Consistent
- ☐ Constant
- ☐ Decisive
- ☐ Detail-oriented
- ☐ Diligent
- ☐ Disciplined
- ☐ Driven
- ☐ Focused
- ☐ Innovative
- ☐ Methodical
- ☐ Meticulous
- ☐ Obsessed
- ☐ Organized

The Entrepreneur Checklist #2: Do You Have the Right Business or Product Idea?

You also have to have an idea that can really take off. If you want to start a business based on your idea, put it to the test:

- ☐ Does it solve a problem?
- ☐ Is it innovative?
- ☐ Can you afford to make it happen?
- ☐ Is there a barrier to entry for others, meaning are you the only one who can do it, or can someone with more money copy it tomorrow and do it better?
- ☐ Is it an original idea?
- ☐ Does the market want or need it?
- ☐ Have you thought every scenario through?
- ☐ Do you know your target audience?
- ☐ Do you have time for it?
- ☐ Do you have the support to make it happen?
- ☐ Do you have the capability to market your idea, getting the word out?
- ☐ Do you have access to distribution channels so people can actually buy your product?
- ☐ Can you easily communicate the idea? If you can't describe it in a few sentences and get people excited, you probably haven't crystallized it enough yet.
- ☐ Do you have connections in your industry? If you've invented a toy, do you have a friend or acquaintance with a chain of toy stores? If you've invented a cocktail, do you have good distribution and media connections? If you've invented a great new office product, do you know any higher-ups at an office-supply company?

LEAN AND MEAN

People like Martha Stewart have giant companies, but I like to keep mine streamlined. People are amazed at how many businesses I have when they see my entire staff: Malini, my VP; Jackie, my assistant; and Cookie, my moral support. My childcare professional, Leslie, doubles as an intern, and we do have one actual intern getting college credit, but that's it. Just us, running a global empire. I like it that way. I cannot mentally handle having Phil down in accounting and Jan over in insurance and having an office supply closet. It's not me. We have to be tight and right. It's just who I am. It ends up costing more because I have lawyers who aren't in house who get percentages, and accountants and tax people and advisers, etc., but it's worth it to me to work out of my home and be a stay-at-home mom. I don't even use the computer. I do everything on my smartphone.

The Pros and Cons of Self-Employment

Every job has its good and bad points, and you need to decide whether the cons are deal-breakers for you, as well as whether the pros would make you happier than you are right now. You could have a great idea and plenty of resources but not really want to be self-employed. Before you jump in, I suggest making your own list, but this is mine:

Pros of Self-Employment

- You set your own hours.
- You decide how much (or how little) to work.
- You decide when to work—after the kids go to bed, before everybody wakes up, in the middle of the night; it's your choice.

- If you work at home, you can go on vacation whenever you want. You don't have to mind the shop. (But you might have to work on your vacation.)
- You don't have to worry about people stealing office supplies.
- You can be in your pajamas all day.
- You don't have to spend money on dumb suits.
- You don't have to sit in rush-hour traffic or on a train with everybody else.
- You can be with your family when you need to be or just want to be.
- You don't have to make small talk.
- You don't have to go to ridiculous office holiday parties.
- You don't have to say hello to everybody in the elevator.
- You don't have to listen to people's bad ideas in staff meetings.
- You don't have to use corporate douche-speak (jargon), like "Let's run it up the flagpole" or "He's a Monday-morning quarterback," and you don't have to use words like "impactful" and "incentive."
- You don't have to deal with some sweaty, fat boss flirting with you or having to pretend you like him so you don't get fired.
- You don't have to play secret Santa and come home with some crappy gift you didn't want.
- No boss is looking over your shoulder.
- You don't have to stress about performance reviews.
- You don't have to suffer through endless birthdays with the same shitty supermarket cake in the break room.
- You might get to make a full-time income on less than forty hours of work a week.

. . . .

NOTES FROM THE SKINNYGIRL TEAM
Malini Patel, VP of Marketing and Strategy

Should you start your own business? My father is a successful entrepreneur, and I happen to work for one of the most famous successful entrepreneurs, so I can say that I have a first-row ticket to this show. The thing people don't realize is that when you start your own business, it is your *own* business. No one will look after it for you. You can hire people to do the bulk of the workload, but you will always be involved because it is yours. You can't wake up one morning and just decide you quit because it is hard or people are annoying or you feel like doing something different. While there are many rewards for having your own business, it is not something you should jump into without thinking things through.

. . . .

Cons of Self-Employment

- If you slack off, you won't get paid.
- If you go on vacation, you won't get paid, unless you work through your vacation.
- You might have to work an eighty-hour week to make a full-time income, and you won't get overtime.
- Your job won't have any structure unless it is self-imposed.
- There is no company to buy your health insurance.
- There is no company to contribute to your retirement plan or 401(k).
- You don't get paid sick leave, maternity leave, or any other kind of leave. Actually, you never get to leave.
- It can be difficult to stay motivated with no boss looking over your shoulder.
- You will pay more taxes than someone who is an employee, even if you are the only employee of your business.

- You might have to compete against businesses that are much bigger than you and have more name recognition, influence, and financial resources.
- You are totally responsible for your own mistakes.
- If you get sued, they are suing *you*.
- You can't be fired, so you can't collect unemployment if your business doesn't work out.
- Many self-employed people have very irregular pay.
- If you work at home, you never get to leave your work behind at the office. It's always there, and chances are you will often be working during times other people have free.
- If the company is your baby, you will lose sleep. Every night. In fact, prepare never to sleep again.

For me, even in the leanest times, self-employment has been worth it, because that's my personality. I just can't work in a traditional setting, but can you? Or would self-employment be worth it, even knowing all the cons? Seriously think about this before you take on the risk, the stress, the investment, and the workload.

• •

HOW BIG CAN YOU GO? HOW SMALL DO YOU WANT TO STAY?

At some point, every business has to decide whether to expand. I recommend starting small, then deciding how you want to scale it. Growth is good, but overexpansion can kill a business through overexposure. Remember in the eighties when frozen-yogurt stores were everywhere? Then there was that episode on *Seinfeld* in the early nineties about how the idea that frozen yogurt was lower in calories was a scam. Suddenly, all the frozen-yogurt stores disappeared. Coincidence? Now juice bars are popping up everywhere. I guarantee they're all going to shut down when something foils the fad. History repeats itself.

The trick is to expand naturally, as your resources and products allow, without going too far too fast. Opening new locations is scary and costly but profitable if you do it when you're actually ready.

· ·

Know If You Have a Barrier to Entry

Another important thing to consider before jumping into business is whether your business idea has a barrier to entry. Is there something keeping anyone else with more money from jumping in and knocking off your idea? Something like the Skinnygirl Margarita has a specific recipe, so there is a barrier to entry, but anyone can make a low-calorie cocktail and call it "Skinny" (and they have). It won't taste the same, but they are still getting into my business.

Most businesses do not have barriers to entry. Consider the new trend of blow-dry bars. Anybody with a blow-dryer and a mirror can blow out someone's hair and charge for it. Now blow-dry bars are popping up everywhere. Actually, I had this idea ten years ago. I wanted to call the business Blow Job. Then I realized that any-one could do a business like that, and as soon as one person did it, everyone would do it and they would all cancel each other out. Sure enough, I think Blow was the first one, and then Drybar came in and did it bigger and better.

Personally, I'd let a monkey on a street corner blow-dry my hair if he were willing, but some people only want to go to the best place. However, it's a blow-dry. How hard can it be? To keep up, pretty soon they'll have to cut their margins and come up with something new, like innovative hair products. Before long, a blow-dry is going to cost three bucks. That's going to be great for me as a customer, but I'm glad I'm not in that business because it's hard to make it stand out. How do you do what Starbucks did and make a culture and a formula out of a blow-dry bar. Everybody's hair is different and every stylist has a different technique, so that wouldn't work. You have to factor in human error.

This is also happening with frozen yogurt. We're in the middle of a frozen-yogurt revival because someone thought to put out a tart frozen yogurt. People think because it tastes tart, it must not be as fattening, even though it has the same amount of sugar and just as many calories. Now anybody can come up with a tart yogurt, so a million places will open. Right now you can fill up a giant bucket of frozen yogurt for $12, but this isn't good for the waistline and people will figure that out. Pretty soon, they'll all be gone again, just like in the nineties.

I can think of many other examples. I remember a business with a few locations in Great Neck, New York, called Steve's Ice Cream. They would scoop ice cream onto marble slabs, add mix-ins, mash it in, stick it in a cone, and it was amazing. Then one day, there was no more Steve's Ice Cream. Ten years later, Cold Stone Creamery emerged, and now everyone thinks of Cold Stone Creamery, not Steve's, when they think about ice cream on a marble slab.

A similar thing happened with spinning, a stationary-bike exercise class invented by a guy named Johnny G back in 1989. I used to go to spinning classes twenty years ago in Los Angeles when the trend first started. I was obsessed. I was Spinderella. The classes were great, with high-energy music. Pretty soon, it was in all the gyms like a regular class. Then there was a new class called Soul Cycle. This was supposed to be a different, more spiritual experience, but I took a few classes and I didn't get it. It was spinning. I would look at my friends and say, "It's just spinning!" and they would say, "No, no, it's totally different!" It became a cult, but it made a lot of money because someone was smart enough to rebrand and reposition the idea.

Then Flywheel opened up, and I have to give them credit. They totally remarketed the concept so successfully that now, in some cities, you have to pay $75 to be able to be in the front row at a spin class. They made it competitive, with rankings and stadium seating, and they took it nationwide. It's spreading much faster than Soul-Cycle.

But what happened to Johnny G? He's not making the money

these other big companies are making now. He had a great idea, but other companies took it farther and made it bigger because anybody with a set of stationary bikes, a boom box, and a loud voice can hold a spin class.

I don't know who first thought of making green juice, but who's making money from this trend? A small company like BluePrint? Around New York we've got Organic Avenue, Juice Press, Juice Generation . . . what's in your town? Anybody can make juice, so I predict they'll eventually run each other out of business. Green juice is everywhere and it's just getting cheaper and cheaper because there is no barrier to entry. Unfortunately, quality will suffer. (Please don't ever drink green juice that isn't organic! It's like mainlining pesticides!)

I've been asked to get into the juice business, but since anyone with money could do this, what would make my green juice any different? How could I be to green juice what Starbucks is to coffee? If I could make it a culture and a system, I might be onto something.

If there isn't a barrier to entry, you're going to have to do something different, like have great service or a culture like Starbucks or remarkable consistency or something else really unique that people want to experience. Think about how easy it will be for others to knock you off. You might do okay, right up until your idea catches on.

This is one of the reasons why I did the Skinnygirl Cocktail deal with Beam. If I had stayed on my own, I might have maybe three or four flavors by now, if I really hustled, and maybe 10 percent distribution nationwide, while bigger companies would be putting out copycat products and making more money. I needed Beam's resources to make the idea into a big idea. I wanted Skinnygirl to be Coca-Cola, not Pepsi. Red Bull, not Monster. McDonald's, not Burger King. Those are all amazing companies, and frankly, if I could be as big as Burger King, well . . . from my mouth to God's ears. But that sale helped me stack the deck in Skinnygirl's favor. I wanted to aim high and be the best I could be, and this was the way to do it.

Your business may or may not have a barrier to entry, but either way, you should know and understand how this can impact your business.

Learn from My Mistakes

I've made a lot of good business decisions, but I've also made a lot of mistakes. Every business I've ever created was basically a start-up. Mistakes are inevitable. I've made tax mistakes, contract mistakes, intellectual-property mistakes, website mistakes, and mistakes that wasted a lot of money.

There are a thousand reasons why you might make a business mistake. The idea might not work the way you thought, or someone else might make a wrong move. No matter how in-charge you are, you will always be dependent on other people when you start your own business—manufacturers, distributors, financial backers, lawyers, accountants, partners, suppliers, vendors, and promotional people. One wrong move on anyone's part can put your business in jeopardy, so you have to be firing on all cylinders all the time and keeping an eye on everything. Even then, mistakes happen, but nobody will protect and defend your business as well as you do, no matter who you hire, so stay alert. I still have to do this every day. I have to be on the offensive constantly. Once you hit it, that's when you really have to watch your back.

But you can learn from my mistakes. Maybe I'll save you time, money, and anguish. Here are some of the many I've had to face in business, and some ideas for how you can problem-solve.

Control Your Quality

You might have the best idea in the world and the resources to make it happen, but what if the product in your head doesn't come out exactly the way you wanted it to come out after you get it produced?

Years ago with my cookie business, I had a great product. Those cookies were absolutely delicious, but eight hours later, they tasted different, then after they were on the shelf, they tasted even more different . . . and then they crumbled in the package. In warm weather, they got moldy. Baking cookies in my kitchen was one thing, but a mass-baking situation was different and there were too many factors to control. I didn't want to use preservatives, but I could see why so many people do. I never completely worked this out, so I had to shutter the business at the time. I just didn't have the resources to get it right back then. I may revisit those cookies someday, now that I've got more resources at my disposal, but at the time, it was a nightmare and such a disappointment.

More recently, when we first came out with Skinnygirl Sangria, it was perfection. Natural, low-calorie, and I loved the taste. However, when we put it into a glass bottle, the color was unattractive. In fact, frankly, I thought it looked like urine. I'm the first one to say we eat with our eyes, and we drink with our eyes, too. The ready-to-drink liquor has to look good as well as taste good, but by the time it was in production, it was too late to change it. I really had to plow through and hustle to sell that batch before we could produce a new run in a better color. Luckily, people bought it and loved it, and the next time, we were able to change the color. It could have turned out much worse, but it was a live-and-learn situation.

A similar thing happened when I first came out with my Skinnygirl cleanse product. The samples were great. They tasted fantastic, and I loved them. I knew other women would love them, too. However, during the first run, something happened between sample and manufacture. The product came out, people started buying it, and then I tried it. It didn't taste good. It didn't taste like the sample. It didn't look good, either. The sample had been a vibrant green, and this color was different. I was livid! This was a horrible moment. We did a recall and I obsessed and tortured yet another partner. How many customers did we lose? I had to get every single packet back, because the product represented me and the Skinnygirl brand. One bad product could ruin the reputation of the whole brand. We had to manufacture it all over again and send everyone who had already bought it a refund.

One of the products I was originally working on was a lip scrub.

It was a fabulous product, but the packaging was wrong, because once it was made, the grains would get stuck in the opening and the lip scrub wouldn't come out of the tube. It also became too solid at cold temperatures. By the time I realized this, the product was already out, and I panicked. It was a flashback to my cookie-baking days. I knew there were people out there trying this product, and the ones who were able to use it loved it, but others never got to experience how great it was because the packaging didn't work. That was the end of the lip scrub.

It might sound like I'm being a Debbie Downer, but if one small aspect of a product isn't working, I obsess. All I focus on is that one thing, and the fact is that one tiny thing can turn people off a great product, and then it's over. Someone could be walking down the aisle at the store and say, "Oh, hey, there's that girl Bethenny's product," but if it doesn't look or taste good, then I've lost a customer. Still, it happens and you need to be ready. What will you do? I think about how Lululemon sold those thousands of see-through yoga pants that revealed the whole butt crack, and what a disaster that was for the company. It happens, but you have to be on it so you catch it as early as possible and can do something about it before it ruins your business.

Obsess Over Everything

One of Steve Jobs's qualities was his tendency to hyperfocus on one thing that bothered him, even when a product was great. I totally understand this. I obsess about every customer I could potentially lose. Never underestimate the price of losing a customer. Once you get someone in the door, literally or figuratively, you then have to figure out how to keep that customer. The customer is always right. If the customer doesn't like something, you apologize and you fix it. It's the cardinal rule of retail.

If anyone ever complains about one of my products, even on Twitter, I make sure the company contacts them, discusses it, and makes it right. I try not to think about the people who are unhappy and don't ever contact us, because I would go crazy. You have to obsess over everything if you want to do well in business. That's just part of the game. No one else will ever think about the details of your product as closely and obsessively as you will. Be prepared to be as obsessed with your business as you are with everything else. That's what it takes.

Maintain Your Relationships

The way you deal with people now can make a huge difference in how you'll be able to handle mistakes or issues later.

When I first developed the Skinnygirl Margarita, my partner and I created the logo of the Skinnygirl together. It was supposed to be based on me, but we both came up with it and owned it. When I came out with the Skinnygirl Daily On-the-Go bars, I wanted to use a version of that logo for those products. I said, "Let's add a tape measure around her waist and have her holding an apple." This all seemed fine and my agent told me I could do the deal, until I realized that my former Skinnygirl Cocktails partner owned part of that logo.

I told my new Skinnygirl Daily partner, Matt, "Listen, I don't know what to tell you. My agent told me I could make this deal, but it occurred to me that the logo isn't completely mine. Let me work this out." Instead of going through my agent or a lawyer, I just called my old partner David and said straight-up, "Hey, I'm doing a deal for the cleanse product and I want to use the Skinnygirl in a different design." He was fine with letting me use the logo. If I had gone through some suspicious convoluted procedure, it might not have turned out so well, but he was a good partner and a good person and we had a good relationship, so it all worked out.

Lawyer Up

There are a lot of ins and outs to trademarks and logos and intellectual property, and it's complicated. Most regular business owners won't understand it, which is why you need lawyers to help you stay on the right side of the law. Don't skimp in this area—with lawyers, as well as with accountants, bookkeepers, and business managers.

When I was first starting out, I hired cheap accountants and lawyers and I ended up making some very expensive mistakes. I was small and didn't know how big I would be, but when you're in business, assume you're going to grow, if that's your goal, and hire the people you will need so you don't make crucial legal or accounting mistakes and end up throwing bad money after good.

The Tax Man Cometh

Taxes matter. They are a major concern of any business owner, and owning your own business makes the tax situation much more complicated than it is if you work for someone else and just get a W-2 and a nice fat refund at the end of the tax year.

The more complicated your business or businesses, the more complicated your taxes, especially when you are selling a business. I made a gigantic mistake during the sale of Skinnygirl Cocktails. Tax forms have different boxes for different kinds of businesses, and years ago when I was on *Housewives*, I checked the box for my current situation. Later, as my business changed, I didn't change that checked box to match my new situation. That one mistake cost me the price of a beach house. I am not kidding you. That was a serious mistake. Make sure you hire good, knowledgeable, honest tax people who will make sure your taxes are done not just correctly but in your best financial interest. If your business is even a little complicated, don't try to do your taxes yourself.

Distribution Is Key

You can have the best product in the world, but if nobody ever sees it, they won't buy it, and you won't have a business.

I have a workout-equipment line that does well where it's available, but it's not killing it because I'm still having trouble with the distribution. The sales numbers aren't yet worthy of the Skinnygirl logo. I'm on it and hustling to get it out there, but it's been a struggle to get that line where it needs to be.

If your distribution isn't in place, you could lose major opportunities, and the other side of that is that you need to know when to pass on major opportunities if your distribution is holding you back. When I first came out with the Skinnygirl Margarita, Oprah's show called and was thinking of featuring it on one of her "Oprah's Favorite Things" segments. That weekend I tortured myself and my partner, but we had to pass. If I had gone on *Oprah*, it would have created demand for a product nobody would have been able to get, and that would have been a wasted opportunity because we had no product to sell.

The same thing happened earlier in my career with my cookies. I had a chance to do a Valentine's promotion in Target, with heart-shaped boxes containing miniatures of my cookies, but I had no way to fulfill that order nor could I guarantee quality at that scale, so I passed. This was a blessing in disguise, because if I had failed Target back then, they wouldn't be interested in carrying my products now.

Jump-start It

When something isn't working, come at it in a different way. The definition of insanity is doing the same thing over and over and expecting different results. When I first came out with the cleanse product, my partner and I realized that people were a little scared of the word "cleanse." They didn't totally understand what it was, and that was a problem. The product was great, but how could I make the concept more accessible? The cleanse is a green powder that makes a lemonade containing both fiber and greens for health. I call it the "Poor Man's Green Juice" because it's a fraction of the cost of a green juice at a juice bar. At first, however, people weren't totally getting the Skinnygirl Daily concept. That's when I came up with the idea of adding the phrase On-the-Go to the product as well as actually marketing it as the poor man's green juice. I'm always out and about and I need things I can take in my purse, like the cleanse packets to add to a water bottle or the Skinnygirl bars for snacking. This was the key to getting this product right—I narrowed down the concept to the problem I had and that I knew other women had. We're busy, we want to save money, we're moving, and we need something we can take with us. When women saw the words "On-the-Go" and "green juice" on the product, they got it, and then they bought it. All that changed was the positioning and the packaging—the message, not the product. It was a whole new way to look at the same product, and it worked to revive the concept in a new way.

Your ideas won't work out every time, but when they do, they can launch your whole business to a new level.

Move It or Lose It

When I first decided to get into the skin-care business, I partnered with some people to manufacture and package a product. They seemed excited and on board with what I was doing, but then they couldn't get me a sample product. I waited for well over a year, seeing no movement. "Guys!" I said. "I got a bottled cocktail on the shelf in eight months and you can't get me an under-eye cream to sample?" I just wanted a prototype. These people were knowledgeable, but they didn't move their asses. I had to end that relationship and go with another company that could get me what I needed before the momentum was gone.

But Don't Rush

You don't want to take too long to get your product or service out there, but on the other hand, you don't want to rush things, either. If you rush to get a product out before it is ready, you could compromise the integrity of your business.

This happens all the time with the *Housewives*. One is coming out with a red velvet Cosmo, another with Moscato, another with a clothing line, another with a kitchen appliance. They go on the talk shows and promote these products but then nothing ever happens—the products never come to fruition because they didn't really have the product in place before they started talking about it. Nobody wants to hear about your product until they can actually buy it. If you can't get it out there, then what's the point of talking about it on television? This is Marketing 101.

When you rush something out and then you can't deliver, it's like watching your dreams float away down the river. It's frustrating because you know customers want something and you want to give it to them, and it doesn't seem fair. Why can't you get it out?

There is a fine line, however. Rushing the cocktails onto television changed my life. I put a (figurative) gun to my partner's head and said, "If you don't get me a shrink-wrapped Skinnygirl Cocktails car to drive on my show, I will shoot you." Now I have a knife to another partner's back about the nutritional bars. I told him, "I'm going to be on a talk show in September, five days out of every week. If you don't have those bars in the stores nationwide, I will stab you." This is rushing with quality assurance. (And drama.)

It is a gamble. Can you afford the stakes? Get your product out fast, but not so fast that you can't fill the orders. I tend to be a person who is permanently rushing. Sometimes you just need to slow down. Thank goodness I realize this about myself now and have people around me who don't let me rush when it's not beneficial to the business.

Know When to Fold 'Em

Sometimes there are good reasons to walk away from a business. After I nailed down a skin-care product line, everything seemed to be going well. I had great products at an amazing price point. They went into Walmart, and business was good—until one of my partners who manufactured the product decided to sell his company to a larger company. He wanted me to just assign my business to them. He assured me he would still be the one in charge, and that all sounded great, but I wasn't sure I wanted to be in business with that large of a company.

At that same time, I was doing my talk show and we had already been approached by several large beauty brands that wanted to be part of the show. (This is called show integration.) They were willing to pay a good amount of money to align themselves with the show, and we had to decline because I was in the beauty business.

I thought about this and realized that this could be my out. I left the matter unresolved for a few weeks, and paid a lot of money for lawyers to talk back and forth, but nothing was getting done. Finally I just picked up the phone to my partner and said, "OK, what do you want, and what do I want?"

I wanted other beauty brands to integrate with my show. He wanted to liquidate my products if I wasn't going to go into business with the new company. He had spent ahead of the brand because we both knew it could do well, but now everything about the deal had changed because of his sale and my talk show.

So we made a deal. I gave him nine months to liquidate the product in any discount store. In exchange, I got the rights back to my license so I wasn't in the skin-care business anymore.

I certainly might go back into the beauty business someday with the right partner. I loved the products I had before. They were high in quality and reasonably priced, and I still use them. I learned a lot during that experience, including the fact that great skin-care products don't have to cost a lot. Right now, however, it doesn't serve my interests to be in this business. It took some wheeling and dealing and stepping outside the box, but everybody came out on top.

Get Real

Sometimes, what you want to do is just a bad idea, and if you aren't being realistic or listening to anyone else, you could make an expensive or painful mistake.

When I decided to go on *Skating with the Stars*, it wasn't exactly a business decision, but it did impact the time I had for all my other ventures. Why did I do it? I had this childlike fantasy. Call it my midlife crisis. People tried to talk me out of it, but I insisted that it was a good decision. Once I got into it, it was the biggest nightmare of my life. It was excruciating and traumatic, flying back and forth from one coast to the other every week with a six-month-old baby.

Every day I was asking myself, "What the hell did I do?" I would sometimes ask the other celebrities on the show, like Sean Young and Vince Neil, "Isn't this traumatic?" They would just look at me with blank stares like I was totally nuts. Finally I realized that the show was something they needed in that moment in their lives, but it was definitely not something I needed. I had to do my best. I couldn't quit or afford to get hurt, and I went to the end and was the runner-up even though by then I could barely walk, but it was a mistake. Now I see it, but at the time I didn't see it, and I didn't listen to all the many smart people who told me it was a bad idea.

Don't Believe in the "Next Big Thing"

One of the most important things every potential entrepreneur has to realize is that there is no "next big thing." Everybody is dying to come up with the next big thing, but it doesn't exist. Great ideas are everywhere but your idea has no power. Your business savvy, ambition, ability to read the market and find good people to help you, and intense follow-through with constant vigilance—those are the things that have the power to create a trend.

Even then, someone can knock off your next big thing and it won't be yours anymore.

Those guys who sued Mark Zuckerberg for stealing their idea didn't get it. Who knows what actually happened, but the success of Facebook wasn't about the idea. Mark Zuckerberg changed the world by making the idea happen, and I'm glad it was him. I live for Mark Zuckerberg. I don't want to believe he stole anything and people talk cavalierly about it, but I also think it doesn't really matter, because if those two putzes had made Facebook, they wouldn't have changed the world. Mark Zuckerberg had the drive and innovation that nobody else had. The success of Facebook was about the execution. Arguably and unfortunately, being the best isn't necessarily the deciding factor. Sometimes, it's about what kind of action you are capable of taking. The real next big thing is what you do with a good idea. Being first doesn't matter.

NOTES FROM THE SKINNYGIRL TEAM
Kevin George, Global Chief Marketing Officer at Beam Inc.

Listen to your customers. Understand that they don't need another "this" or "that" but are looking for a true solution. Also, you must have a very simple story to tell people why they should buy this product. It shouldn't take a PowerPoint presentation to explain it. With Skinnygirl Margarita, all you have to do is simply tell a girlfriend on the back deck: "The average restaurant margarita we love has five-hundred-plus calories. Skinnygirl is a simple, great-tasting ready-made cocktail that only has one hundred calories per serving." Done. Simple.

• •

Getting Started

So this is what it's about. Know what you're getting into, do your homework, be brave, and get out there and enjoy the stressful-but-liberating life of the entrepreneur. Or, if that sounds like too much for you, then don't. There is absolutely nothing wrong with succeeding at a job you love for a company that supports you and takes on the stresses and risks you don't need.

But if you really do think self-employment is for you, your big idea is big enough, you have the right personality, and you've got the capital, then great. You just might make it after all. Before you quit your day job, however, make a plan and do some research.

Confession: I never made a business plan, and it hurt me financially. You need a plan. You need to know how much money it's going to take so you spend it where you need to spend it. Imagine going to the mall without a plan. If you have a hundred bucks to buy an outfit, but you see a tank top you like, then some lip gloss, then a headband, before you know it, you're going to be halfway through the mall with no money and no outfit. If you go to the mall with a plan, you can allocate your wad of money instead of randomly throwing it away where it isn't going to help you.

You don't need an official plan, unless your business loan or investors require it. You don't even have to write it down. Put it on a series of Post-it notes. Just have a plan. Have some sort of blueprint. You don't need a Harvard MBA, but you do need a map. Even when I didn't have a good plan, I at least knew the direction I wanted to go. I just wish I had paid more attention to where I should have been spending my money.

After you've got a plan, don't get mired in it. Stay flexible. Network. Tell people about your business in a simple, clear way. You never get a second chance to make a first impression. Are you stuttering? Are people's eyes glazing over? Then go back to the drawing board. Make a business plan and write it out until you have an elevator speech (you can explain clearly, in a few words, about your service or product in a way that gets people excited). Make business cards and give them to everyone. Build your Rolodex, and be the best at your job. Keep your eye on your industry, stay realistic, work hard, stay organized, and never stop moving forward.

If you do that, then you might just have a chance at making it work.

Chapter Fourteen

Money Management and Finances

Managing money has been a challenge for me. For years, money gave me anxiety because I never had enough. Just a few years ago, I could barely pay my rent. Then I sold Skinnygirl Cocktails and wound up on the cover of *Forbes* magazine, which was a surreal experience because I never thought of myself as a money person. Yet, I realized that over the years, I've learned a lot. I've also learned when to call in the experts to guide me on the things I don't know enough about. Whether it's managing your personal finances or funding your start-up, money matters, and the more you know now, the better off you'll be later.

Money is so important for women to understand. If you have your own money, you have a measure of personal power you cannot have without it. Whether it's right or wrong, money garners respect in our society, and you don't need much of it to get that respect—you just need to understand it and use it wisely.

I've always had money noise—I had it when I didn't have money, and I have it now. However, I've learned to control it and recognize it when it pops up. This is what I hope every woman can learn to do: recognize the money noise and master it. You might never get rid of it entirely. Sometimes it might even flare up and surprise you. However, if you let your money noise negatively impact your business, you're going to get in trouble. If you let it keep you from saving anything for the future, you're going to regret it. If you let it convince you to burn through every paycheck at the mall, you're letting it control you, and you should be the one calling the shots.

You need to get the money side of things figured out and straight in your head. There is nothing romantic or glamorous about budgeting or paying bills, but it's the cold hard reality. It's numbers and decimals and dollar signs, and it matters. You can't ignore this part or dream it away, but you can hire it out. Here's my advice, based on personal experience, about what you need to know about money.

KNOW YOUR MONEY NOISE

We all have it, but every person's money noise is unique. If you know what yours is, you can arrange your financial life in a way that works better for you.

- If you know you would never be happy being financially dependent on someone else, start saving and managing your own money now, and keep your own bank accounts, even if you get married. You might have one joint checking account for bills, but you should be able to have your own checking account for personal expenses, savings account for a backup, and even your own investments. Get this stuff in your own name now.
- If you know you will feel resentful if someone else is spending your money, right or wrong, know yourself and don't get that joint checking account. Decide who pays for what. Each person can put his or her own contribution toward the bills and other expenses.
- If you know you will feel obligated if someone else pays for you, right or wrong, agree beforehand to go Dutch, whether for dinner or a vacation. Blame it on your own quirkiness, but know yourself well enough to know that doing otherwise will cause a fight later.

- If you know you are a compulsive shopper, take action. Don't keep your credit cards readily available. Put them somewhere that takes effort to retrieve them, so you have to take at least a little time to consider your purchase. Or always pay in cash so you really feel it. Ouch!

- If you fear losing your money, let your fear drive you to save and be a deterrent to excessive spending. Set up a safe, low-risk investment and/or savings account and add to it every month before you do anything else. When you get afraid, just remind yourself you have those funds, you're committed to them, and you're going to be okay.

- If your weak spot is facing your financial situation, hire a financial adviser to help you see the truth. Collect the information they ask for and listen to what they say. Depending on your income and debt, you might even be able to find free financial advice in your area, or at least free credit counseling.

Money Management

It doesn't matter how much money you have. If you have a job and you have an income, you have to start managing it so you know exactly where it's going. I don't expect you to write down every penny you spend. With credit cards and online payments, that gets too complicated. However, there are some very smart ways to keep track of how much is coming in and how much is going out:

- **Make a budget.** I never did this when I really needed to do it. Now that I have more money, I do it because I realize the value of a dollar more than I ever did before. A budget doesn't have to be annoying or complicated. It's just a very basic list of how much you bring in each month, what you absolutely have to pay, and what expenses are discretionary, like shopping or even food (you need food, but how much you spend on it can vary greatly). At least have a rough idea of how much you have free for spending after your basic obligations are paid, so you never get too far in the hole. It can help you see where you should be cutting back.

If you ever want true financial independence, you're going to have to pay closer attention to how much is coming in and how much is going out. This is how you start.

- **Use financial accounting software.** I'm not a computer person, but financial accounting software isn't complicated. Set yourself up with something like QuickBooks (for business) or Quicken (for personal) and just start keeping track. You can sync many programs with your bank account so your bank statement is downloaded each month. Keep your receipts and once a month, go through and verify that everything looks correct. It's simple, and then you can generate reports to see where your money is going and design budgets to help you shift your spending and saving in a direction you want to go in. Nothing gives you a reality check like a good pie chart that demonstrates to you in bright colors exactly how much you've been spending on mochas or shoes.

  If you're really not that type (I'm not either), you could also have someone help you set it up. If you are using it for business and it's even a little complicated, enlist the services of a bookkeeper. A good bookkeeper can save you thousands of dollars in potential mistakes.

- **Keep your receipts.** Put personal receipts and receipts related to your business in separate files, organized by month. When you use your accounting software and you're trying to figure out what a charge was, you'll be able to look. You might need those receipts come tax time if they are deductions, but even if they aren't, keeping close track of where your money goes will help you realize when you're spending too much on something stupid, and if someone makes an error (a store, or even your bank), you will have evidence to back up your claim.

- **Pay off your credit cards.** Credit is confusing. When I was in my twenties, I didn't care how it worked. I got all these preapproved credit cards at 3 percent interest that would then suddenly change to 18 percent interest, and I had no idea what that even meant. I would pay just the minimum or a little more to make myself feel better, but I had no idea how many thousands of dollars I was paying just to be able to have those cards and not pay my bills right away.

Let me give you a mini lesson right now. Let's say you carry a balance of $5,000 on a credit card, at an interest rate of 18 percent. If your minimum payment is $125, and you only make the minimum payment every month without ever charging anything else on that card, it will take you almost twenty-three years to pay off that five grand, and you will end up paying $6,923.14 in interest. Stupid, right? Why would you do that if you know?

Even if you only have a $1,000 balance and you get an awesome rate, like say 8 percent, and you pay a minimum balance of $16.67, it will still take you over seven years to pay that thousand bucks off, and you'll end up paying $319.86 in interest. That's three hundred bucks you could have spent on groceries or your electric bill, and that's seven years of worrying about what you did in one extravagant day at the mall.

Some people think credit is just the "American way," but there is nothing American about throwing away the money you worked so hard to get. Just stop using it, if you possibly can. Pay down your cards by making the largest payments you can, even before you save, because credit is costing you a lot more than you will earn in interest in any savings account. Make this a priority, and wise up. Once your credit card is paid off, never carry a balance again.

I don't even want to think about how much money I wasted by using credit cards over the years. Today, a lot of credit card statements actually tell you how much you will pay in interest and how long it will take you to pay off your balance if you pay just the minimum, so take advantage and read your statement. Stop hiding from your money and start keeping more of it!

- **Don't miss payments.** I know. You have a lot of bills—rent or mortgage, utilities, student loans, car payment, credit card payments, quarterly taxes if you're self-employed, etc. These are called *fixed expenses*. They are not optional or discretionary expenses that you pay after you see what you have left from shopping. Not only will bills paid late negatively impact your credit, but you could end up paying hundreds of dollars in unnecessary late fees, and that's just throwing your money away for no good reason.

- **Start saving.** Nothing feels better than having a savings account as a cushion in case some unexpected expense arrives, but how do you afford that cushion? Saving is a habit, and you might think you need every penny you are making right now, but if you just start small, you'll catch the bug and realize how good it feels. Even fifty bucks out of every paycheck will make a difference. Funnel it to a savings account automatically so you never even see it. This can save you when you get into a fender bender and you have a high insurance deductible, or you suddenly need to fly to Vegas for your best friend's secret wedding. Life is full of these little surprises. If you've got a cushion, you can relax a little.

- **Know your banker.** Go into your bank frequently. Let them get to know you. Open a checking and a savings account, and maybe a CD to start saving some money. Form relationships and talk about what you are doing with your money. You might get some free advice, and if you ever need a loan, those friendly relationships could pay off.

● ●

NOTES FROM THE SKINNYGIRL TEAM
Malini Patel, VP of Marketing and Strategy

Are you getting paid what you're worth? Knowledge is power. Do your homework and know the general pay for someone who has the job you have, in your area, with similar years of experience. You need to keep refreshing this knowledge, as it changes from time to time. If you know what the market would pay for your skills, you can assess whether or not you are being fairly compensated for the work you do.

But keep in mind that salary should not be viewed in a vacuum. Look at your total compensation package and determine what you value the most. For instance, some people are the sole breadwinner in the family, so health insurance provided for the family may be worth more than $10,000 extra in salary or in a bonus. On the flip side, if your spouse has the insurance covered, you may be able to waive that and negotiate for a higher salary or even more vacation.

If you think you aren't getting what you're worth, you can negotiate to get more. It won't work every time, but it often will. If you think you bring an extra skill set to the table, then by all means ask for more than average, but be ready to back it up. Know what you absolutely must have and what you are willing to give up. This allows you to have a more dynamic negotiation that is not based on salary alone.

If you can't get the exact salary you want, try to build in performance-based metrics so you can make more money if you achieve your goals. Most bosses don't have a problem rewarding someone who has done great work, but the bottom line here is just because you *want* a raise doesn't mean you deserve it or will get it. But if you make a strong case and you have success to support you, you have a good shot.

Finally, understand your position. Do you absolutely need

this job? Do you absolutely want this job? Are you willing and able to walk away from your current job if you can't get what you think you deserve? Are you sure you really want that new job, or are you just exploring whether or not you should make a move? Consider your circumstances before making a major career decision, because if you end up out of a job, it can be hard to get back into the workforce. Just getting back in again may be all you get in the next round of negotiations.

· ·

Wisdom from My Financial Manager

I got a great deal smarter about money after I hired a financial manager from Merrill Lynch. I learned a lot from him and he has generously agreed to share his top tips for money management:

- **Establish good credit.** If you are just starting out, establish good credit. Whether you are single or married, you as an individual should have good, solid credit in case you want to make a major purchase someday, like a house. Do not get specialty credit cards, like for department stores or home-improvement stores. These are not very helpful for your credit and they have very high interest rates. People don't realize that 20 percent off a purchase if you open an in-store card isn't a good deal if you carry a balance, because the rates they charge are significantly higher than the national average. Instead, get a major credit card, but don't pay it off every month initially. This sounds counterintuitive, but let's say you spend $1,000 and then you pay it off. That does nothing to establish your credit. Instead, pay $500, then pay $500 the next month. You only need to do this partial payment once or twice—don't use this as an excuse to carry a balance for the rest of your life. After two or three months of this, get back to your good habit of paying off your balance every month. Now you're getting somewhere.

- **Start saving for retirement now.** I don't care if you are twenty. It's never too early. It's also never too late. At most companies, you can start a 401(k), even if you are only putting 1 percent or 2 percent of your paycheck in it. It's something, and if the company matches your money, as they often do, that's free money. If you don't work for someone else, consider a Roth IRA. If you earn over $5,000 per year, you are eligible to open one. This is the best kind of retirement account because you don't deduct what you put into it on your taxes, but when you take it out at retirement, when tax rates may be much higher, you get that money without having to pay taxes on it. It's the best deal.

- **Have your own money.** I don't care if you are blissfully wed for all eternity. Many women don't have their own credit card or retirement plan, let alone their own bank account. Have your own money, your own credit card, and your own IRA. Not to be unromantic, but you never know when you might want to rent your own apartment one day, or buy your own house, or start your own business. You will want those assets in place.

- **Check your credit score.** You are allowed to do this once per year for free. The government made this mandatory. There are three major credit reporting services. Go online, search "check my credit," and don't get sucked into one of those pay plans. I trust annualcreditreport.com. Do not give out your credit card number. Credit reports often have errors or things you forgot about, like an old gym membership or a small credit card balance at a specialty store. Get these errors cleaned up and taken care of so they are off your credit report. This will pay off later in lower interest rates when you need a major loan, like a mortgage.

- **Don't spend more than you bring in.** It's common sense, but it's really hard to do. Imagine if you were Apple Inc., for example; you couldn't spend more making computers than you got from selling them, or you would go out of business. Don't put yourself out of business. Pay yourself, put a little in your retirement account, and *then* go to the mall. Manage your money like you're a business and you won't ever get into debt, have poor credit, or lack savings—or you will soon get yourself out of these situations.

- **Invest.** You can do this. It sounds scary and confusing, but if you dip your toe in, you can learn as you go. There is no "when" or "how" to invest. Just start. Put in what you can afford to spare and don't move it or take it out. Everyone who got out of the market in 2008 missed the over 140 percent increase in the market since then. Stay in! Just ask yourself: What do I need this money for? If you're thirty-five and you aren't retiring next week, just keep it there. An investment is like a bar of soap. The more you touch it, the smaller it gets, and the more people who touch it, move it, massage it, the sooner it will become just a sliver.

  A good place to start is with index or passive investing, or by buying exchange-traded funds (ETFs). These are funds that contain a lot of different kinds of securities, like mutual funds do. The advantages of ETFs are that they have no minimum investment, have very low fees, and the way they trade means you don't need to pay taxes every time the contents are traded.

  You don't have to understand exactly how they work, but they are a good place to start. You can just go online to a place like Vanguard or T. Rowe Price and set up a brokerage account, then buy ETFs online through that account, or you can go to any individual ETF site and purchase them. If you want more information, a broker can answer your questions, but these funds are pretty low-risk and simple ways to start.

Once you're in the market, don't obsess about what your investment is doing. Just stay put and start learning more about it. If you put $100 a month into an index fund, that may sound boring, but it will often end up being a more successful investment than some hedge-fund online-trading ventures. Just take all the noise out of the equation. Then, if you decide you want to start investing in stocks, which are higher risk but potentially more profitable, you'll know a little bit about how the market works. And if you ever decide to hire an investment adviser to do your investing for you, you'll know what questions to ask and you'll already be ahead of the game.

You don't even really need a financial adviser until your investable assets are up over $100,000. Until then, you should do these simple things every month:

1. Pay yourself first.
2. Put a little in your Roth IRA.
3. Put a little in your passive index fund.
4. Then and only then, spend your money at other people's cash registers.

Tips for Smarter Spending

Now that you've got a handle on fixed expenses and saving and even a little bit about investing, let's talk about the part you probably already know a lot about: spending. It's addictive, it's fun, and it can suck you dry, but I'm not going to tell you to quit shopping. Instead, let's talk about how to spend smarter:

- **Spend like you eat.** I believe that your diet should be like your bank account, but I've also realized that your bank account should be like your diet. If you splurge, then you need to pull back. If you've been saving, you can afford a few extra luxuries. Spending is a balance, even if you never "count your calories," or keep a budget. You have to at least keep an idea in your head of where you are and what you can and can't do.

- **Stop binge-spending.** Excessive spending, whether insane shopping sprees or bouts of Internet shopping where you can't stop ordering things, is actually very similar to a food binge. You spend like crazy and you feel high. You think you have to have these things you never even knew existed hours before, like they're the last things you're ever going to be able to buy. It's like an alcoholic going into a bar. Then you come down and you feel guilty. You've got major buyer's remorse, which is like a binge-spending hangover. Now you're broker than ever, or you've maxed out your credit card. I guarantee that the new pair of shoes or dress or necklace or overpriced designer handbag won't look so great tomorrow once the rush of acquiring it is over and the remorse kicks in. Now you're wondering if you even like the stuff that much, and you've overdrawn your bank account.

  The truth is that almost everything you think you want right now will still be there tomorrow and will go on sale eventually. You can wait. Not binge-spending is just as important as not binge-eating. It's time to tell yourself you are through with that. And if you do find yourself gravitating toward the mall or the strip or the Internet with your credit card at the ready, at least limit yourself to stores with simple, free returns so you can get the money credited back to your card when you realize you didn't want to buy that thing after all.

  When the urge to spend hits, I have a better idea than shopping. Go back to chapter 7 and totally reorganize your closet. If you've already done that, then go put new outfits together. Put a pair of shoes you've had for years with an interesting bag you never use and a pair of earrings you forgot you had. Make a list of the new outfit ideas you get. This can get the urge for something new out of your system without costing a dime.

- **Buy with intention.** Before you ever pull out that credit card, decide what you want, make sure you don't already have it (you'll know because you're organized now), and then shop around. Never buy the first thing you see. An enforced waiting period will help you head off a spending binge.

- **Pay in cash.** If you pay in cash, you know exactly what you are spending and it will feel more like what it really is: you trading your hard-earned money for something you supposedly want. I know this isn't always possible for people who need to track their spending on a credit card, but I know that I would never have allowed myself to buy even half the stuff in cash that I've put on a credit card.

- **Never pay retail.** If you've decided you really need something, comparison-shop in stores and on the Internet. I've found deeply discounted designer items I really liked on eBay, at flash-sale sites, and at sample sales, and I've found things I liked just as much at discount stores for a fraction of the price. Almost nothing is actually worth the retail price, so why overpay? Even if you really want the genuine article, it's going to go on sale eventually. Sign up as a member on your favorite shopping sites so you get an alert for twenty-four-hour 80 percent off sales and similar promotions. If that thing you think you need never does go on sale, then maybe you weren't meant to have it. If you make it a rule that you can't have it at full price, then you'll save tons of money.

- **Assess the differential.** This is another concept I use with food that also applies to money. If you really care about something, like high-quality shoes or organic, shade-grown, free-trade, locally roasted coffee beans, spend money on those things. However, don't waste money where it doesn't matter. Do you really care if your sheets or toilet paper or nail polish remover came from a discount store? When the difference between an expensive item and an inexpensive version of essentially the same thing doesn't matter very much to you, go for the inexpensive. You will save a lot of money this way, if you're used to just picking up the first thing you see without looking at the price or thinking you have to have the "best" of every single thing you ever buy.

. . . .

BUY UNSEASONALLY

Buy your food in season, but nothing else. Every category of merchandise, from clothes to cars to houses, has a season where it is the most expensive and a season where it's at the lowest price. For clothes, if you buy at the end of a season for the following year, you'll pay a fraction of the price. If you're afraid it will be out of style by next season, you shouldn't buy it anyway, unless it doesn't cost much. Remember: Invest in classic, timeless pieces, and spend less on the trendy stuff. I've also read that you should:

- Buy cars in the summer or at the end of the month, when salespeople are trying to reach quotas.
- Buy electronics between January and March.
- Buy computers in spring or fall.
- Buy appliances in fall or on Black Friday (the day after Thanksgiving).
- Buy air conditioners in the fall and furnaces in the spring.
- Buy cookware after wedding season or the holidays (July or January)
- Buy a home in the fall, because people don't want to move in the winter.
- Buy gym memberships in the summer when nobody wants to be stuck inside a gym (unless you also don't want to be stuck inside a gym).

Less Is More

Another way to control spending is to get by with less. This isn't deprivation. This is freedom. The less stuff you have, the less you will have to worry about it, clean it, maintain it, and wonder if it's good enough.

However, you need things, and sometimes you really just want something. I'm not going to deny you a new outfit or a double latte if that's what you want, but I do have some ideas for how you can pay less for the things you buy—and see how much money you can save by saying no to a purchase now and then.

Let's look at some specifics:

- **Rethink your latte habit.** How much money do you spend on lattes every month? Instead, you could invest in a nice coffee machine, get an eco-friendly ceramic travel mug, and enjoy your coffee exactly the way you want it. This has been a problem I've been eager to solve, so I am working on a Skinnygirl coffee line—so we can feel like baristas in our own homes, without the seven-thousand-dollar espresso machine.

. . . .

SORRY, STARBUCKS

How much are those lattes really costing you? Let's work this out. If you spend $4 on a latte every day, you'll be paying $28 a week, about $120 a month, $1,460 a year, $7,300 in five years. Is that really where you want to spend seven grand? At Starbucks? I bet that coffee machine is looking a little more appealing . . . but that's not all. According to a finance article I read recently, if you invested that latte money at 9 percent over thirty years (9 percent is high right now, but maybe not in a few years), you would have $239,891. In forty years, you could have $634,428. You could buy a house or retire early. I don't know how accurate these numbers are, but it's something to think about the next time you think you can't live without a mocha.

. . . .

- **Manage your hair.** If you're having your hair colored every four weeks, you can stretch it to six or eight by doing your own root touch-up at home, if you have dark hair. I do this with the Clairol root touch-up kit. It's easy and pennies on the dollar compared to the salon. You could save $50 to $100 or more every month.
- **Cancel the gym membership.** Are you paying for a gym membership you don't use? Save money and your health by exercising in ways you actually enjoy and will really do. A few DVDs you can do at home (like my *Body by Bethenny* or *Skinnygirl Workout* DVDs or something more vigorous like Tracy Anderson's DVDs) are a lot cheaper than a gym membership. A walk costs nothing.
- **Don't buy in bulk.** Costco is my church, but people think those big bulk discount stores are inexpensive. Actually, buying in bulk can be a big waste of money. Like buffets, they aren't always a bargain. Produce goes bad, or you just get bored of those particular kinds of fruit snacks or cheese balls, or you realize you have no room for fifty rolls of toilet paper so you start giving them away to everyone you meet. Either split bulk items with friends or restrain yourself. If you can't, don't even buy a warehouse-store membership.
- **Profit from your closet purge.** If you are cleaning out your closets based on chapter 7, you probably have a lot of clothes and other household items you've realized you don't really need. You could donate them (tax write-off, get the receipt) or give them to friends, but if you want to make some cold hard cash, sell it on eBay or on consignment at a nice consignment store. The advantage of consignment

is you can usually get more in credit than you can in cash, so you can use that credit to buy clothes you'll actually love and wear. It's like shopping for free!

RESIST THE BLUE BOX

People love getting the blue box or a present from a fancy store with the name of the store prominently featured. These stores definitely have some nice things, but for a major investment like a diamond, all you need is an authentic GIA certificate and a reputable diamond dealer. A diamond ring will always have value. It doesn't matter if it came from a high-end store. Once it's used, it will never go down in price again. Get it at a discount, or buy from someone getting divorced (unless you believe in bad energy). Nobody will take a loss like a woman trying to get rid of a diamond. Buy your own fancy box and save the markup.

- **Drive less.** In the city, I see people wasting money on cabs and car services when they could easily walk somewhere or take the subway. In the suburbs, people will drive half a mile, or even drive to the mailbox. All that driving is costing you, in gas, car maintenance, and cab fees. If you walk or bike more often, it's efficient: you get somewhere and get a workout at the same time.
- **Eat out less.** I love to eat out and I would never swear off it, but if you do it every night, you're spending hundreds more than if you made your own lunch or cooked dinner at home. You'll also appreciate restaurant meals more if you have them less often. Once a week, get excited about going out for lunch or dinner, to keep you from falling into a food rut. You'll be healthier eating your own food on the other days. I just read a statistic that said brown-bagging your lunch every day at work could save you $25 per week,

$1,300 per year, and more than $50,000 over the course of a forty-year career!

- **Save on nights out.** I used to almost die of anxiety when I went out with my friends, for fear they would want us all to split the bill. Here are some good ways to enjoy a night out on a budget:

  - Have your aperitif at home. *A before-dinner drink can cost triple the price in a bar or restaurant. Invite friends over, toast each other, and relax before you head out (if you all end up drunk, just stay in and order a pizza! Please never drink and drive).*

  - Find the free stuff. *Most cities have a lot of really great cultural activities for free. Instead of paying a ridiculous club cover charge every single weekend, look for other opportunities: free concerts in the park (bring a blanket, a picnic, and wine), free movies in a public green space, free nights at the museum, free (or inexpensive) wine tastings or whiskey tastings with free appetizers at local stores, free Latin dance lessons sponsored by local studios trying to get new students, or the good old-fashioned tried-and-true ladies' nights. You might end up having more fun than you would have doing the same old thing.*

- **Don't pay a restaurant for food you could make yourself.** It's easy to make a bowl of pasta or grilled chicken or the food your kids like. Save the restaurant meals for exotic things you couldn't or wouldn't make yourself, like Indian, Thai, Japanese, or Vietnamese food.

- **Have potlucks.** Potluck dinners are great if you make them fun. Invite friends or neighbors over and ask each person to bring one component of a meal: hors d'oeuvres, entrée, side dish, bread, salad, dessert, drinks. This is a nice way to socialize without having to bear the whole expense or do all the planning and cleaning. Each person's contribution becomes a conversation piece and you can often get away with making nothing.

- **Work out for free.** A lot of gyms, yoga studios, and fitness centers have introductory free weeks or free classes to get people to try things out. In a big city, you could probably gym-hop for months and never pay a dime.
- **Use your credits.** If you shop online or you use department-store credit cards and you've returned merchandise, they may only give you store credit. Use it! If you have gift cards, don't let them expire. Don't buy anything you don't want, but use them for gifts or things you need.
- **Date for cheap.** A lot of people go online to meet people these days, and many dating sites arrange mixers that people can do for free. Why not try one? They are a great way to meet people without a lot of one-on-one pressure.

The Cost of Doing Business

There are many parallels between your personal finances and the finances of a business—you have to know how much money you have, where it's coming from, and where it's going—but keeping track of business expenses is even more important, especially to the IRS, if you are deducting expenses. If you own your own business, record-keeping goes to a whole new level.

The costs of running a business can seem high, even if your business is simple. You will have legal fees, tax bills, accounting fees, bookkeeping fees, trademark fees, business card costs, marketing costs, advertising fees, and printing costs. You've got to register your business, register your website (not to mention create and design your website, or have someone else do this for a fee), pay for website maintenance, and a million other things, depending on the nature of your business. Does your business need insurance? Do you need to rent office space? Can you deduct money if you work from home? Do you need to buy office supplies? It all adds up, and dealing with all this is complex. Do you have enough coming in to cover it all and also make a profit?

If this sounds daunting to you, don't let it scare you out of business, but do let it sober you up. Here is what I've learned about business finances, plus advice from several people on the Skinnygirl team who have a lot of experience.

. . . .

FINANCIALLY SAVVY HOUSEWIVES?

People ask me whether any of the other Housewives are smart or good at business. To be perfectly honest, most of them love the bells and whistles of business, but they don't really know what they are doing. They grab everything they can for short-term gain, but most of them don't have a plan and they often make all the wrong moves. I will say there are a few—two, to be exact— Housewives who I think are making some good moves.

The interesting thing I've noticed is that the people who make all the right moves aren't always the most marketable or charismatic people. The ones everybody notices are more likely to make decisions that make you scratch your head. Take Ryan Lochte. The guy is a gorgeous eleven-time Olympic medalist with five golds. So what does he decide to do next? He goes on *90210*. And then what does he do? He decides to do reality TV. I did reality TV when I was broke and starving. Why does an Olympic gold medalist need to do reality TV? He's going the wrong way. As I write this, his show hasn't launched yet, but mark my words: It's not going to do well. He's making the wrong move.

The truly rare combination is a charismatic, marketable person with a head for business. It's the magic formula for leveraging an opportunity like being on television to build a career.

. . . .

Treadmill or Up-front?

One of the first things to consider is whether you have what I call a treadmill business or an up-front business. Knowing which kind of business you have can help you plan your business finances.

If you have a treadmill business, you have or make a product and you hold inventory. Your business is to sell the product, but you are constantly laying out money before you get paid. You have to keep making your product, no matter how well it's selling. This applies to industries like the garment business and the restaurant business, as well as any business where you have a thing to sell rather than a service to provide.

Let's say you're in the garment business. You buy fabric, buttons, and zippers, and then you create your product and put it out there, but before you even get your money back, you have to buy more fabric, buttons, and zippers for the next batch. I experienced this with my pashmina business. Once I got started, it was hard to get ahead because I was funneling the profits into the next shipment. Buyers pay in 30, 60, or 90 days.

When I had my cookie business, I was buying ingredients, hiring people to help me make the cookies, and selling the cookies. Whether I was paid or not, I still had to keep buying oat flour, raw sugar, and dark chocolate chips.

You have to have the money to stay afloat until you hit that sweet spot where you get ahead of your treadmill and more money is coming in than you are laying out. You need to think about how long you can last before you turn a profit. It's easy to get sucked under when you get on the treadmill and you feel like you can't get off because there is a constant flow of unrelenting expenses.

The other kind of business is an up-front business. This is a business where you get paid before you start spending, and it's more common for service businesses than product-based businesses. Caterer, photographer, massage therapist, hairstylist, manicurist, and event planner are some examples. These jobs are usually subcontracted. You aren't an employee of the person who hires you and you don't hold any inventory. You are subcontracted labor doing something for someone else. You get paid and you walk away, and it's up to you whether you take on the next job, for the same client or someone completely different.

When I was an event planner, I ran a business like this. I would make a truly comprehensive P & L (profit and loss) statement to cover every possible expense. Then I would add my fee and charge the client half upon signing the contract and half on the day of the event. I would pay all the vendors out of this money and I never had to lay out any money up front. For example, let's say an event for Disney would cost $150,000. They would give me a budget, and I would back out all my costs and add my fee. I would be obsessed with that P & L statement. I would add every foreseeable expense—taxes, coffee, everything. On the day the contract was signed, they would pay me $75,000, which I would deposit into my business bank account. I could use this money to cover any of the costs that I had to pay during the planning stages. Then on the day of the event, I would require the remaining $75,000 or the event didn't start. Out of that final payment, I paid all the vendors and took my fee. I wrapped the event and closed the book.

That's good business. If you have a good relationship with your vendors, you tell them that they all get paid when you get paid. All you need is an office and infrastructure. You aren't constantly laying out money for production before you make any profit.

The downside of an up-front business is that you may not be able to make as much money. An event planner can only do so many events on one day, even with good staff, so business may be steady and lucrative, but it may not have the potential of really taking off like a treadmill business could.

Before you launch your business, no matter what kind it is, make out your own P & L statement. What are your start-up costs? How much is running this business going to cost you? How soon can you expect to turn a profit? Some things to consider as you draw up this important document:

- List all start-up costs. Do you need to rent or buy a facility, or will you work from home? Do you need materials? Do you need to invest in training? Do you need employees? What about a website, software, computers and printers, and other equipment?

- Can you do everything yourself or do you need to hire employees?
- How much will you need to pay an accountant to do your taxes? Can you get a friend's mom to do it in exchange for something you can offer?
- Will you need to hire a bookkeeper to keep track of your income and expenses, or can you take a QuickBooks class and learn how to do it yourself? Will you have time to do it yourself?
- Do you need to have a business lawyer to deal with contracts and legal issues? What about insurance and workers' comp?
- Do you plan to incorporate? Depending on whether you decide to be an LLC, an S corporation, or a C corporation, there will be costs to set up this legal structure.
- If you have investors, how will that impact your profits later? If you have an agent or someone who put the deal together, factor in the commission you have to pay when you consider your future profits.

. . . .

NOTES FROM THE SKINNYGIRL TEAM
Ron Nash, Skinnygirl Business Manager

What type of business should you start? This requires research. There are many charts available that outline the differences in choice of entity, and the discussion of the pros and cons of each type of business entity can be rather in-depth depending on the sophistication of the needed structure. For example, will there be many owners? Will those owners be equal or will there be multiple classes of owners?

Generally, acting as a sole proprietor is the easiest and cheapest form of business entity and is most commonly used when first starting out. However, this form isn't appropriate for every business. Each case needs to be examined with an eye toward the future growth possibilities so the structure can handle these changes, but here are some basic principles:

- A sole proprietorship (including "doing business as," or DBA) is the simplest form of business entity and requires the least administration but affords no liability protection.
- A partnership is similar to the sole proprietorship structure but, as the name implies, has more than one owner, though it also affords no liability protection.

One of the most important factors to consider is whether to limit the personal liability of the business owner(s). If so, that essentially leads to two choices: a limited liability company (LLC) or corporation (either S corp or C corp).

- LLCs are very flexible structures that do provide liability protection but may not be appropriate for businesses that are providing services from the owner(s).
- S corps are commonly used for service providers but do not have the flexibility to allow for multiple classes of shareholders or foreign shareholders.
- C Corps are the most complex of the structures but may not be appropriate for most start-up businesses as there are limitations on how profit is distributed. They are also costlier to administer.

Securing Capital

Almost every business requires some capital to get started. You could need a little or a lot, but if you don't have it, you might have to be creative to find it. I've had some people get into business with me because they liked my ideas. Others backed my projects because they liked me personally. Some backed me because I flirted with them. Some backed me out of the goodness of their hearts, just because they wanted to help me, and you know what? I took it.

Figure out who might be willing to support you financially as you get your business going. Go to friends, family, and banks. Go to those who might be interested in your line of work. Ask once and ask right because you only get one shot. If you are passionate enough about your business to make it work and practical enough to do it smartly, then you are a good investment.

. . . .

NOTES FROM THE SKINNYGIRL TEAM
Ron Nash, Skinnygirl Business Manager

Get enough capital. Most businesses fail because they are undercapitalized in their formation stages. If you plan to raise capital from a third party, a business plan is essential. The more money you need, the more sophisticated the plan should be. Start with family and friends, but also network to find potential financing sources. You could even try "crowd funding," a new way to raise capital via websites like Kickstarter, GoFundMe, and Micro-Ventures.

. . . .

Bookkeeping: Do It Right

You might do it yourself or you might have someone else do it, but bookkeeping is one of the most important things that happens for your business.

Keep track of everything that you can write off: part of your rent for your home office, continuing-education costs, trip expenses related to business, office supplies, book purchases relevant to your business (it's research), relevant trade and consumer magazines, and meals and drinks with clients or colleagues. Save everything and log it all. Every time you throw away a deductible receipt, you are throwing away money.

If your business gets too complicated, you might want to hire a bookkeeper. Find someone you can trust with great references, and check the references.

If you do hire a bookkeeper, don't let that be an excuse to be blind to your financial situation. Randomly check up on the reports. Does everything look right? Do you know what your bookkeeper is doing? Ask questions. "What's this?" "I noticed this—why is it like that?" Your bookkeeper needs to know you are paying attention. If you show that you know some things, they'll think you just might know everything. Even if you don't know every detail, you should understand your general financial picture.

Should You Partner Up?

Another thing to consider when assessing your finances is whether or not you should have a partner. A business partner isn't just a partner on paper or "the money." It will be a relationship, and you have to take that into account: Can you handle that? Do you prefer it? Or are you better working alone?

There are many pros and cons. A partner with the skills you don't have can be a huge benefit to your business. If you and a friend have all the same skills and love all the same things, you might not be good business partners. However, if your potential partner can butt heads with you in a good way, offer a point of view you wouldn't think of, or has a head for bookkeeping and contracts but not for being the front person like you are (or vice versa), then it might be a good match.

Sometimes, one person pulls all the visible weight and makes all the money, but the other person handles logistics and keeps the internal operation solid. That could work, unless the person on the front lines has an ego and doesn't appreciate what the other partner does or value the other person's contributions. Don't make the mistake of believing that the rainmaker does everything. Sometimes, the person holding down the fort, doing the books, paying the rent, looking at all the details, following the law, and making sure you're not getting sued is doing just as much, if not more. The person behind the scenes may sometimes feel the frustration of not being the one making the public decisions, but without that person, the whole thing could shut down.

If you're the rainmaker and you don't want to or can't share the power, then contract out your weak points and forget the partner. However, if you can say, "I'm going to bring in all the business and you're going to make it all work behind the scenes," that's a good partnership. I've seen it work both ways, and I really respect those long-term partnerships when people have worked together for twenty or thirty years. Just look at Elton John and Bernie Taupin. It's a very challenging thing, and it says something about the character, integrity, and business savvy of the people who can do it. I also take it as a good sign when a potential colleague has great relationships with former assistants, ex-employers, and past business associates. That says something about how a person does business.

When I was younger, I wasn't great with partners, but now I have many successful working relationships because I know how to manage them. I know that ultimately, I have to have the final say. I have to be the boss. An agent once said to me after I told him one of my ideas, "Let me run that by creative." I was like, "Are you fucking kidding me? You're not running anything by creative. I *am* the creative." But that doesn't mean I can't take advice. As long as it's clear who has the final say, I can work well in a partnership because I know that I can't do everything.

When I was working with a partner building my Skinnygirl cocktail brand and we ran out of stock, I said to him, "Listen, this brand is going to blow up. It's going to be the biggest thing that ever happened to anyone, so when this goes on TV, you need to spend ahead of the brand and get as many bottles as you can." He was a conservative businessman, and he wasn't willing to do that. Understandably, it could have buried us. On the other hand, if it were my money, I would have bet the farm. He said he didn't want to spend ahead of the brand and end up with excess stock, because what if I was wrong? What if my show *Bethenny Getting Married* got canceled? What if nobody liked the cocktail? He would have been sitting there with a million bottles. He wouldn't take the risk.

This was an interesting situation because we were both right. The bottles were sold out nationwide and people couldn't get them because he hadn't spent ahead of the brand, and I would scream at him every day, but I couldn't have guaranteed this would happen. This is what happens when you have a partner. They won't always do exactly what you want them to do, and that's when you have to realize that sometimes a system of checks and balances is in everyone's best interest. Maybe you're too rash or too conservative, and your partner will push you a little toward the middle—and you might push your partner, too. The result can be better ideas or smarter moves than either one of you might have come up with alone. It's like a marriage.

My Skinnygirl Cocktails partner and I were actually a good team because I pushed him to take more risks than he would have, but he reeled me in, so I was more careful than I might have been. One of the things I've respected about him is that he would complain about spending six dollars for a latte, but he would never complain about hundreds of thousands of dollars in legal fees. After months of negotiating to sell Skinnygirl Cocktails (and incurring the previously mentioned legal fees), when push came to shove, at the last minute, I told him I wasn't sure if I wanted to sell it, and he said, very calmly, "Then we won't sell it." I loved that. It made me feel calmer about what was going on. There was no pressure, and that helped me think clearly about the deal and helped me to realize I would sell the brand.

I've gotten much better at accepting what other people are saying, but I'm still the person who puts the fire under everyone's ass. There is nothing wrong with the fact that I am the leader, and there is nothing wrong with the fact that some people work better with a leader. You just need to know which you are. If you are a leader, you'll never be happy under someone's thumb. If you need a leader, you will never be happy or truly comfortable being in charge.

Partners should be able to rely on each other. I know I'm not the person who can open up a computer and fix it. If you paid me ten grand, I couldn't create an Excel spreadsheet. I can't do taxes and my eyes glaze over when people start talking about the technical details of a business deal. Know thyself. I do know that 90 percent of my ideas are good. I'm the creative marketer, the salesperson. If we build it, they will come. But now I'm wise enough and experienced enough to know that I can't do it all.

To accomplish this, I've become particularly aware of how diverse personalities can benefit a partnership. When I was hiring executive producers for my talk show, I decided to hire a straight married woman with a news background who tends to be cautious and conservative. She lives in the suburbs with her husband and children, and she knows women very well. Then I hired a charismatic, high-energy gay man with a more manic, passionate personality who is very creative and already has experience running a talk show. He's quick to jump at any new opportunity.

When I first got these two producers together for dinner, everyone said they could not possibly work together. They were too different and definitely not a match made in heaven. They would never have picked each other as partners, either. That night, I woke up in the middle of the night and said, "That's exactly why I want them!" I think they will push each other. I don't want yes-men. I want different points of view behind the scenes at my show. I want variety and multiple perspectives and a whole range of people in the audience, so I decided that precisely because they are so different, they will be a great combination.

Only time will tell!

. . . .

DON'T GIVE IT ALL AWAY

When you're trying to accumulate capital to start your business, err on the side of caution. Don't give up too much in the beginning. Before you're making any money, it sounds like nothing to give someone 5 percent of your business to do your PR or 20 percent of your business for an investment of capital. You might think it doesn't matter because 95 percent of something, or even 80 percent of something, is better than 100 percent of nothing. I get that, and when you need capital or a good PR person, this kind of deal could make sense. If your business is at risk of failing, you do what you need to do, but be conservative. When you're profitable, you will kick yourself if you gave too much away.

. . . .

Hiring Good Employees

Some businesses never consist of more than one person, but most grow to the point where they need at least one employee, and often many. An assistant, a receptionist, an accountant, a lawyer—some of these people may be personal contractors and some may be regular employees. Before you hire anyone, you need to know what paperwork is required and what the difference is between different kinds of employees, accounting-wise and tax-wise.

You want to hire people you can trust, not people who take more time putting together their outfits and choosing their heels and putting on their makeup than they do thinking about what has to get done. I see this in Manhattan all the time—all these personal assistants are walking around the city like they are working at Bergdorf's, but can any of those people get down and dirty when it counts? If you're working at a makeup counter, maybe looking polished will be good for your career, but I need someone who looks like she can work hard. Not to be judgmental, but if you're working because Daddy told you that you have to pay for your own nail polish, you're not going to be a very good employee.

So forget looks unless it's your front-desk person and you need your business to make a certain impression. Instead, get someone you feel like you can trust who has great references—then check the references. There are a lot of lunatics out there.

I've had my share of hiring disasters. I had an assistant whom I used to treat to manicures and pedicures every now and again. Sometimes we would go to lunch. Then one day I found out she was taking spa days and taking her friends out to lunch on my business credit card. Another girl left me high and dry while I was running that sweatshop of a bakery. She didn't show up on a crucial day, and I was alone with thousands of cookies to package. Her ass got canned.

For people out there looking for a good job, my advice is to take your job seriously and give it all your effort because you never know what's going to happen. One day you could realize that the former boss you screwed over turned out to be Bethenny Frankel, and then you might show up at her book signing crying and apologizing for what you did. Sorry, bitch. You left me sweating my balls off that day. Apology not accepted.

This chapter gives you a lot to think about, but on the other hand, it barely scratches the surface. This is just a start, but I hope I've got your gears turning. Just work on your money noise, know everything you can about your business, plan well, and manage your money with both eyes open, and then you can concentrate on bigger and more interesting things, like making your product, offering your services, and building your great reputation.

Chapter Fifteen

Work-Life Balance

It's still hard. Balancing work and life is something I'll probably always struggle to get right, but I've come a long way since I wrote my first book. I've learned a lot about what's really important and what can too easily be lost when it's not prioritized. I've always been the person who wants to do it all, have it all, be it all, but to be honest, all I ever really wanted was to be able to pay my rent, afford a taxi, and not sweat bullets when the server puts the check on the table.

The rewards of success are great. If I have an idea, I know people will listen to me now, with confidence that it's a good idea. I've been vetted. I've learned how important it is to stop and appreciate those moments in life when things are good. I am grateful: for trustworthy friends, girls' night out, snuggling with Bryn, belly rubs with Cookie, and all the lessons I've learned and the ways I've changed for the better. Sometimes I think I'm even growing up a little bit.

But success has a price as well. I'm certainly not one who likes to hear celebrities complain about being celebrities. Truthfully, I have a great life and I'm very lucky that many of my dreams have become a reality, but part of fame is gray hair, wrinkles, aging, and stressing out. I used to think I was pretty cute until I became famous and people started telling me how ugly I was. When you are famous, you are constantly under the microscope. You worry about aging because of its direct impact on your career. When you walk down the street, people judge everything about you. You have no privacy and your body language changes as you start to close yourself off. You keep a smaller, tighter circle of friends. Like anything else, fame has its pros and cons. It's a rose with petals and thorns. All you can really control is how well you live your life, how well you do your work, and with how much grace you can handle the pressure.

Listen, I don't have all the answers. Sometimes I talk like I do, but I don't. I have good days and bad days, but right now, this is what I know: *You can have it all, just not all at once.*

In that spirit, I want to leave you with a list of mantras I say to myself all the time, one for every year of life I've lived so far. Steal them, memorize them, use them, take them to heart:

1. This is not a dress rehearsal.
2. Do what you can.
3. Be your best.
4. Go for yours.
5. Don't hate the player, hate the game.
6. Don't make it so important.
7. Don't overthink it.
8. Don't take yourself too seriously.
9. Just do it.
10. Just enjoy it.
11. Keep it moving.
12. Use it or lose it.
13. Always stop at a lemonade stand.
14. Never diet.
15. Never pay retail.
16. Clean out your closet.
17. Laugh.
18. Dance.
19. Play.
20. Let yourself feel hurt.
21. Do the right thing.
22. Thank people.

23. Don't beat yourself up.
24. Tell the truth.
25. Sleep.
26. Cherish your friends.
27. Enjoy a cocktail once in a while.
28. Have passion.
29. Have integrity, even when no one is looking.
30. Never let them see you sweat.
31. It's a marathon, not a sprint.
32. It's the journey, not the destination.
33. Don't get stuck in the mud and the minutiae.
34. Find the yes.
35. Get involved.
36. Don't let good enough be good enough.
37. Use what you have.
38. Expect the unexpected.
39. Own it.
40. Go there.
41. Play your own game.
42. Live your own life.

Thanks for sticking with me. I often say, "Don't seek credit," but here I'd like to take the opportunity to give *you* credit. You all have taken me to this place, and I am thrilled to continue on this journey with you. You are always in my life, and I can't wait to continue the conversation.

Acknowledgments

Thank you to Cookie, aka "dabooboo," my furriest of family. I love you for exactly who you are. You were my first child and you have now had to accept becoming a dog when Bryn came around. You remind me a lot of myself in many ways, both negative and positive. You are complicated and lovable and the most loyal bitch a girl could ever know.

Thank you, Jackie, my assistant (who will be working for me over at the talk show by the time this is published). You are honest, loyal, dedicated, and hard working, and you will always be part of "the team." You always jump in and do whatever you can, especially when the chips are down.

Thank you, Malini, for your wisdom, insight, for protecting what is important in business, and for jumping into very stressful and overwhelming circumstances.

Thank you, Leslie, for your support, calm nature, honesty, love, and morality.

Thank you to my girlfriends: Corey, Sarah, Amy, Teri, Connie, Louie, Jake, and Chuck. You are helping me through an enormously difficult time and you answer every phone call.

Thanks, Warren. You have been a loyal and trusting friend and I will never forget it. Xo.

Thanks, Turch, for the daily phone calls and the great advice—and "for giving me tooth."

Thank you, Carrie Gordon. You are the best that there is. Whether it is the fanciest of fancy or the grittiest of gritty, you are in the trenches.

Thank you, Amanda. You have been so strong and so supportive. I consider myself lucky.

Thanks, C., for being patient with me.

Thanks, Kate, for doing nothing. Xo. Just kidding, but I couldn't resist.

Thanks, Dr. A., for everything.

Thank you Bryn, my love, my life, my peanut, my everything. You taught me what true love really is, in its purest unconditional form. You show me what is important and meaningful and give me a reason for doing everything I do. You have helped me to learn so much to pass on to other mommies. You are the most special strawberry in the world. As I said the minute you were born: "You are a nice girl."

Thank you, Zach Schisgal, for embarking with me on my career as an author. I never forget.

Thank you, Stacy Creamer, for being a great partner, a great springboard, for loyalty, for stretching yourself even when you're nervous, and for a great home as my publisher.

Thank you, Matthew, for your knowledge, tenacity, passion, and hard work. You are wonderful to work with.

Thanks, Eve, for your ability to keep up with me, to understand me, and to have always listened and trusted me from day one. Xo.

Thank you, Hilary. You are a rock who believes in me no matter what the deal or the day is.

Thanks Ed, Mary, and Andy. Because I love you.

Thank you, Ellen, for believing in me, for welcoming me into your home to connect with women, and for giving me the opportunities that I hope to give to others.

Thank you to all of my friends—I have never appreciated you as much as I do now. I am so lucky. You have taught me how to be a better person and a good friend in return.

Finally, thank you to the women who inspire me to come from a place of yes every day, no matter how difficult that is.

Index

About the Author

Bethenny Frankel is the four-time bestselling author of *Skinnydipping, A Place of Yes, The Skinnygirl Dish,* and *Naturally Thin*. She has a daily talk show set to launch in the fall of 2013. She is the creator of the Skinnygirl brand, which extends to cocktails, beauty, fitness, and health, and was the star of her own Bravo TV show. In 2011, Bethenny won a *Glamour* Women of the Year Award and was named one of the Top 100 Women in Entertainment by *The Hollywood Reporter*. A graduate of the Natural Gourmet Institute for Health and Culinary Arts, Bethenny lives in New York with her daughter, Bryn, and dog, Cookie. Visit Bethenny.com.

DON'T MISS ANY OF
BETHENNY'S
NEW YORK TIMES BESTSELLERS!

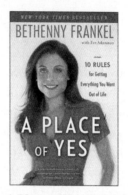

Plunge into Bethenny's fiction debut, *Skinnydipping*, a devilishly dishy and hilarious roman à clef about a woman who sells her soul to reality TV for a chance to have it all.

In *A Place of Yes*, Bethenny takes us on an empowering journey and provides more of her no-nonsense advice for getting the most out of life.

Naturally Thin started readers on the Skinnygirl journey—then Bethenny served up the next step in learning how to cook fearlessly and make the foods you love in *The Skinnygirl Dish*.